SPEAKING
MY MIND

OTHER BOOKS BY TONY CAMPOLO

SPEAKING
MY MIND

TONY CAMPOLO

W PUBLISHING GROUP
A Division of Thomas Nelson Publishers
Since 1798

Published by W Publishing Group, a division of Thomas Nelson, Inc., P.O. Box 141000, Nashville, Tennessee 37214.

Unless otherwise indicated, Scripture quotations used in this book are from the King James Version of the Bible.

Other Scripture references are from the following source:

The New King James Version (NKJV®). Copyright © 1979, 1980, 1982 by Thomas Nelson, Inc. Used by permission. All rights reserved.

ISBN 0-8499-1817-0 (hardcover)

Printed in the United States of America

To my son-in-law
Marc Goodheart

He is an answer to my prayer that
my daughter Lisa would marry a good man.

Contents

CONTENTS

Foreword

Recently, Tony Campolo had a serious stroke. Afterward, in our regular prayer group conversations over coffee in the back room of Joe's Place, Tony demonstrated more impatient concern than usual when discussing the church. It was a loving concern, expressed within the context of a high view of the church as Christ's body—a body anointed to preach the gospel to the poor, to set free the captive.

Indeed, his zeal reminded the four of us who share such time with Tony not only of Jesus's Lukan reading from Isaiah, but also of the observation of one of the disciples during the Lord's cleansing of the temple: "The zeal of His Father's house has consumed Him" (see John 2:17).

This book grew out of that loving concern and consuming zeal for the church. If read in its entirety, it will strike the objective reader that the author cares deeply about both the people who make up the church and the Lord of the church. Reading only snippets, as Tony's detractors will make certain happens by quoting selected lines out of context, will result in a regrettably distorted and fragmented view of this prophetic Christian and his beliefs. It would be advisable, in my opinion, to begin the book by reading the last chapter, then proceeding to chapter 1.

Virtually no week goes by without someone, after learning where I work, telling me that Tony was instrumental in his or her becoming more deeply committed to Jesus and His teachings. More often than not, these people observe that they did not want to be moved by Tony because they disagreed with his political views. Yet, as they listened, they were inspired to understand the kingdom of God more deeply and fully than ever before. Political differences were transcended by the common ground around the cross and empty tomb and by the Scriptures illuminated by the Holy Spirit as Tony preached.

A nagging concern of Tony's while writing this book was that the surgical dissection and selective reporting of its lines by his critics would further isolate him from the conservative evangelical community he regards as family. In the final analysis, he believed that he owed the community a full explanation of how his journey with the Lord for more than half a century has shaped his beliefs.

As always, when he preaches or writes, Tony issues invitations to faith and service. This book is no exception. However, it goes further, inviting those who share his longing for a church that is reflective of the Christ who lived out the Sermon on the Mount to join him in conversations about such a church.

Last year, my father had a series of mild strokes in a rather abbreviated number of weeks. With each stroke came a temporary loss of memory. To jog his memory, Dad would recite the names of immediate family members. Following one particular stroke, try as he might, he could not remember anyone's name—not even Mother's. After straining to call her by name but failing, he began to recite the first verses of the book of John: "In the beginning was the Word, and the Word was with God, and the Word was God . . ." (NKJV). Although we in the family needed no such evidence, it was a reminder that nothing could separate that saintly fellow from the love of God that he shared in Christ Jesus. It is my hope that this book will convince many people of the truth that gave my father the assurance of salvation and his confidence in a gracious God.

In conclusion, I am grateful for the courage Tony shows in addressing controversial questions that most thoughtful Christians have prayerfully, but privately, pondered. They need to be discussed in the light of day. May you and trusted prayer group partners do so, just as a handful of people have done for many years in the back room at Joe's.

DAVID BLACK, PHD
President, Eastern University
St. Davids, Pennsylvania

Preface

Just for the record: I did not choose the subtitle of this book. That phrase was the publisher's idea. A prophet is, by my definition, someone who has a word straight from God and declares it to the world, knowing that the message has divine legitimation. Such is not the case with me or with what I have to say in this book. I spent many hours in prayer, seeking God's direction in what I would write, but I received no specific revelation that would allow me to declare, "Thus saith the Lord!" At best, I am a detective. I see myself as someone who works hard trying to ferret out the truth about what God is doing in the church and in the world, and the part we are to have in that work. What you have on the pages that follow is the thinking of a struggling Christian who is trying to figure out what is right and wrong within the community of Christians he loves as it strives to relate to the world.

As I wrote this book, I fought within myself, trying to make sure I wrote honestly about what was going on in my heart and mind. Parts of what you read here will probably seem somewhat inconclusive. That is because I am still unsettled about certain things myself. However, I am convinced that if I waited until I was absolutely sure about everything, I would say very little, if indeed anything at all. My faith journey is not complete, by any stretch of the imagination. My thinking about many of the issues discussed in this book is still in process. Over the years, I have had to change opinions and beliefs that I once held with dogmatic fervor. Now, there are fewer and fewer things about which I am absolutely certain. However, I hold those things with an ever-increasing tenacity. And this one thing I *do* know, in accord with the apostle

Paul, and that is Jesus Christ—crucified, risen, and coming again. The more I feel the certainty of who He is and what He did for me, the more I love Him.

I once had a conversation with Bono, the lead singer for the rock band U2. I wanted to know how he could put together a song entitled "I Still Haven't Found What I'm Looking For," since I knew he was a firm believer in Christ. Bono answered, "Being a Christian hasn't given me all the answers; instead it's given me a whole new set of questions." The more I think about his answer, the more I think it applies to me too. It is as a struggling Christian that I try, in these pages, to make valid cases for some of the most pressing concerns of our times. As I lay out my arguments, I leave it to you to be the jury that discerns, decides, and then returns the verdicts on what I have to say.

In the first part of the book, I provide my personal observations as to how evangelicalism moved from being a struggling sectarian movement that was only a side eddy to the mainstream of American religion to the role of dominance that it holds today. I will outline what factors contributed to the decline of mainline Christianity, on the one hand, and on the other hand, what made for the great successes of evangelicalism over the past fifty years.

Then, in the second section of the book, I will raise a variety of issues and problems that evangelicalism must face and resolve if it is to continue its winning streak into the twenty-first century. This second part of the book will deal with matters that are sources of arguments among evangelicals, but they are matters that cannot be ignored.

There is a carefully planned progression to the book. I do my best to lead the reader to consider four distinct concerns, which I believe evangelicals should contemplate seriously at this particular time in American history. A sensitive working through of these concerns is essential, if we are to speak relevantly and helpfully to a world that is growing increasingly suspicious of Christians and feels threatened by much of what we say and do. The four areas of concern with which I deal here are

> Do evangelicals have an image problem?
> What is happening to our theology?
> How well do we relate to the rest of the world?
> What does the future hold in store for us?

Welcome to the world of religious controversy, because this book is full of it. Some books are written to comfort troubled Christians, but this is not one of them. Rather, this book will disturb and trouble the comfortable. Evangelical preachers and writers sidestep many subjects because they polarize the Christian community. It is about these controversial subjects that I have written here.

There will be those who contend that I have been a little too daring in this book, that I went a bit too far in honestly expressing what I do and don't believe. To people who think that way, let me say that I subscribe to T. S. Eliot, who states that "only those who risk going too far can possibly find out how far they can go." I believe that we evangelicals have a long way to go if we are to be respected as a people who are willing to engage the world with something other than the pat answers that it has come to expect from us.

There is a common perception among those outside our community of faith that we evangelicals are clones, and that when they have spoken with one of us, they have spoken with us all. Too often they see us as people who have a single way of thinking and talking. Recently, I heard someone refer to evangelicals as "cookie-cutter Christians." To be credible, we must demonstrate that we are a body of individuals, each of whom can think for herself or himself. I have made an attempt in this book to do that.

Whenever a book is put together, the author needs to thank all those who made it possible. This book is no exception to that rule. Thanks go to the secretaries in my office: Jessica Maiorana, who helped me in many ways, and especially Valerie Hoffman, who did a wonderful job of deciphering my handwriting, typing up what I had written, and working with my wife on the editing process. I also want to thank Biju Mathew, who was my research assistant. David Black, Allen Carlson, Mary Darling, Ken Medema, and Beverly Vander Molen read my manuscript and made some very helpful suggestions.

I am grateful to my son, Bart, who critiqued this book and forced me to rethink what I said and how to say it. I am most appreciative of the support and help of the people who worked with me at W Publishing Group, especially senior editor Laura Kendall and Holly Halverson, who edited my manuscript.

Most of all, I want to thank my wife, Peggy. She spent almost as much time editing what I wrote as I spent writing it. If I seem like a somewhat literate person on the pages that follow, it is because of the work she did.

Lastly, I'd like to thank you for being willing to read this book and giving me a chance to share my thoughts and my convictions with you. I hope you are challenged by what you are about to read, and I also hope you enjoy it.

TONY CAMPOLO
Eastern University
St. Davids, Pennsylvania

PART ONE

The Evangelical Takeover

1

Whatever Happened to Mainline Denominations?

We are all aware that mainline churches are rapidly losing members and that many of them are drifting into nondenominational evangelical churches. The statistics speak for themselves: whether we look at the membership rolls of the Presbyterian Church USA, or those of the United Methodist Church, the same disturbing evidence is clear. They, like all the other mainline denominations, are in decline, and when we analyze this problem, it is easy to see that whatever independent evangelical churches have done to make themselves attractive, it is what mainline denominations have done to themselves that has been responsible for so many of their members leaving them to join nondenominational evangelical congregations.

If some strategists had sat down and planned how mainline churches could go from being the dominant expression of American Christianity to churches struggling for survival, they could not have come up with a more effective scenario than what has been evident in the practices and policies of these churches over the last quarter of a century. First and foremost has been that, in their attempt to be *relevant* (the "in" word) to what they perceive to be the mind-set of the prevailing culture, much of the preaching heard in these churches has become devoid of the kind of personal mystical spirituality for which so many Christians hunger. Those who analyze what has been going on in what has come to be called the "postmodern world" make the point that the rationalism of liberal modernistic preaching has failed to meet the basic subjective longings of vast numbers of churchgoers. From the time of Sören Kierkegaard, the nineteenth-century Danish existentialist writer who reacted against the systematic logic of Friedrich Hegel, and Dostoevsky, the Russian novelist, there have been those who declared that scientific rationalism could not satisfy the quest for inner contentment that drives people to God. Nevertheless, the theologians and biblical scholars who dominated the thinking of mainline denominations in the middle of the twentieth century tried their very best to develop modes of Christian preaching that would appeal to those nurtured in secularity.

Langdon Gilkey, in his book *Naming the Whirlwind*, traced the ways in which these theologians tried to make Christianity acceptable to those whose modernistic thinking led them to scoff at anything that had even a tinge of the mystical and miraculous. Rationalistic skepticism about such doctrines as the virgin birth of Jesus and the idea that there really are such things as miracles became common among students at many mainline denominational seminaries.

Numerous leaders of mainline denominations promoted a theology that "demythologized the Bible" (to use Rudolf Bultmann's expression). The dynamics of personal conversion experiences, so common in American revivalism, were often written off as a lot of emotionalism. In place of "the old-time religion" of fundamentalism, these self-declared avant-garde church leaders fostered a Christianity marked by a deep commitment to rational moralism and social justice, but often lacking in subjective emotional gratification. Pastors fed many of those who attended mainline churches a steady diet of sermons that had little or no emphasis on the need for sinners to have a "born-again" experience. Mainline church leaders just didn't get it when their people began to complain and say they wanted something more. While many sophisticated members of the clergy, who were trying to prove themselves acceptable in the halls of academia, were making cynical critiques of mass evangelism, congregants were flocking to Billy Graham crusades. And when these members began leaving their churches to seek out a more evangelical message, their pastors counted the rejection of their preaching as evidence that their preaching was being socially prophetic. They tried to convince themselves that from ancient times, people have always rejected preaching that made them uncomfortable about the racism, sexism, materialism, and militarism that marked their lives. It was the *truth* of their messages, they told themselves, that was causing people to vote against their preaching with their feet, as they walked away from mainline Christianity.

There may be some truth to such conclusions, but there is still the reality that denominational leaders did not pay enough attention to people who were subjectively aware of their own sinfulness and longed for a message of deliverance. These leaders often failed to give sufficient recognition to people's need for something more than a religion that made sense in the face of the scientific rationalism of modernity and addressed the painful social crises of the times. Too often they overlooked the fact that people craved a feeling of connectedness with God that gave them the sense of being inwardly transformed. In the pews of mainline churches were men and women who wanted to feel a cleansing from sin and experience the ecstasy of being "filled with the Spirit," but mainline theology and preaching marginalized such dimensions of Christianity.

OPPOSED ON SOCIAL ISSUES

To make matters worse, church members often diametrically opposed the positions on social issues articulated from the pulpits of mainline Protestantism. Sociologists have conducted studies validating the fact that church members generally have more conservative stances on political and social matters than do their denominational leaders, or even their clergy. The differences between clergy and laity became especially pronounced between the late 1950s and the mid-1970s, when the United States was traumatized by the civil-rights movement and the antiwar movement. As mainline church leaders lent their voices to these movements, they often encountered a laity committed to resisting their socially liberal rhetoric. When the national assemblies of denominations related to the National Council of Churches passed resolutions, the people back home in local congregations increasingly deemed themselves under attack by the leadership of their churches. To conservative lay Christians, it seemed almost as though their denominational leaders were taking positions that were designed to appeal to those persons who were least likely to attend their churches.

It has been said that eleven o'clock on Sunday morning is the most segregated hour in American life. That being the case, those who were committed to keep it that way became upset with preachers who made racial integration a basic Christian commitment.

The ordination of women, along with many of the proposals feminists set forth, upset those conservative church members who believed that there is biblical legitimization for traditional roles for women.

The antiwar sentiments church leaders commonly articulated ran contrary to the convictions of the people in their pews who were supporters of the government's Vietnam policies.

More recently, the growing support that the gay and lesbian civil-rights movement has gained in mainline denominations has greatly disturbed most rank-and-file members of mainline churches. As leadership has made moves to ordain homosexuals as clergy, and even as bishops, vast segments of mainline denominations have claimed that things have gone too far to the left, or they have threatened to leave their liberal mainline churches and make their spiritual homes elsewhere. There is evidence that the division over how to respond to homosexuals in the church is likely to bring about church schisms on a scale that will redefine the structure of American Christianity for a century to come. Those who exit gay-friendly denominations will likely make their way into evangelical congregations that preach that homosexual eroticism is against the will of God. On the other hand, there are probably more people than one would suspect who support gay marriages and/or have homosexual friends and relatives who are likely to join mainline churches because of the positions those denominations are taking on this issue.

FINANCIAL SUPPORT FALLING

Even those who agree with the liberal positions many of the leaders of mainline churches have taken will have to admit that such liberal positions on those matters I have cited are not conducive to fostering growth in church membership or increasing financial support. Thus, it is not surprising that for the last few decades, church membership in mainline denominations has declined, and giving has dropped below what is needed to sustain denominational programs. My own denomination, American Baptist, has cut its staff in draconian fashion. Much of the land and office space that housed our national denominational offices has either been sold off or rented out. And what is true of my denomination is true for others.

The Interchurch Building on Riverside Drive in New York City, which serves as the headquarters of the National Council of Churches, was once bustling with staff running a host of interdenominational social justice programs. Today, the failure of church members to put up the money to run such programs has resulted in such huge cutbacks that only a skeleton crew remains. Some office space is rented out and much space simply is left unused. The National Council of Churches has seen better days. I think it is safe to say that, were it not for the dynamic leadership of its new general secretary, Bob Edgar, the whole organization might be bankrupt right now.

Those who want to save mainline denominations—and perhaps revive them—all agree that the ministry styles of their churches bear significant shortcomings, and that they have somehow lost the ability to win new converts or to call their members into the kind of zealous commitment that is so evident among members of evangelical congregations. The vitality and growth of evangelical megachurches such as Willow Creek Community Church in South Barrington, Illinois, or Saddleback Church in Orange County, California, are not the result only of the charisma of their pastors. In reality, the success of these churches is dependent upon having a membership that is empowered and enthused about winning friends, neighbors, coworkers, and family members to Christ through personal evangelism.

CONVERSION VERSUS SOCIALIZATION

Evangelical churches put a great emphasis upon individuals making personal decisions for Christ, and such decisions require a high level of commitment to participating in the mission of the church. There is, within evangelicalism, a theologically prescribed expectation that every member be a missionary. The responsibility for reaching the lost with the gospel belongs to every single member. The zeal to carry out this mission is the consequence of having church members who have been *converted* into the Christian faith rather than *socialized* into it, as is the case with most members of mainline congregations. The majority of members in mainline churches grew up in their respective denominations. They are American Baptists, Methodists, Presbyterians, or Episcopalians primarily because their parents had these affiliations. In most cases, joining their churches was simply a part of the growing-up process, and it seldom was marked by any real independent decision-making process. Contrast such Christians with those who join churches as converts.

At an anniversary celebration of the Willow Creek Community Church, which now has as many as twenty thousand in attendance for weekly worship services, someone asked how many of the members had no active membership in a church prior to making a decision for Christ and joining the Willow Creek congregation. The thousands in the audience gave an overwhelming response. These were *converts,* and sociologists from Ernst Troeltsch through Reinhold Niebuhr have constantly pointed out that converts bring to their religious lives a zeal and a commitment for evangelizing others that are seldom evident in those who have been socialized into the memberships of traditional mainline denominations. Mainline churches need more zealous converts if they are to have the kind of laity that will foster church growth.

FROZEN IN LIMITED METHODOLOGY

Still another prominent reason that mainline denominations are dying is because they are usually frozen in methodology and styles of programming that do not foster the kind of successes that mark the evangelical movement. Take foreign missionary work, for instance. Mainline denominations have had a long-established process of recruiting and financing those who go to foreign fields and into domestic church planting. They have limited themselves to academically qualified persons, who in most cases are those who have seminary degrees. They have raised financial support for these missionaries by having local congregations send contributions in to their denominational headquarters. Then, after executives and committees do careful planning and budgeting, they parcel out the money to the workers and missionaries on the field.

The mainline denominational missionaries recruited and financed in this manner have done a brilliant job over the years. As they labored on the field, they did not have to worry about whether or not funds would be forthcoming to enable them to sustain their ministries. I can report from personal observations that the work missionaries of my own denomination are doing is among the most responsible and effective work I have seen any missionaries do anywhere.

The problem is that this way of recruiting and supporting missionaries very much limits what can be done when compared with the methodologies of independent evangelicals. As a case in point, while my own historic mainline denomination, American Baptist Churches USA, has less than two hundred full-time workers serving as international missionaries, an independent evangelical organization, Youth With A Mission, which is less than fifty years old, has more than thirty thousand missionaries serving across the world. Operation Mobilization, another highly evangelical ministry, has more than ten thousand workers on the field.

Such independent evangelical groups are able to deploy so many workers in so short a period of time because they ask their workers to raise their own financial support. Each missionary makes pleas to his or her friends, relatives, and especially the members of his or her home church. If any missionary recruit doesn't raise enough support, he or she doesn't go to the field. It is amazing how well this works. It is easy to understand that people are much more ready to give sacrificially to a young missionary whom the givers know and who maintains close contact with them through letters and personal visits, than to some denominational agency that finances missionaries who are only names to them. Furthermore, the independent missionary organizations, unlike mainline denominations, do not require that their workers have an array of academic qualifications. A willingness to go, a sense of calling, an orthodox theology, some good recommendations—and yes, the ability to raise the necessary financial support—are usually all they require for a committed Christian to go out as a missionary to some needy land.

Incidentally, one of the many reasons mainline denominations are having budget problems is that these independent organizations are siphoning significant amounts of money away from the members of their churches, who would rather support some young, independent, zealous evangelical missionary than give to a somewhat impersonal church bureaucracy.

The results of all of these differences between the methodology mainline denominations employ and that independent evangelical missionary groups use are obvious to anyone who has visited mission fields. Missionaries from evangelical organizations *vastly* outnumber those mainline denominations have placed on the field. Their sheer numbers across Africa, Latin America, and Asia enable evangelicals to win many more converts, plant many more churches, and develop many more indigenous church leaders than mainline denominations possibly can match.

THE SHIFTING OF POWER

All of this impacts what goes on here in the States. As evangelical churches and Christians in the southern hemisphere become more numerous, they begin to exercise a greater influence on what American denominations are and can do. The dominance of developed nations in the northern hemisphere over world Christianity is coming to an end, and Americans, especially, find that they are less and less able to dictate what goes on in the worldwide activities of their denominations. This development has become dramatically evident with the recent controversy in the Episcopal Church over the ordination of a homosexual bishop in the state of New Hampshire. The way in which American bishops voted on this matter is one the churches in the Third World are not about to accept. The Archbishop of Canterbury, who is the leader of the worldwide Anglican church, which includes American Episcopalians, faces the fact that African bishops, who represent the growing edge of his denomination, are not going to lie back and accept what the American bishops have decided about homosexuals in roles of church leadership. As the archbishop faces the power shift to those in the Third World, he cannot ignore their demands.

The Presbyterian Church USA is facing much the same problem. Its membership statistics would show even steeper declines than are now evident, save for the fact that huge numbers of Presbyterians are coming to this country from Korea. These immigrants come with a fundamentalist theology that is a challenge to the moderate beliefs of their established American church. These Koreans are joining the Presbyterian churches across America, and they are planting a host of churches of their own. To say that they are making their presence felt within Presbyterianism is an understatement. Their influence, according to many observers, may lead to a major schism in their denomination in the days that lie ahead, because their fundamentalist theology is in conflict with the theology that prevails within the denomination's hierarchy.

All of this is to say that what goes on in missionary work today is highly permeated by evangelical Christianity, and this is generating a feedback here in America that is making things rough for mainline denominations.

To the many who question whether or not mainline denominations even have a future, I answer with a resounding *yes!* But their future lies in imitating much of what has made evangelicalism so successful. They need to study the programming and marketing techniques that evangelicals have employed in order to vault them into being the dominant religious movement of our time. Mainline denominations have a lot to learn from evangelicals when it comes to winning souls for Christ. The demographics of mainline churches indicate that their membership rolls are skewed toward the elderly. Unless these churches can figure out how to bring in baby boomers and Generation Xers, their future is bleak.

Simply put, if mainline churches cannot do as well as evangelical churches when it comes to attracting members, the answer might be to join them—that is to say, for mainline denominations to become more evangelical. However, before considering that option, it would be wise to take a good look at evangelicalism, and that is what the next chapter is all about.

2

How Did Evangelicalism
Get So Big?

Evangelicalism is on a roll. Mainline denominations have been sidelined as evangelicalism has grown in size and significance across the American scene. Fundamentalism, which most sociologists predicted would fade into oblivion by the beginning of the twenty-first century, has done just the opposite. Reclothed under the more respected label of *evangelicalism,* fundamentalist Christianity has shown surprising signs of vitality and gained dominance over American church life.

There used to be those who distinguished evangelicalism from fundamentalism, claiming that only the former had a social conscience that made its proponents into progressive social activists. These activists worked for justice in the world while viewing fundamentalism as being so steeped in rigid categories of thinking and legalistic behavioral patterns that it was irrelevant to the prevailing culture. Today, any distinctions between evangelicalism and fundamentalism have all but disappeared, as fundamentalists have usurped the word *evangelicalism* and made it their own. Certainly, to the world outside the church, these two labels now are used interchangeably.

But it is something that has developed *within* fundamentalism that has done the most to make the differences between it and evangelicalism hard to perceive. Fundamentalism has developed a strong social conscience! No longer can it be said that those in this movement are devoid of social concerns. Fundamentalists, who once wrote off those Christians who got involved in politics or spent time and effort in meeting the material needs of the poor, are now among the most committed servants of the victims of poverty. They are reaching out, not only to the homeless here in America, but also to the hungry in Third World countries.

Furthermore, these once socially disengaged sectarians have organized themselves into the most powerful special-interest groups in American politics. In addition to their influence upon the decision-making processes of government, they are diligently working to change the culture, boldly holding up their end of social policy arguments and campus debates, making sure that their voices are heard via television talk shows, movies, and books, including novels with broad public appeal. Whereas it was once their style to withdraw from the world, the fundamentalists now have an almost triumphalistic commitment to change it into their version of the kingdom of God.

Perhaps what is most noticeable to those who study evangelicalism is that evangelical churches are growing by leaps and bounds. Almost every community in the country can point to some evangelical megachurch that has just put up a new building to hold its growing congregation. These churches have drawn in large numbers from the hitherto religiously disaffected, and it is interesting to note that as they have done so, they have subtly cast off some of the characteristics that once made them unattractive to outsiders. They have quietly abandoned legalisms that absolutely forbade wine drinking, dancing, and smoking and replaced the anti-intellectualism that once pervaded these churches with a reasonable faith and intelligent apologists. These new churches not only connect with hordes of people who previously had little or nothing to do with Christianity, but they also attract members away from mainline churches where many had begun to feel there was too much in the way of liberal politics and too little in the way of Bible-based gospel.

The media have widely noted the effect of those new churches on American culture. Some years ago, the popular magazine *Time* ran a cover story entitled "Is God Dead?" Two years ago, the Easter edition of that same magazine ran a story on angels. That should tell us something about how much evangelicalism has changed the tenor of our culture.

Evangelicals have become public-opinion makers in a big way, and there are those who now fear them, especially when they talk in a determined fashion about "claiming the nation for Christ" and making America into a truly "Christian nation." Evangelicals always talked about transforming the country and bringing it under the lordship of Christ, but few people took them seriously until the last couple of decades. Now the fear of such a takeover is so great that groups specifically committed to preventing this are forming.

How did this happen? How did this seemingly irrelevant and often ridiculed religious movement evolve from a small, struggling sect that many assumed was doomed to extinction to become the most vibrant form of Christianity in the land? What were the ingredients of its success, and what did it have going for it that mainline denominations lacked?

In this first section of the book, I will try to answer such questions from a subjective point of view. Through this last half-century, I was an observer participant (to use a sociological term) to the success story that evangelicalism has become. I not only saw it all happen; I was a part of it. I came to know many of the major players personally and got a closeup look at those things that made them powerful presences on the religious stage of America. I reiterate that what I offer here is a subjective view of these developments and personalities. I do not claim that it is objective or comprehensive.

For any who do not know, I consider myself an evangelical, and my admiration and love for this movement will be evident in these pages. However, because I have had such a closeup view of things, I have seen the warts and blemishes—the shortcomings of this movement. I know some of its vulnerabilities and have my own convictions as to the issues and problems that must be dealt with if evangelicalism is to continue its incredible winning streak.

In the second part of this book, I will endeavor to set forth my own judgments and reflections on the definitive issues with which evangelicals will be forced to deal if they are to insure themselves a bright future. But for now, let us focus on what has happened to evangelicalism over the last half-century and take a brief look at those factors and key persons who have been instrumental in making it into what it is today.

I believe that evangelicalism has done so well at outdoing mainline denominational churches in growth and development for the following reasons:

1. It has an abundance of charismatic entrepreneurial leaders.

2. It is more effective at marketing religion.

3. It has learned how to exercise political power.

4. It has addressed the individualistic needs of Americans, avoiding taking positions on social issues that would alienate its constituencies.

Allow me to elaborate on each of these contributing factors.

EVANGELICAL ENTREPRENEURSHIP

Over the past fifty years, evangelicalism has been blessed with a host of innovative entrepreneurs. It has drawn into its ranks those whom the famous sociologist Max Weber would have called "charismatic personalities." Most famous among these leaders is Billy Graham, but there are others. James Dobson has created a vast radio audience with his program, *Focus on the Family.* Jerry Falwell began with his nationwide television show and has created a large university and a powerful political action group called the Moral Majority. The well-known television evangelist Pat Robertson also formed a reputable university that now has its own law school. He was the driving force behind the organization of the Christian Coalition, a political lobby that can sway national elections and made possible Robertson's own reputable run for the presidency. Another evangelical star is D. James Kennedy, who, out of his church in Fort Lauderdale, Florida, created Evangelism Explosion, a program of visitation evangelism that thousands of churches across the country utilize. More recently, Bill Hybels, a moderate voice in evangelicalism, has made his Willow Creek Community Church the model for a whole movement that is transforming churches around the world by using new worship styles that he calls "user-friendly."

A giant among evangelical leaders was the late Bill Bright, creator of Campus Crusade, which has become the most extensive evangelistic movement ever on college and university campuses across the country. Also included on this list of brilliant evangelical entrepreneurs is Loren Cunningham, the founder of Youth With A Mission, and George Verwer, the founder of Operation Mobilization. Their organizations have generated tens of thousands of young missionaries. The list goes on and on.

RATIONAL-LEGAL LEADERS VERSUS CHARISMATIC LEADERS

Mainline denominations, in contrast, find such charismatic leadership threatening. Those who rise through the ranks of denominational bureaucracies to roles of leadership are generally what Max Weber called "rational-legal leaders." In his book *The Theory of Social and Economic Organization,* Weber contrasts "rational leaders" with those whom he labels "charismatic personalities."

According to Weber, the charismatic leader gains authority through the dynamism of his or her own personality, whereas the rational-legal leader is specifically trained and gains a position of leadership by having prescribed credentials and living up to the role expectations set down by the organization. The rational-legal leader is a nonthreatening person who never rocks the organizational boat.

Weber contrasts the charismatic risk-taking leader, who is capable of initiating a new movement, with the "safe" rational-legal leader. While the charismatic leader professes, or at least suggests, that he or she has some special leading from some higher authority, such as God, the rational-legal leader gains a position of leadership by being elected via a constitutionally prescribed system and by having paid the proper "dues" to the organization through loyal service.

It is generally the rational-legal-type leaders who are appointed to the key leadership roles of mainline denominations. Consequently, it is not surprising that these denominations lack the kind of daring, innovative thinking and programming that can market religion. They do not connect well with our fast-moving, consumeristic society, marked by people who are attracted to exciting new approaches to things and who are more than ready to nurture "the cult of the personality."

Most of the evangelical leaders who have dominated the American scene over the past half-century have been colorful, bigger-than-life individuals who could electrify their followers with a "can-do" attitude and their ability to communicate a sense of God's having uniquely chosen them. Denominational leaders, on the other hand, usually come across as being good, decent people who have the background and training to qualify them for their jobs and who know how to maintain a smooth-running bureaucracy and keep the various factions within their respective denominations from causing schisms. This latter type of leader is very necessary for maintaining organizational stability and efficiency, but he or she is not the kind of person who bravely innovates, creating the kinds of programs and ministries that meet the needs of a quickly changing world. Rational-legal leaders play things safe, and it is that conservative disposition that prevents denominational leaders from making the changes that would enable their churches to be functionally adapted to a cultural system that is suffering from what Alvin Toffler called "future shock."

Contrast the organizational conservatism of denominational leaders with the bold charismatic entrepreneurship that has characterized the leadership of the evangelical movement. These charismatic-type leaders, to use Weber's label, step out in faith. With little, if any, financial resources, they do such things as start radio stations to broadcast the gospel in Third World countries; reach hundreds of thousands of teenagers by starting evangelistically oriented clubs such as Young Life and Youth for Christ on high-school campuses; found companies to produce evangelical films, videos, and books; establish entire nationwide networks for television and radio broadcasting; sponsor religious festivals that attract tens of thousands of people; and set up citywide evangelistic crusades.

The seminary-trained rational-legal leaders of mainline denominations are staid compared with the entertaining communicators who have become the superstars of evangelicalism. Charismatic leaders are a lot more interesting than the sincere, competent, but too often plodding leaders of mainline churches.

AVOIDING DENOMINATIONAL LABELS
AND DULL PREACHING

Of course there are exceptions to these ideal types outlined by Weber. There are some charismatic leaders within denominational leadership systems. It is not too difficult to find dynamic speakers within mainline churches, but to be honest, these leaders are usually highly evangelical, and they generally stay within their denominational churches in the hope of moving their denominations into more evangelical commitments and ministry patterns. It should be noted that there are still many growing congregations within mainline denominations, but these are churches that, for the most part, have a highly evangelistic message that calls listeners into "born-again" conversion experiences.

My friend Wil Willimon, dean of the Duke University Chapel and a prime example of a charismatic leader, who nevertheless possesses all the credentials of a rational-legal leader, says that the last person to join a mainline church probably did so somewhere around 1958. By no means is he suggesting that nobody has joined any mainline church since then. He is stressing only that over the last forty-some years, people have not been joining churches *because* of denominational labels. When people move into new neighborhoods, they do not necessarily look for the church that has the denominational label that was part of their family tradition and in which they were raised. Instead, they usually go church shopping and try out all the churches in town. They look for a church that will best fit the needs of their children. Usually, they end up in highly evangelistic churches, because these churches are most likely to have exciting programs for young people and interesting worship programs. That such churches often lack familiar denominational labels and go by such generic designations as "community church" or "family life center" is of no consequence to most church shoppers. Sometimes such vital churches are a part of mainline denominations, but if they are, their programs usually have very little in them that comes from denominational headquarters.

Leadership is the key to everything that makes for success. An academically qualified and properly ordained preacher can secure a pulpit within most mainline denominations. Hierarchal denominations such as the United Methodist Church and the Episcopal Church will somehow find pulpits for those who go through the ecclesiastically prescribed hoops. The net result is that mainline denominations have far too many churches being pastored by preachers who can deliver properly structured homilies but lack the ability to stir people to action or elicit intense commitment. On the other hand, the independent churches that characterize evangelicalism have pastors whose primary credential is the ability to draw and hold crowds of people. The boring, prosaic preacher has a short life in independent evangelical Christendom. Those who cannot cut it as pulpiteers soon find other lines of work, whereas denominationally placed preachers are moved from pulpit to pulpit, often to increasingly larger churches whether they can thrill a crowd or not. It is easy to figure out what the consequences of these differing types of leadership have been and will continue to be.

AT LAST: EVANGELICALS ENTER THE INTELLECTUAL ARENA

What has taken most observers of contemporary religion by surprise is that evangelicals have become effective combatants in the intellectual battle for the minds of Americans. There was a time when it was easy to write off evangelicals as fundamentalist buffoons who really didn't know much and who certainly were no match for the well-educated liberal thinkers who had graduated from such prestigious theological training centers as Harvard Divinity School, Union Theological Seminary, and the University of Chicago Divinity School. But that is no longer the case. Today, most evangelical scholars have top academic credentials and are more than capable of holding their own in clashes with those who would attack their conservative theology.

The transformation of the intellectual stature of evangelicals owes much to the writings and lectures of Francis Schaeffer. In the mid–twentieth century, this colorful, articulate scholar established a study center in Switzerland, where he held seminars and personally directed the studies of evangelical men and women who wanted to have some intellectual buttresses to support their shaky faith. Instead of simply defending evangelical theology, Schaeffer went on the offensive. He carried on a frontal attack on existentialism, which was the popular philosophical fad of the 1950s and '60s. His critiques of Marxism and secular humanism are still taken seriously by scholars.

Some have severely criticized Schaeffer's work. Many have contended that either he did not really understand what existentialism is all about or he dealt with it unfairly. But when all the critiquing has been said and done, everyone will have to agree that his great contribution to evangelicals was in establishing a model of how to engage successfully both liberal theology and secular philosophies. Following Schaeffer's example, evangelicals no longer ran away and hid when secular scholars tried to laugh off their orthodox beliefs and doctrines. Schaeffer showed that Christians could effectively confront those cultured despisers of evangelical thought in the intellectual marketplace. In today's world, evangelical scholars are everywhere, and they are holding high the colors of their faith. They have, as Scripture has instructed them, studied to show themselves approved unto God, rightly dividing the word of truth. But all of them owe a debt of gratitude to Francis Schaeffer, who set an example for evangelical scholars who want to do apologetics.

So well has this new breed of Christian scholars earned credibility that some of the well-established citadels of liberal thought have begun to bring them onto their faculties. Mark Noll of Wheaton College, that bastion of evangelicalism in Illinois, became a visiting professor at Harvard Divinity School, and Miroslav Volf, who was on the faculty at the evangelical Fuller Theological Seminary, has been recruited by Yale Divinity School. At Yale, Volf joins a one-time faculty member of the very evangelical Calvin College, Nicholas Wolterstorff.

A network of Bible colleges and Christian universities endeavors to train leadership for the evangelical movement. Parents once viewed these schools as safe havens for young, impressionable evangelical Christians. Afraid to send their children to secular institutions where they might be seduced by "worldly" professors, evangelical moms and dads regularly chose to send their children to these Christian schools. There, they believed, their children would be safe from seductive, secular doctrines, such as Darwinism and socialism. Today these schools do much better than that. Once looked upon as inferior academic institutions, many of these schools have gained high standing in academia.

There are now more than a hundred highly accredited evangelical institutions of higher education, many of which are listed in Barron's guide to America's top colleges and universities. Schools such as Gordon College, Westmont College, and Calvin College are listed among the very best in their respective regions. My own Eastern University has a faculty that stands head and shoulders above those at many secular schools. Wheaton College attracts a host of merit scholars to its student body each year and has a greater proportion of its graduates going on to earn PhDs than any other undergraduate school in the country.

While evangelical colleges and universities are reaching great heights academically, the colleges and universities founded by mainline denominations have become so secularized that it would be a mistake even to call some of them Christian institutions. Bucknell University and the University of Redlands, which were once American Baptist institutions, have given up their denominational identities. The same could be said of many Methodist and Presbyterian colleges and universities. Oberlin College, which once was the center for the revivalism of Charles Finney in the nineteenth century, is far removed from its Christian roots. Williams College, site of the historic Haystack Prayer Meeting that gave birth to the modern missionary movement, seems to have only a dim memory of its spiritual origins. I must recognize that a few mainline denominational schools, such as Whitworth College and Grove City College, still embrace a vital Christian emphasis, but most denominational colleges have, over time, become fully secularized.

If you are looking for places where Christian faith and academics are integrated into a unified world-view, it is best to look at the elitist evangelical schools, because they are where it's happening. Now, when it comes to vigorous orthodox Christian scholarship, elitist evangelical colleges and universities have taken the lead. Out of these institutions are coming a host of well-trained leaders who are going to take charge of the direction of American Christianity in the twenty-first century. This will prove to be significant for the future of evangelicalism. It guarantees that this movement will have the leadership it needs to promote its expansion.

EVANGELICALS MARKET BETTER

It has been said that Christianity started in Israel; was exported to Greece, where it was made into a philosophy; taken to Rome, where it was made into an organization; sent to Europe, where it was made into a culture; and sent finally to America, where evangelicals made it into a business enterprise.

When it comes to marketing their message, evangelicals come close to being geniuses. They have figured out how to market their message in attractive and entertaining ways that mainline denominations have never come close to matching. Evangelicals are the ones who developed contemporary gospel music and made pop stars out of their recording artists. They are the ones who made the book publishing business into a multimillion-dollar success, while denominational presses were struggling to stay in business. It was the evangelical leaders who had the entrepreneurial daring required to create the big "Jesus festivals," which look like Christian versions of Woodstock and draw hundreds of thousands of teenagers together at various places across the land. Evangelicals are the ones who have come up with innovative ways of proclaiming the gospel, such as their wide promotion of the *Jesus* film, which has been an instrument for converting hundreds of thousands to Christ across Africa and Asia.

Consider the fact that evangelicals own and run most of the Christian bookstores in America and see the marketing of Christian literature as a calling from God. Their stores generally sell only books by authors who are regarded as evangelically "sound." Authors know this and therefore are disinclined to write anything that the evangelical community would deem theologically suspect or dangerous. The gigantic annual Christian Booksellers Convention is an extravaganza that features only evangelical authors and speakers. The popularity of such authors is astounding. The Left Behind novels written by Tim LaHaye and Jerry Jenkins have sold over 140 million copies. Bruce Wilkinson's *Prayer of Jabez* is one of the bestsellers of all time. Frank Peretti has sold millions of copies of his novels featuring stories of Christians who struggle to stay faithful in spite of the onslaught of demonic attacks.

The Christian publishing business has consistently offered an array of books that not only promote a basically fundamentalist message but are easy reading and very enjoyable. Mainline denominations, on the other hand, often offer heavy theological tomes and deep biblical studies that appeal only to a specialized audience. Given those realities, religious publishing has become an evangelical domain, and what the evangelical press sells is impacting church people everywhere.

When it comes to the production of videos, once again evangelicals have left mainline denominations so far behind that comparisons are just about impossible. Bill Gaither has sold more than 20 million copies of his Homecoming videos, offering brilliantly produced southern gospel music to millions of mostly middle-aged and older listeners. The VeggieTales videos, featuring Christian morality plays starring animated vegetables, are wildly popular with children. Any Christian bookstore has for sale hundreds of talks and videos by key evangelical communicators.

The Internet has become the newest instrument employed by evangelicals to carry out their mission. Already they have created Web sites and Internet magazines by the scores. In evangelical chat rooms, inquirers can get a taste of the gospel, and there are attempts to create virtual-reality churches. Mainline denominations are not even in the picture when it comes to using this electronic tool, which is destined to dominate the future of religious communication.

THE GROWING POLITICAL POWER OF EVANGELICALISM

There was a time when evangelicals had little to do with politics and thought that the whole business was too dirty for Christians to touch. They were disengaged from the political process, and unlike the leaders of mainline denominations, they thought they could accomplish nothing worthwhile for the kingdom of God through government. But then everything changed. Evangelicals created a politically active constituency largely as a reaction to some of the things that were happening in Washington during the 1970s. This change came about, to a large extent, because of the Supreme Court's *Roe v. Wade* decision, which made abortion legal across the country.

When the Supreme Court voted in favor of Roe, it pushed a hot button among American evangelicals. They had always been concerned about the liberalization of sexual mores in America, but for them, making abortion legal pushed things too far. Television evangelist Jerry Falwell, who up to that time had gained very little national attention, was able to lead a crusade against abortion rights that made him one of the most well-known fundamentalist Christian leaders in America. Falwell used this issue as a rallying point for a new evangelical-based political movement that he called "the Moral Majority."

AN IMPORTANT APPENDIX

In discussing evangelicalism, it is important to recognize that what I've said here and found in the results of most surveys of evangelicalism pertains only to white

Christians. African-American churches do not fit the profiles generally drawn of evangelicals.

Almost all African-American churches have an evangelical theology and strongly affirm conversion experiences that bring people into personal relationships with Jesus. But unlike most white evangelicals, these believers have not allied with the conservative wing of the Republican Party. African-American Christians are deeply committed to addressing the concerns of the poor and oppressed, and most of them believe that the Democratic Party is more sensitive to these concerns than is the Republican Party. They view Republicans as being opposed to affirmative action and other entitlements that, over the years, have benefited African-Americans. Whether it is the Republicans in South Carolina who insist on keeping the Confederate flag emblazoned on their state flag or the Republicans in the White House who cut funding to the Leave No Child Behind program, African-Americans view Republicans as being opposed to their interests.

Another distinction between white and African-American evangelicals is that the separation between a Christianity that concentrates on winning souls to Christ and a Christianity that concentrates on social justice issues has never existed in most African-American churches. These churches have stressed the need for individuals to be "born again," but their preachers have made serving the poor and oppressed the responsibility of these "born-again" Christians. Conversely, white evangelicals have often tended to neglect social justice concerns and white liberals have been prone to ignore personal evangelism.

African-American churches, with their strong commitment to social justice, have been the breeding grounds for almost all of the leaders of the civil-rights movement. In most cases, those leaders have come from the ranks of their clergy. Rev. Al Sharpton, Rev. Jesse Jackson, Rev. Ralph Abernathy, and most important of all, Rev. Martin Luther King Jr. have all been Baptist preachers. Even those leaders who have not been members of the clergy have gained their training and experience for leadership within African-American churches.

For many years, in just about every case, prominent African-American Christians found their political home in the Democratic Party and viewed the religious right as being opposed to their interests. However, in recent years, this close connection between African-Americans and the Democratic Party has shown some signs of weakening. Many key African-American church spokespersons have sent a loud and clear message to the leadership of the party that their support had better not be taken for granted. They point out that the

Democratic Party, in trying to appeal to moderate voters, has been ignoring many of the concerns that are high on the African-American agenda.

Even more threatening to the Democrats is that President George W. Bush has made concerted efforts to broaden the base of the Republican Party by reaching out to people of color. Utilizing his faith-based initiative program, President Bush has made millions of dollars available to African-American churches to help finance many of their social programs. Church-sponsored tutoring programs, charter schools, and job training and day-care programs have been the recipients of generous government funding from the Bush White House. It remains to be seen if the help the president has given to these churches will translate into political support for his party and overcome the negativism toward Republicans that African-Americans have demonstrated in the past.

One possible enticement that might lure African-American Christians into the Republican camp is that party's embracing of what has come to be called "traditional family values." For the most part, African-American Christians have viewed the gay rights movement as anti-Christian, in spite of the fact that both Sharpton and Jackson have made being pro-gay part of their political agendas. There is, among most of them, a deep resentment toward the idea of treating the efforts to achieve social and political rights for homosexuals as part of the civil-rights movement. This puts African-Americans in harmony with spokespersons of the religious right such as Focus on the Family's Dr. James Dobson, who overtly promotes the Republican Party as the savior of traditional family values.

I have written this short aside about African-American Christians in order to point out that, while they hold to all that evangelicals believe theologically, they do not conform to the sociopolitical profile that characterizes most white evangelicals.

OTHER ETHNIC EVANGELICALS

Hispanic evangelicals generally are politically conservative. Those who have left Catholicism for Protestant Christianity usually have experienced conversion via the ministries of white evangelical missionaries. Consequently, Hispanic evangelicals tend to conform to the white evangelical profile and to have an affinity with the religious right. In this respect, they contrast with the Roman Catholic majority of the Hispanic community who are very much in the camp of the Democratic Party.

Asian Protestants also are highly evangelical and likewise identify with the conservative agenda of the Republican Party. The Asian emphasis on traditional family values aligns them with the religious right, and their work ethic is such that they find the entitlement programs of the Democratic Party unwarranted. Asian evangelicals fit very well within the framework of white evangelical Christianity. When they make their homes within mainline denominations, they usually exercise a strong evangelical influence on those denominations. As I have already pointed out, the United Presbyterian Church USA is having its liberal tendencies powerfully challenged by Korean members who have come to America after having been nurtured in the evangelical Christianity in their homeland.

White evangelical missionaries are primarily responsible for most of the conversions to Protestant Christianity in Eastern Europe and Africa. Consequently, Christians from these parts of the world who emigrate to America generally bring with them strong evangelical commitments. This is one more factor that adds to the strength and significance of evangelicalism within American Christianity.

In summary, ethnic evangelicals, apart from African-Americans, conform to the profile of white evangelicals and generally are embraced warmly by the socially and politically conservative white evangelical churches.

As brilliantly as evangelicalism has engineered its way into being the dominant expression of Christianity, it shows some danger signs. Increasingly, people are voicing resentments against the triumphalistic spirit of evangelicalism. Many of its key leaders have staked out positions on the crucial issues of our times in a way that makes them come across as right-wing, legalistic religionists.

To the secular society, evangelicalism generally appears to be a narrow-minded movement full of members who believe that they are the only truly "saved" and the only ones whom God will accept on Judgment Day.

Evangelicalism still has a great deal of momentum, but some wonder whether it harbors within itself the seeds of its own destruction. That question demands attention. The survival of evangelicalism is dependent upon its coming up with new ways to respond to those issues that it has been handling badly. In the next section of this book, I will endeavor to analyze and address some of those issues.

3

Do Evangelicals Have
an Image Problem?

A recent study by the Barna Research Foundation in Ventura, California, indicates that non-Christians have a very low opinion of evangelicals. On a list of people they respect, evangelicals ranked eleventh, followed by prostitutes in twelfth place.

While on Harvard's campus, I asked one of the professors why the folks there were so negative toward evangelicals. I said, "The Jews respect the Muslims, the Muslims respect the Jews, and everybody respects the Dalai Lama. But there are sneers of condescension if someone says, 'I'm an evangelical Christian'!"

The professor answered, "Imagine yourself at lunch. Seated at the table with you is the leader of the gay-lesbian task force, an ardent feminist, and an angry neo-Marxist African-American. You propose playing a game in which each of them is to respond to a word with the first word that comes into their minds. You say, 'evangelical.' How do you think each will respond?"

I said, "Given those three people, I suppose I would hear them say things like 'bigot,' 'homophobe,' 'male chauvinist,' and 'reactionary.'"

The professor then asked, "Now, to these same three, you say the name 'Jesus.' What reactions will you get to that?"

I paused a moment and then said softly, "Caring, understanding, forgiving, kind, empathetic . . ."

"Does it bother you, Tony," he asked, "that the name of Jesus elicits a completely opposite reaction from the name 'evangelical'?"

That does bother me. However, when I explained how bothered I was to a fellow evangelical, he said, "I really don't care what people like that think about us!"

Of course, that's the point. While evangelical Christians should never compromise what they believe in order to gain the approval of the secular community, we should care if people out there see little, or nothing, of Jesus in us. That being the case, we need to ask some very serious questions about ourselves.

WHERE EVANGELICALS AND OTHER BELIEVERS PART COMPANY

A friend of mine is part of a support group for parents whose children have AIDS. As this circle of brokenhearted mothers and fathers shared their concerns, one mother said, "My other two sons don't know about their brother having AIDS. I'm not worried about the older one, because he's so kind and affirming. But my youngest son has become an evangelical Christian, and from what he's already said about homosexuals, I know he'll be filled with contempt when he finds out why his brother is sick."

Last year, I had a debate with Gary Bauer on the campus of a leading evangelical college. In the course of our exchanges, I happened to say that America should show as much concern for justice for Palestinian people as they do for the security of Israel. I lost the evangelical crowd on that one.

I always try to point out to critics of evangelicalism that many of us do not fit their stereotypes. While we do tend to be overwhelmingly pro-life, when it comes to other issues, a significant minority of us are not part of the religious right. We are critics of the Bush tax cuts, which we see as a bonanza for the rich that necessitates cutting services to the poor (e.g., ending after-school tutoring programs for half a million children). We want universal health care, advocate legal protection for homosexuals, oppose what we see as a growing militarism in America, and are appalled by this administration's environmental policies.

Unfortunately, the religious right controls the microphone. They own almost all of the thousands of religious radio stations across the country and put on most of the religious television shows. Jerry Falwell and Pat Robertson are the celebrities of evangelical broadcasting; hence, they are primary definers to the rest of the world of what it means to be evangelical. Those of us who do not buy into their agenda have to either find a way to tell the world that there is a broad spectrum of evangelicals or come up with a new name.

DON'T MAKE UP YOUR MIND FOR ALL TIME

One of the first steps we must take to redefine ourselves is to overcome the primary generalization that secularists make about us—that is, that evangelicals are closed-minded. They see us as people whose minds are made up, who refuse to be confused with facts. When there is solid evidence that we might be wrong on an issue, we come across as people who dig in our heels and refuse to budge from our a priori declarations.

I believe that if we are to be taken seriously, we must be ready to recast our opinions on a variety of issues when the evidence suggests that we are wrong, even as we hold tenaciously to the core truths of the Christian faith. If we are going to carry on an honest dialogue with the rest of the world, we have to entertain the possibility that we might be in error even about some of those things about which we were so sure in the past. We will earn respect for our basic gospel message only if we do that.

As a case in point, I believe the Promise Keepers enhanced the credibility of evangelicalism when they publicly admitted that evangelicals had been wrong and repented of the racism that evangelicals had supported in the past. Evangelicals rise in stature when they confess that they were off in declaring the entire environmentalist movement to be a New Age plot. More and more Christians nowadays support this movement even while critiquing it.

I am pleased that, for the most part, the evangelical community has confessed that it was wrong ever to say that the horrendous pandemic of AIDS was some kind of special judgment of God on homosexuals. Those who still maintain this erroneous view ignore the fact that worldwide, in the overwhelming number of cases of AIDS, heterosexuals are spreading the disease. In Africa, 67 percent of those with AIDS are women and children, who got it through no fault of their own.

We hurt the testimony of the church when we hold on to opinions even when all the evidence proves otherwise. For instance, the church is still being ridiculed for its condemnation of Copernicus and Galileo and its insistence that the world was flat, when the two astronomers offered proof that the earth is simply another planet circling the sun.

In this book, I am going to argue that we evangelicals may have been wrong on some crucial social issues, even that we should question some of our theological assumptions. I believe that our credibility depends upon our being honest about our mistakes and open to new perspectives. We must not be like the little boy who, when asked to define "faith," answered, "Faith is believing what I know isn't true." We have to do much better than that. We must have a reason for the hope that lies within us (1 Pet. 3:15).

I AM AN EVANGELICAL

Right now I deem myself very much within the evangelical camp. My theology, my convictions about the authority of Scripture, and the self-transforming relationship that I have with Jesus are the credentials I offer to make this claim. However, there is much that I find worrisome and disturbing about some things a few prominent evangelical leaders have said over the last couple of decades, as well as some of the beliefs and practices these leaders have declared to be normative for evangelical churches. But these men and women, regardless of what faults and hypocrisies I find in their words and actions, and what faults and hypocrisies they find in mine, are still my brothers and sisters, and I want to embrace them as such for as long as they will let me. And I hope that they, in like manner, will want to embrace me. I do not want to be alienated from this community of Christians.

Fellowship, however, cannot be built on lies. Thus, I cannot lie about what I believe and think just to stay within the evangelical fold. I pray that my brothers and sisters in this faith community will have the grace to accept me, even when some of the things that I say and write are unacceptable to them.

I do not want you, the reader, to get the idea that I hatched the ideas that follow in isolation. I have discussed just about everything in this book with other Christian thinkers, some of whom are very well known in the evangelical community. I have listened to their critiques and given close attention to their suggestions. To my surprise, when I shared what I was thinking with these fellow evangelicals, I found much more agreement than I expected. Over and over again I heard words such as "I wish I could say those things, but it would be far too risky. I have a ministry to protect, and my ministry would lose the support of a lot of people—but I am glad that you are willing to step out there and say them."

THIS BOOK: AN EASY AND ARDUOUS TASK

This has been both the easiest and, at the same time, the most difficult book that I have ever written. It was easy to write because I have thought through, long and hard, each of the topics I touch upon here. The views and convictions that I have outlined in the pages that follow are the result of my own intense struggles, in which I have tried to resolve some of the most perplexing issues in my life. Despite long hours of reflection, however, I still come away with only limited clarity in my conclusions, so any confusion in what you read will be the result not only of my less-than-perfect efforts to express myself, but also of the fact that I have not finished thinking about the topics addressed in this book. I expect to wrestle with some of them as long as I live and am able to think.

On the other hand, writing this book has been very difficult for me because some of the things I have written may offend many of the fellow Christians whom I love and respect. Like most people, I want to be loved and affirmed, and I know I am risking losing relationships with some Christians who are near and dear to me by stating my opinions.

I am willing to take the risk of upsetting some of my most precious friendships because I believe that what I have to say is important. I know that some of the explanations of what I believe, think, and feel and have written about in this book have helped some people along my way. It is for the sake of others who might be helped that I have written these things. By sharing the ways in which I have thought through many of the issues that trouble Christians in our society, and by dealing in a straightforward manner with some of the problems that perplex those of us who are honest about our doubts, it may be that some sincere seekers will find aid. I would not put this book into print if I did not believe that my writings would assist many of those who presently verge on disillusionment and are losing confidence in a church that seems to evade essential controversy. I would not risk incurring arguments and losing friends if I were not convinced that what I say here could be important to some struggling Christians.

MY GOAL IS TO SAVE AND RESTORE, NOT DEMOLISH

Above all, among the fears and trepidations that I have about this book, there is one overriding concern that drives me to publish it, and that is the future of evangelicalism. I believe that if evangelicalism becomes frozen in practices and thought patterns that are not biblically founded, it will die. What worked in the past—as we "circled the wagons" and tried to ward off the attacks of biblical criticism coming out of German universities during the late nineteenth century and the modernist theologies that spread across America in the early years of the twentieth century—will not work in the years that lie ahead. New times bring new challenges, and evangelicals must be willing to take the risks that go with the creativity that is essential for dealing with those challenges.

I am not suggesting that I am some kind of special thinker who is re-creating evangelical theology and ethics in forms that will handle the challenges of the "brave new world" in which we must serve Christ. I am saying simply that I am taking risks in this book. I believe they are the kinds of risks that must be taken to keep evangelicalism alive. If I have pushed the envelope too far, please be forgiving, and correct me with gentleness. Know that, whatever the results, I have tried to do the right thing.

In *Thus Spake Zarathustra*, Friedrich Nietzsche wrote about a tightrope walker who slips and falls to his death. In the story, Prince Zarathustra praises the dead tightrope walker for having been a man who dared. Risk taking is a noble calling, and Nietzsche saw it that way. I accept that calling, and in accord with the instruction of the apostle Paul, I am trying to work out the implications of the salvation I have in Christ "with fear and trembling" (Phil. 2:12).

It is my hope and prayer that others will also take the risks that are necessary to make evangelicalism the innovative movement that it must be in order to live out its mission for the twenty-first century. In the eyes of so many, our churches have become the vital expression of Christianity, and it is far too easy for us evangelicals to think that we are all set for the challenges that lie in the years to come. Such is not the case!

If the coming generation is going to be in our fold, we must be the kind of dynamic, creative people who offer viable answers to their questions, and above all, we must be honest Christians. I am praying that what follows might offer a small contribution to such ends.

PART TWO

What Problems Lie Ahead?

4

Is Evangelicalism Sexist?

I got into big-time trouble when I declared to the 2003 gathering of the Cooperative Baptist Fellowship (a split-off from the Southern Baptist Convention) that those who prevented women from being ordained to the preaching ministry were perpetrating an evil practice. They were heated words, and some of my friends and relatives thought they were ill-advised. Looking back, I wish I could have found better ways to express what I felt, because I know that many basically good Christians disagree with me about this. It may have been that anger got the best of me. But behind my words, poorly chosen as they might have been, were some valid concerns, deep convictions, and strong feelings.

A host of negative reactions were forthcoming from the leaders of the Southern Baptist Convention, a denomination that a few years earlier had concluded a long-established practice of ordaining women. Not only did the Southern Baptists end the preaching and teaching ministries of many women who had been occupying Baptist pulpits and holding faculty positions in their theological seminaries, but they extended their opposition to women preachers overseas. The very day I made my strong statements against those who would keep women from the preaching ministry, I had met with some missionaries from Japan who were beside themselves because women clergy who had been faithfully pastoring churches in Japan were now being "defrocked," so to speak. A good bit of the passion for what I said stemmed from my reactions to what the Southern Baptists were doing to these missionaries.

Some will contend that my remarks in that sermon were too extreme. They suggest I should have limited myself to simply saying that I had a difference of opinion with my Southern Baptist brothers and sisters; that, in my opinion, they were wrong on the issue of women preachers. What my critics do not consider is that when it comes to the ordination of women, I am convinced that what we are dealing with is much more than just a debatable issue. Those who push women out of church pulpits are denying them what is crucial to their identities as persons. They are contributing to the dehumanizing of these women in ways that chauvinistic males are not likely to understand. Allow me to explain.

Preaching is my vocation. Part of my identity is wrapped up with this calling. In this respect, I am trying to imitate John the Baptist who, when he was asked who he was, did not answer, "I'm John, and my mother is Elizabeth." He didn't give his name or even his family connections. Instead, he gave his inquirers his calling. He told them, "I am a voice crying in the wilderness." John's identity was wrapped up in his calling, and I am somewhat like that. Take away my preaching, and you negate a good part of who I am.

I tell you all of this as a way of giving you some idea of why it is so destructive for those women who have a sense of calling to preach to be barred from that calling, especially for those who have spent years in training to live out that vocation. To these women, it means the destruction of who they are as persons. That's why I call it evil when a denomination wipes out the ordination of women.

SEXISM AS A PRINCIPALITY AND POWER

I believe in Satan, and I believe that the evils Satan wills to exercise in this world occur often through those social structures that the apostle Paul calls the "principalities" and "powers" (Eph. 6:12). In the theology of Walter Wink, these principalities and powers are much akin to what the classical social theorist Émile Durkheim called "social facts." They are, as Durkheim says, social structures that emerge from the interactions of people and have two characteristics: (1) they are external to the individual, and (2) they are endowed with the power of coercion by reason of which they control the feelings, acts, and thinking of individuals. These principalities and powers include the folkways and mores as well as the various institutions of a society. Within their domain is certainly the stratification system that assigns people their designated roles within the social order, along with the behavioral patterns that go with those roles. These principalities and powers exercise great control over people and significantly determine how they will think and act.

Racism is such a principality and power, and who can deny that it has had a dehumanizing effect on both the victims of racism and the racists themselves. The consumeristic value system that pervades our society, along with the commercialistic interests that feed it through television and the other instruments of the mass media, are also examples of how principalities and powers can exercise awesome influence over human behavior.

But it is sexism that is the focus of my attention as I write this chapter. And it was sexism that I was referring to when I called evil the effects on the women preachers now barred from their callings because of decisions made by the Southern Baptist Convention.

The ridiculous extremes to which the rejection of women preachers can go were evident at a gathering of Baptist leaders where the speaker was Anne Graham Lotz, the daughter of the famous Billy Graham. Anyone who has heard this woman will have to admit that she has inherited her father's gift for evangelistic preaching. Incredibly, when she got up to speak, a good number of men in the audience turned their chairs around so that she had to preach to their backs. It was their way of showing their contempt for women preachers.

I don't want to convey the idea that the Southern Baptist denomination is the only one that keeps women out of the ordained preaching ministry. Many other denominations do the same, including the fast-growing Assemblies of God. It is just that the Southern Baptists once allowed women to exercise that high calling, but now they have taken away that right. We could point to the Roman Catholic exclusion of women from the priesthood as being an example of another Christian denomination that limits the calling of women.

SPIRITUALIZED SEXISM LEADS TO HAVOC

When another theologian, Hendrikus Berkhof, did a scholarly exegesis of the Pauline use of the expression "principalities and powers," he contended, like Walter Wink, that demonic forces could use these institutionalized attitudes to wreak havoc among us. According to Berkhof, the evil one does harm to people through these superhuman agencies and often makes them into instruments of oppression. Such principalities and powers are the sexist attitudes that deny women the right to express their vocational gifts as preachers, and it is in this context that I assert that the denial of that right is evil.

Among contemporary theologians, such arrangements that diminish the dignity and humanity of persons by frustrating the will of God in their lives are referred to as "structural evils." A structural evil is one that exists apart from the conscious willing of specific individuals, but nevertheless exercises controlling influence on how groups of people think and act. For instance, slavery as an antebellum institution was a structural evil, in that it was a demonic means for the crushing of the freedom and well-being that God intended for the many people who fell under its curse. Individual Christians who had been born into the society that sustained that horrendous institution did not consciously decide to oppress the victims of slavery, nor could it be said that they were demonically possessed. But it is unlikely that many of them suffered any guilt over their participation in maintaining this institution. Nevertheless, the work of Satan was carried out through slavery, and lives were destroyed by it.

Other forms of structural evil can be found in the idolatry of the state that resulted in Nazism, as well as in the creation of what Dwight D. Eisenhower called "the military-industrial complex," which has fed the arms race around the world. Whenever I go to Durham or Winston-Salem, North Carolina, I encounter structural evil in a tobacco industry that helps to kill 450,000 Americans each year but has solid "born-again" workers keeping it going.

So it is that the sexism that oppresses women is another form of structural evil, and though its demonic character is not so obvious, it is still responsible for much destruction of the hopeful aspirations and the self-worth of many women. Sexism is especially reprehensible when it is carried out in the name of biblical Christianity.

A CLOSER LOOK AT SCRIPTURE

Those who defend the practice of barring women from the preaching ministry of the church claim that they do so in obedience to the authority of Scripture. Of all the passages of the Bible they are likely to quote, the one most often cited is 1 Timothy 2:11–12: "Let the woman learn in silence with all subjection. But I suffer not a woman to teach, nor to usurp authority over the man, but to be in silence."

Most of my fundamentalist friends set aside this same kind of commitment to literal obedience to the Scriptures with respect to behavioral requirements in the verses that immediately precede this passage. I refer, of course, to those verses that prohibit women from cutting their hair or wearing any form of jewelry: "In like manner also, that women adorn themselves in modest apparel, with shame-facedness and sobriety; not with broided hair, or gold, or pearls, or costly array" (1 Tim. 2:9).

I suppose that a literal interpretation of what Paul wrote in these verses would also have to apply to the wearing of wedding rings. I applaud the Amish for their consistency, even if I do not agree with their ordering the abolition of wedding rings from the fingers of their church members. But what perplexes me are those Christians who champion an adherence to a literal interpretation of Scripture when it comes to women preaching and teaching, then ignore what it says in adjoining verses about wearing wedding rings. Of course, this latter group of Christians will argue that we have to understand what the apostle Paul wrote about hair and jewelry in the context of the ancient sociocultural setting in which he wrote it. *Exactly!* And so must we understand Paul's words about women preachers.

The apostle Paul made clear that Jesus's death on the cross abolished the second-class religious status that women had in Judaism (Eph. 2:13–22) and that for Christians, the old divisions that favored circumcised Jewish males were no more: "There is neither Jew nor Greek, there is neither bond nor free, there is neither male nor female: for ye are all one in Christ Jesus" (Gal. 3:28).

Almost all restrained people who suddenly breathe the air of newfound freedom have a tendency to abuse that freedom, and so it was with many of the women of early Christendom. Social historians tell us this was true in the days of the early church. With their freshly discovered equality, women made exaggerated use of their right to speak at church gatherings. They often used the opportunity they suddenly enjoyed to speak to assemblies of fellow believers in ways that were disruptive to the church and humiliating to their husbands.

These women even took the occasions of church meetings to discuss the foibles and shortcomings of their husbands and to lecture them on what they should and should not do. Historians tell us that Paul spoke against such behavior; he told women that if they had such things to say, they should say them at home. This is one way to historically contextualize these verses so often used to prohibit women from preaching. Thus we allow for the declaration that the gifts of the Spirit, which include preaching (Eph. 4:11–12; 1 Cor. 12:8–11), were intended not only for men but for women to exercise as well.

Evangelical feminists point out that most of those who use 1 Timothy 2:11–12 to deny women the right to preach interpret this passage in a far too simplistic manner. The word translated here as "subjection" is a Greek word that means "to refrain from domination." Paul, they claim, was concerned that the liberation of women had gotten out of hand and that the men who used to be the oppressors were themselves beginning to be oppressed. He feared that some women were usurping authority from men instead of sharing it with them as equals. Furthermore, when Paul said that women should learn in silence, he was saying simply that they should show respect when men were preaching and teaching and not interrupt them, as some women supposedly were doing. What he gave as instruction about remaining silent was for *all* learners in the ancient Jewish world, whether male or female, and here Paul was reminding women that this rule still applied.

There can be no question that according to what the Bible states in Acts 2, the outpouring of the Holy Spirit on the church on the Day of Pentecost had led to women receiving the call to preach. "And it shall come to pass in the last days, saith God, I will pour out of my Spirit upon all flesh: and your sons and daughters shall prophesy, and your young men shall see visions, and your old men shall dream dreams: and on my servants and on my handmaidens I will pour out in those days of my Spirit; and they shall prophesy" (Acts 2:17–18).

Consequently, if there are women who have the gift of preaching, they ought not to "neglect the gift that is within them" (see 1 Tim. 4:14). To do so would be sinful, and those who perpetuate institutional practices that keep women from exercising their gifts for preaching are, probably unconsciously, doing evil.

BORN OF PERSONAL EXPERIENCE

All of this has special importance to me arising out of my own personal history. Undoubtedly, the most significant influence in leading me into a relationship with Christ was my mother. Both in words and in deeds, she showed me what Christianity was all about, and she motivated me into a life of vocational service to the church. In addition to that, she was the best storyteller I have ever encountered. She was able to take ordinary, everyday happenings and describe them in ways that made them seem bigger than life. She had an unparalleled gift for communicating what she believed and a brilliant story to illustrate any point she wished to make. There could be no doubt that God had given her the gift of preaching, but this was a gift that the church in her day would not allow her to exercise.

As I was growing up, she often talked about how she, as a teenage girl, had thought about running away from home and joining a small evangelical sect head-quartered in Zarephath, New Jersey, called the Pillar of Fire Mission. She told me that what kept her from doing so was that she was needed to take care of her several younger brothers and sisters, who were struggling to survive in the care of her widowed mother.

One day I asked my mother what was so special about the Pillar of Fire Mission, and she told me, "They let women be preachers." Then it dawned on me: my mother not only had the gift for preaching, but also had a sense of calling. Evil was the ecclesiastical ruling that kept her from living out that calling, and poorer was the church that was deprived of her extraordinary gifts.

THE DEEPER DAMAGE

Denying women the right to preach affects more than just those who are gifted and called to do so. This denial sends a message to all women, and especially to young girls who are trying to figure out who they are, that they are inferior to men. Oh, those Christian leaders who say otherwise will make their case by stating that just because women have different callings from those of men, they are not inferior. But I argue that when they tell women that they are barred from the high calling of God to preach because they *are* women, these leaders have made a sexist statement that drowns out any theological tap-dancing they may do on this reality.

Some sexists further argue that according to Saint Paul, there actually is an inferior status for women as the result of God's curse, because of what Eve did in bringing about the fall of Adam in Eden. I can only refer them to Scripture that tells us that in Christ, we have a new humanity, and in this new humanity the curse of the Fall has been undone (Rom. 5:14–21).

It is not as though no women held key roles of leadership in the history of the church. In the church at Philippi, we find that Euodias and Syntyche filled significant leadership roles. In Romans 16:7, we read how Paul sends greetings to Junia, a woman, to whom he refers as *a fellow apostle*. It should be noted that some recent translations, which have a male bias, have changed the name of Junia to Junias. To me it looks as if they wanted to conceal the truth that one of those who held the highest office in the early church was a woman.

We read in Acts 18:26 that Priscilla was one of the persons who instructed the young preacher Apollos about the work of the Holy Spirit: "And he began to speak boldly in the synagogue: whom when Aquila and Priscilla had heard, they took him unto them, and expounded unto him the way of God more perfectly." This is further evidence that women had a teaching role in the early church.

Thomas Cahill, the author of the best-selling book *How the Irish Saved Civilization*, points out that later in the history of Christianity, during that time when barbarians had overrun Europe, women again exercised key roles of leadership in the church. One of the last outposts of Western Christianity, in what was called the Dark Ages, was held in the north of Ireland. It was there, points out Cahill, that women sometimes controlled monastic communities. It was these women who often were the only spokespersons for the church.

In the history of the United States, we find that women were regularly preachers on the American frontier. Ironically, Baptists, who in their contemporary fundamentalist sectors now bar women ministers, had more female preachers than any other denomination. Women pastored almost half of all Baptist churches in the state of Maine in the mid–nineteenth century. This was also the case in half of the Baptist churches in Michigan and Wisconsin.

A study of Presbyterian missionary work on the American frontier shows that women carried out most of the pioneer excursions with the gospel to Native Americans living in the Dakotas. These heroic preachers ventured into territories fraught with danger. Ignoring threats of death, they faithfully carried out their calling to preach the gospel. The records show that these women often endured physi-cal hardships that would have caused most men to give up and go back to where life was safe and comfortable. There are accounts of how tribal chiefs became open to the gospel because the courage of these women preachers so impressed them. There are stories of how these women missionaries trudged through snow up to their waists in order to bring the message of Christ's salvation to their Native American brothers and sisters living on the plains of America. About none of these practices did the men in the wealthy prestigious pulpits back east complain.

For that matter, men have never seemed to object to women going off to difficult missionary assignments in the far corners of the earth. The matter of women preachers became a problem only when women wanted to be pastors back home, in the sometimes affluent neighborhoods that typically had churches pastored by men.

It seems odd to me that there are men, both in the past and even in the present, who have no problem with the idea that women can be sent overseas to difficult mission fields to preach the gospel, but these same men go ballistic when it comes to allowing women to preach to nearby audiences in their own country. There may be more than male chauvinism operative in all of this. There may be racism evident here.

Consider that there could be an unarticulated hierarchy established in their minds with whites at the top and blacks and other ethnic groups lower down. Consequently, white men can preach to anyone, but white women, while not free to preach to white men (their superiors), can preach to black men (in racist thinking, their inferiors). Black men, given this hierarchy, are able to speak down to black women. Black women, who are at the bottom of this social ladder, are not allowed to preach to anyone, save other black women. A great many questions need to be raised about such a pecking order.

THE *S* WORD: SUBMISSION

Male chauvinism has an even fuller expression among evangelicals when it comes to the matter of the interrelationships they often promote for husbands and wives. Some in the evangelical community use Ephesians 5:22–25 to make the case that wives must be submissive to their husbands. At first glance at this passage, it is easy to see how they might come to that conclusion. The passage reads:

> Wives, submit yourselves unto your own husbands, as unto the Lord.
> For the husband is the head of the wife, even as Christ is the head of
> the church: and he is the saviour of the body. Therefore as the church
> is subject unto Christ, so let the wives be to their own husbands in every
> thing. Husbands, love your wives, even as Christ also loved the church,
> and gave himself for it.

What men often ignore is that the verse immediately preceding this passage of Scripture calls upon married couples in the church to submit "yourselves one to another in the fear of God." Yes, it does say that wives should be submissive to their husbands, but doesn't this chapter of the Bible also say that husbands are supposed to love their wives *as Christ loved the church and gave Himself for it*? Every Christian who studies the Bible should know what that means.

Perhaps the best description of how Christ loved the church appears in Philippians 2:5–8, which reads:

Let this mind be in you, which was also in Christ Jesus: who, being in the form of God, thought it not robbery to be equal with God: but made himself of no reputation, and took upon him the form of a servant, and was made in the likeness of men: and being found in fashion as a man, he humbled himself, and became obedient unto death, even the death of the cross.

All Bible scholars know that the word translated here as "servant" in the King James version is in the original Greek language the word *doulos,* which is better translated as "slave." From that we can conclude that if a Christian husband wants to love his wife as Christ loved the church, he has to define himself as her slave. What wife would have trouble becoming totally submissive to someone who considered himself her slave? What all of this amounts to is a living out of each serving the other in love, even as Paul instructs them to do (Gal. 5:13).

You can imagine that in an ideal Christian marriage, the wife might say to her husband, "Honey, my dreams and aspirations are not as important as you actualizing your dreams and aspirations. I am willing to sacrifice all that I am, and all that I have, to help you to become all God wants you to be."

Then imagine him responding by saying, "Oh, no! It's the other way around. I'm ready to sacrifice all that I am and have to help you to become all that God wants *you* to be. I want to give myself to helping you live out the dreams and aspirations God has made part of *your* calling."

And then she says, "Oh, no! It's the other way around," and they have their first fight. It is the only kind of fight that Christians are allowed to have with each other, according to the Scripture that tells us to outdo one another in love, "but in lowliness of mind let each esteem other better than themselves" (Phil. 2:3).

Needless to say, this interpretation of what Paul is saying in Ephesians 5 does not fly well in many evangelical circles, and especially among those who want to use the Bible to legitimate the oppression of women and make them secondary to men in the hierarchy of the family.

You can hear the "submission of women" message broadcast daily on most of the thousands of Christian radio shows that blanket the country these days. Well-endowed evangelical ministries feed this line of thinking to hundreds of thousands who attend regularly held seminars on family life. These seminars draw people who are hungry for some help in trying to save their disintegrating families and are looking for some God-ordained instructions as to what to do.

THE ROLE PROMISE KEEPERS HAS PLAYED

These are tough times for those of us who champion the equalitarian relationships between husbands and wives and advocate what sociologists call the "democratic family structure"—a structure in which husbands and wives have an equal voice in the decision-making process. Even Promise Keepers, which I regard as the most constructive movement of our time in the building up of men to be good fathers and husbands, has a tendency to articulate a hierarchical structure. I can't say enough good about the overall impact of Promise Keepers on American family life. It has done an incredible job in re-creating responsible men. At a time when males, especially white, Anglo-Saxon males, have had to endure name-calling and put-downs, it is a relief to have this movement empower them to live out their obligations to their families and to the church. But the Promise Keepers' remarkable and wonderful accomplishments do not put them beyond a critique in this one area that has to do with male dominance.

A family system that disempowers wives may seem benign in Promise Keepers, because this movement has brought so many men into a saving relationship with Christ and has done so much good in inspiring husbands to become men who keep their marriage vows. But teachings about men being head of the house and exercising control over their wives have, in the wrong hands, had ugly and painful results. I know of situations wherein men have been led to believe that it is right to beat their wives if their wives do not do as they are directed to do. Those who run shelters for abused women can tell horror stories about women who believe they deserved the battering they received at the hands of their tyrannical husbands, because the pastors of their churches told them that Scripture supported submitting to such treatment. Thank God that Promise Keepers is a men's movement that is totally against that kind of submission teaching, despite the fact that they support a hierarchical marriage structure. Unfortunately, not all of the teachers and preachers in the evangelical community are as loving as Promise Keepers are in their attitudes toward women.

Recently I had a chance to support the claim that I really like Promise Keepers, in spite of my concerns about what they say about "headship" in the family. It happened when a reporter from a major newspaper called and asked my opinion of this movement. He was doing an article on Promise Keepers that would be syndicated in papers all across the country. He had called sociologists from various prestigious universities and had gotten a lot of negative feedback on the movement. One angry feminist, who taught women's studies in an Ivy League school, had told him that Promise Keepers was nothing more than an evangelical plot to put down women and to reestablish the old societal system with its oppressive male dominance.

Other sociologists explained the Promise Keepers phenomenon as a reaction to the constant battering of white, middle-class, capitalistic males by the rhetoric that blamed them for everything that is wrong in the world. The reporter had been told that white, Anglo-Saxon men in particular were fed up with being made the culprits for everything from racism and militarism to homophobia and the oppression of women and that Promise Keepers was the beginning of a countermovement against all of that. Evidently, someone had said to this reporter that to make his story complete, he ought to interview at least one evangelical sociologist for some comments and reflections. And that is why he gave me a call.

As I listened to what the reporter had heard from others, I asked if he himself had ever attended a Promise Keepers weekend. After a long and poignant pause, he slowly answered, "No." Then I asked him if he thought it fair to write about Promise Keepers when he had never experienced firsthand what they were all about—when he was depending on the opinions of others who had not attended any of these gatherings either. Fortunately, there was a huge Promise Keepers get-together in Colorado just a few days later, and I told him that he could get in on it.

At my urging, this reporter attended his first Promise Keepers weekend. I say it was the first because what happened to him so impacted his life that he went to others over the next couple of years. He himself became a committed Christian, and he concluded that while he had to disagree with what Promise Keepers said about men being the final authority in the decision-making processes of the family, he had come to believe his wife welcomed the changes that had taken place in his life because of these meetings. She said that the results in her husband were superb; she could not say enough good about the transformation in both her husband's attitudes and his behavior.

AT THE HEART OF THE CONFLICT

From time to time, I am asked to speak on the topic of marriage and the family at churches and other Christian gatherings. During the question-and-answer sessions that usually follow these presentations, it is not unusual for some man to stand and say, "You haven't answered the *real* question." And when I ask, "What *is* the real question?" he answers, "Who's supposed to be the head of the house?"

When I hear such a question, I am inclined to say, "If you were really a Christian, you wouldn't ask a question like that. The Christian never asks who's going to be master. Instead, the Christian asks who's going to be the servant. A true Christian never asks who's going to be first in any hierarchy but rather asks who's going to be last."

Fortunately, I don't have to be that tough in my answer. All I have to do is read what Jesus said about all of this when He taught His disciples: "And he sat down, and called the twelve, and saith unto them, If any man desire to be first, the same shall be last of all, and servant of all" (Mark 9:35).

Then I simply ask how he could apply this Scripture in answering the question he just asked.

FEMINISTS VERSUS EVANGELICALS

Feminists have generally regarded evangelicals as their enemies. It did not help the relationship when evangelicals provided some of the most extensive opposition to the Equal Rights Amendment of the U.S. Constitution, which would have guaranteed women a host of rights that the promoters of the amendment believed were being denied them. Supporters of the amendment were concerned over such things as women finding it difficult at times to establish credit with banks and securing proper treatment from insurance companies.

Just as it seemed that the last few states were about to ratify the amendment to make it the law of the land, some leaders of the evangelical establishment took notice and mobilized against it. Christian radio stations blared out condemnations of the amendment, calling it "antifamily." Prominent women speakers and authors who carried the banners in the fight against the amendment became the darlings of the evangelical conferences and conventions. Marabel Morgan and Phyllis Schlafly became household names in evangelical circles, and it wasn't long before a juggernaut of opposition ensured that the amendment would be defeated—and it was.

The inflammatory rhetoric that put the opposition to the amendment in high gear included warnings that the amendment could lead to women being drafted into the military in times of war, leaving husbands and children behind. Another hot button that stirred reactions in the evangelical community was the claim that if the amendment passed, women would have equal access to men's public toilets. That really caused a lot of excitement in the evangelical camp.

Without going into the pros and cons of whether the amendment was a good or a bad thing, I can say there is no doubt that battle lines were drawn, with feminists on one side and evangelicals on the other. To claim to be an "evangelical feminist," as I do, was and is an oxymoron to most people, and it will take a long time before rapprochement between evangelicals and feminists will become any kind of a reality.

Adding to the conflict is the extreme difference over abortion rights. The feminists, for the most part, are pro-choice and have made their claim to complete access to abortion-on-demand a keystone of their agenda. Evangelicals, on the other hand, have made being pro-life a defining requirement for any who want to be accepted within their camp.

These differences have made it very difficult for those Christian feminists who belong to such groups as Evangelicals for Biblical Equality to explain themselves to either side. On the one hand, most of those who belong to this group, being evangelicals, are pro-life. This makes them suspect among most other feminist groups. But their strong commitments to the rights of women (which includes a woman's right to be a preacher) put them in questionable standing with their other evangelical brothers and sisters.

ONE OF THE FIRST FEMINISTS

It is a strange turn of events that feminists and evangelicals should stand in such diametrical opposition to each other, since it was evangelical Christianity that gave the feminist movement a great deal of its initial impetus. Going back to the nineteenth century, we find in Charles Finney a strong advocate for women's rights. Finney, the dominant American evangelist at that time, called for people who committed themselves to Christ to follow through with this commitment by working for the justice that he believed Christ wanted to actualize in the world. His message was about a holistic salvation and is best known for its opposition to slavery. Lesser known was his strong support for the liberation of women.

Finney wanted women to be able to actualize all their God-given potentialities. This preacher, whom many have called the Billy Graham of his day, contended that women should be free to exercise all their gifts in all sectors of society. He believed that women should be free to be leaders in the political and economic sectors of society, as well as in religious institutions. When people committed themselves to Christ, Finney wanted to know whether they would join either the antislavery movement or the newly emerging feminist movement. Not only did Finney give religious legitimation to the feminists, but his revivals became a major source of recruits for their movement.

Those of us in the twenty-first century who seek to bridge the chasm between evangelicals and feminists need to talk about the roots of feminism in evangelical revivalism, but we have to do much more than that. We must also offer some ideological alternatives to what seems to be an ongoing impasse to any meaningful reconciliation between feminists and evangelicals. We need to provide alternatives to the rhetoric that sets these two groups against each other. I want to offer up one such alternative here, which might contribute to this end. It is a way of talking about becoming complete persons in Christ and doing so in a way that I hope feminists will find attractive. It is an approach that offers a liberating alternative to the cultural oppression that both females *and* males endure daily. It is about what it means to become members of a new humanity created through the power of the Holy Spirit.

BECOMING WHOLE AND COMPLETE PERSONS IN CHRIST

In Colossians 2:9–10, we read these words: "For in him dwelleth all the fulness of the Godhead bodily. And ye are complete in him, which is the head of all principality and power."

As we reflect on this passage, we must ask ourselves what it means to become "complete in him." I have been intrigued with that question ever since I read the fascinating theories about human personality set forth by the great psychologist Carl Jung. According to Jung, the process of socialization has distorted all of us into being incomplete persons. Jung goes on to say that the psychological maladies that plague so many of us are in one way or another related to this distortion. He argues that men are socialized to suppress those dimensions of their humanity that our culture assigns to women. Likewise, Jung contends that those traits of being human that our society has ascribed to men are traits that we require women to suppress. In other words, members of both sexes are skewed persons, in that society requires each to suppress traits of humanness that only the other sex is allowed to express.

Interestingly, ancient Chinese philosophers set forth exactly the same theory of personality in their description of how what they call *yin* and *yang* are manifested in our lives. Yin, say these ancient philosophers, is akin to what we mean by feminine personality traits. On the other hand, yang comprises personality characteristics that we associate with masculinity. We can achieve holistic health and well-being, they say, when yin and yang are in perfect balance with each other. Following this formula, if we are to be "whole" persons, men must recover the yin that they have been required to suppress, while women must recover their yang.

There are those who are critical of using concepts from an ancient Chinese philosophy to provide insights for a Christian understanding of human personality. I must remind such critics that the apostle Paul used teachings of pagan Stoic philosophers, as in Acts 17:28, when he found them useful in making his case for the gospel. All of us have heard preachers refer to ideas and insights provided by Plato and Aristotle in their sermons, and scholars are well aware that John Calvin developed much of his theology in line with Plato's teachings, even as Thomas Aquinas leaned heavily on Aristotle in developing his. Surely we are not so Eurocentric as to believe that truth can be found only in Western philosophers.

To those who ask, "Aren't the yin and yang concepts incorporated into the New Age movement?" I ask in return, "Isn't the same true of teachings from Plato and Socrates?" The New Age movement, like all heresies, steals truths and uses them to propagate its falsehoods. I contend that there are insights in Chinese philosophy that can help us, and we should not allow those insights to be the sole prerogatives of the New Age movement.

I find much that is attractive in the way that the concepts of yin and yang help us to understand the call to wholeness in Jesus. I think it helps us to overcome the cultural disfiguration of both men and women that culture has imposed on us. I think that it can also help us transcend some harmful stereotypes of femininity that the evangelical community too often reinforces. I believe that by using insights from Jung and the ancient Chinese, I can come up with a model for humanness for each of the sexes that will galvanize feminist tendencies in evangelicalism and enable feminists to see some positive possibilities in the evangelical camp. What I am proposing is that culturally prescribed distortions can work themselves out in women, as well as in men, through transformations of personality that can come as a work of the Holy Spirit. I believe that as members of both sexes submit to the changes wrought by the Spirit, we will become more and more like Jesus, whom the Bible declares the perfect person—the only complete human being who has ever balanced the yin and the yang, or as Jung would refer to these dimensions of being fully human, *"anima* and *animus."*

PERFECT BALANCE: ILLUSTRATION #1

To define the differences between yin and yang and to give some clarification to make these rather abstract concepts more concrete, I think it might be helpful to offer some illustrations. First of all, yin, according to Chinese philosophy, is very person-oriented, while yang is principle-oriented. That means that sensitivity to how other persons will be affected tends to determine the ways in which women react to the situations of everyday life. They tend to be more concerned about how people around them are thinking and feeling. In diametrical opposition, men tend to be more strongly guided by principles. As a case in point, let me describe a situation in which the feminine and masculine played themselves out against each other.

A friend of mine and his wife went for an evening's entertainment to the Valley Forge Music Fair. This no-longer-existing venue for Broadway musicals was for Philadelphia suburbanites who did not want to venture into the city. Being middle class, they arrived at about 7:45—fifteen minutes before showtime. Sociologists will tell you that middle-class Americans are like that. Generally, they try not to arrive late, nor do they arrive very early. Middle-class folks, say sociologists, usually arrive between fifteen minutes and five minutes before showtime. That meant that at 7:45, a thousand cars suddenly appeared on the highway leading to the theater, lining up to squeeze through the one and only entrance to the parking lot. My friend was in one of the first cars in line.

The parking lot attendant came over to his car and said, "Fifty cents to park here, mister!"

My friend picked up the newspaper that advertised the evening's show and pointed out the line that read "Free parking."

The parking attendant responded, "Look, mister, you don't give me the fifty cents, you don't park here."

"That's fine!" my friend answered. With that, he rolled up the windows of his car, turned off the ignition, folded his arms, and just sat there. His car was blocking the only entrance to the parking lot. Cars were backed up in both directions on the highway. People were shouting all kinds of things at him. Yea, they were saying all manner of evil against him, but he was not budging.

In the meantime, his wife had crawled under the dashboard and was pleading, "Give him the fifty cents! It's a lousy fifty cents! For fifty cents, you're ruining my evening. Everybody's *looking* at us."

Please note that she was concerned about people—how the people in the other cars were reacting and what they were thinking. He, on the other hand, could not have cared less about the people as he shouted, "It's not the fifty cents! It's the *principle* of the thing."

She based her reactions on the people around her—she was person-oriented. On the contrary, principle guided his reactions—he was principle-oriented.

PERSON, PRINCIPLE, AND JESUS

The individual who is "complete" is perfectly balanced between being person-oriented and being principle-oriented. Such an individual is Jesus. He is the flawless balance between the feminine and the masculine. That is why both men and women can find in Jesus the incarnation of what each sex is meant to be. In Jesus is a person who, for males, has overcome the cultural pressures to suppress the yin qualities of humanness. On the other hand, Jesus offers to women the model of someone who is able to counterbalance yin qualities with yang and be more assertive. That is why I can tell women to be like Jesus, just as I can tell men to do the same. He is the picture of the fullness of humanity that transcends the cultural stereotypical categorizations of masculinity and femininity. Thus, in accord with Colossians 2:10, each of the sexes becomes complete in Him.

In the New Testament, we find many illustrations of how Jesus lived out this balance, but His dealing with the woman caught in adultery is my favorite (John 8:1–11). In this story, the Pharisees dragged the woman before Him and threw her at His feet. They reminded Him that according to the principles Moses laid down in the Torah, they should stone the woman to death for her sin. They waited to see if Jesus, whom they knew to be compassionate, would allow His feelings to negate the Mosaic principle.

Everyone knows what happened next. Jesus stooped down and began to write in the dirt, saying, "Let the one who is without sin throw the first stone." There is no indication of what He wrote, but I suspect that He listed the names of the men who stood around with rocks in their hands, including alongside their names the sins they had committed that also called for stoning. One by one, these Pharisees slipped away. Then Jesus asked the woman, "Where are your accusers?"

The woman lifted her head and was stunned when she realized what had happened. She answered, "They're all gone, Lord!"

His empathy in her time of disgrace and fear constrained Him to give her another chance. That was an expression of yin. However, He followed that up with the reaffirmation of the principles of the Torah by saying, "Sin no more!" Over against the softness that our society assigns to women, Jesus demonstrated a firmness for the principles of biblical law.

It is that kind of balance that both men and women in our society must strive to achieve as they seek to become "complete" persons.

PERFECT BALANCE: ILLUSTRATION #2

A second dichotomy that illustrates the differences between yin and yang is that yin is very oriented to being conscious of the physical side of life; hence, women pay great attention to the physical conditions around them as the five senses register them. Yang, on the other hand, is focused on the abstract and ideological dimensions of life. In other words, men are trained not to pay much attention to the physical dimensions of life, but to live out their lives in a world of abstract concepts and ideas.

This dichotomy has especially worked itself out in the life of the church. When men dominate church life, all attention is given to prepositional truths. Abstract theological concepts, such as justification by faith, substitutionary atonement, and doctrines related to predestination versus free will, become the primary concerns of church life. This is a yang emphasis.

On the other hand, when women are allowed to express themselves in the life of the church, the emphasis changes to the physical needs of life and the ways in which the Christian church should address those needs. With yin comes the social concerns of Christianity, and then we have a church that concentrates not so much on theology, but on the need to feed the hungry, clothe the naked, and care for the needs of the downtrodden. Theology becomes quite secondary in this yin mind-set.

Another way of thinking about these differences is balancing the yang of Calvinism, with its logical deductive system of doctrines, and the charismatic movement, with its emphasis on *feeling* and experiencing God's presence. Whereas Calvinists focus on addressing the need for right beliefs, charismatic Christians, with their tendencies toward yin, make healings, speaking in tongues, and other "manifestations of the Spirit" their major concern.

Again, we find in Jesus a balance between the two. In Jesus, we encounter a God who reaches out to us both with truth that meets the needs of the mind and with healings that meet the needs of the body. In Christ, we find a God who not only offers us doctrinal truths to comprehend, but also makes meeting the social and material needs of people (through what some have called "a social gospel") a basis for judgment when God shall judge the nations (Matt. 25:32–46).

PERFECT BALANCE: ILLUSTRATION #3

A third expression of the dialectical tensions between yin and yang can be found in the awareness that the masculine requires the establishment of order and structure, whereas the feminine is likely to embrace spontaneity. We find this differentiation in a variety of examples within the expressions of Christian worship. For instance, in prayer, those with a yang emphasis require a format to their prayers. A good prayer, given a yang disposition, incorporates a definitive structure that requires the following components: adoration, confession, supplication, and intercession. *The Book of Common Prayer* in the Anglican, Lutheran, and Presbyterian churches has such structured prayers in its liturgies.

Contrasted with yanglike praying is the kind that is emerging in charismatic churches. With these particular Christian communities, prayers, to the outsiders, might seem chaotic. These Christians pray "in tongues." Their prayers express "groanings" that cannot be put into the words of our normative languages: "Likewise the Spirit also helpeth our infirmities: for we know not what we should pray for as we ought: but the Spirit itself maketh intercession for us with groanings which cannot be uttered" (Rom. 8:26). The prayers in these churches are spontaneous outpourings of the heart and soul, and they follow no established forms prescribed by ecclesiastic authorities.

There are other ways of praying besides those expressed by charismatics that are demonstrations of what we mean by yin or what the culture might designate as being feminine that are found in the prayers of such medieval saints as Teresa of Ávila and Julian of Norwich. Contemplative prayer, for instance, is very much in accord with what could be considered yin. This contemplative praying, which we find fairly common within Catholicism, is growing in popularity among Protestants. In my own life, I try to start each day with a kind of prayer that is less structured and more of an experience of surrendering to the flow of the Holy Spirit. For several minutes I get "centered down" on Christ. I drive out of my consciousness, as much as possible, all the thoughts and concerns of the coming day that rush into my mind the moment I wake up. What I seek is quietude—the creation of what the Celtic Christians called "the thin place."

The thin place is a condition in which the presence of the sacred becomes so real that the mundane becomes unreal. It is a sense that "the Holy" has flooded the room. In the stillness of such a time, I *feel* myself penetrated by the divine. I experience Jesus invading my heart, mind, and soul. I feel in these special times, at their best, something of what the sociologist/theologian Rudolf Otto called "the *mysterium tremendum*." I am not quite sure exactly what Otto meant by this expression, but whatever it was, he verbalized the sense of being encompassed by that which is sacred. This is the kind of prayer the prophet Isaiah proposed when he wrote: "But they that wait upon the LORD shall renew their strength; they shall mount up with wings as eagles; they shall run, and not be weary; and they shall walk, and not faint. [God speaking:] Keep silence before me, O islands; and let the people renew their strength: let them come near; then let them speak" (Isa. 40:31–41:1).

Someone once asked Mother Teresa what she said to God when she prayed. She answered, "I don't say anything. I listen!"

When the interviewer followed that up by asking, "Well, then, when you pray, what does God say to you?" she answered, "God doesn't say anything. God listens, and if you don't understand that, I can't explain it to you."

I do understand what Mother Teresa was saying. She was talking about the kind of praying that I do at the start of the day, wherein I do not make any requests or petition God for anything. Instead, in the stillness of the morning, I simply surrender to the unseen but spiritually felt presence of God's love.

PRAYER AND JESUS

With Jesus, once again, we find the balance. He taught His disciples a disciplined prayer that we call the Lord's Prayer (Matt. 6:9–13). That prayer is perfectly structured with a simple but encompassing listing of all that theologians contend goes into a "sound" prayer. But in addition to that yanglike prayer was

His admonition to His disciples to "go into a closet and shut the door"—and in the stillness and darkness of that setting to meet God in secret (see Matt. 6:6). Jesus Himself went apart from everybody else to have such times of aloneness. In His quietude, He experienced a renewal of all the dynamism coming from His heavenly Father.

MASCULINITY, FEMININITY, AND CHAUVINISM

My reason for spelling out this very incomplete listing of the complementary but different characteristics of yin and yang is to give one way evangelicals might move beyond the male chauvinism and sexism that are so often evident in our ideologies and practices. I am not advocating what might be called "the feminist agenda," with any of its variant expressions. What I am suggesting here is that evangelicals abandon the stereotypical differentiations of male and female and find in Christ the declaration of a new humanity that He incarnates for all of us. This new humanity revealed in Him would liberate us from playing culturally prescribed roles and help us achieve the balance that goes with the complete dimensions of personhood that Jesus incarnated.

We need an alternative to both the male chauvinism that too often has expressed itself in evangelicalism and the radical feminism that, in my opinion, simply tries to imitate the imbalanced traits of yang-oriented males, which are all too evident in our society. That alternative is allowing ourselves to be transformed into what He is: "Beloved, now are we the sons of God, and it doth not yet appear what we shall be: but we know that, when he shall appear, we shall be like him; for we shall see him as he is" (1 John 3:2).

5

Are Evangelicals Handling the Gay Issue All Wrong?

Arguments over homosexuality have become one of the most divisive problems in Christendom. Whether it's at the international gathering of Anglican bishops at the Lambeth Conference or the meeting of Presbyterian leaders at their General Assembly, this issue is certain to be a major source of conflict. It seems that every major denomination is on the verge of schism over whether or not to allow persons who are in homosexual liaisons into their pulpits, or even into church membership.

Heated discussions go on in local congregations. There are conflicting opinions on this issue even within my own family. My wife, Peggy, believes that the church should legitimize gay marriages because she thinks that lifelong commitments by people who love each other enhance their humanity. I hold to a more conservative view, believing that same-gender eroticism cannot be reconciled with Scripture.

What makes matters worse is that on each side of the argument, people demonize those on the other side. For many evangelicals, this is a defining issue, and they say that to approve of homosexual marriages is to throw out the Bible. They even question whether they can stay in a church or a denomination that does not agree with their stand.

While I believe that this is an important issue, I do not think it is a defining one. We must not allow ourselves to think that those who differ with us on the matter of homosexuality are less Christian or even less committed to Scripture than we are. Differences over this issue should not be the cause of church schism. My wife and I are evidence that it is possible to have opposing opinions on this subject without getting a divorce.

I define an evangelical Christian as one who takes the Bible seriously as an infallible guide for faith and practice, who believes in the doctrines the Apostles' Creed sets forth, and who has a personal spiritual relationship with the resurrected Savior. As far as I am concerned, other issues are secondary. As each of us strives to work out his or her understanding of what is expected in Christian living, we must do it "with fear and trembling." We must learn to be humble enough to realize that we only "know in part"—and must wait for that time to come when the fullness of truth will be revealed.

I often address the homosexual issue in my sermons, and I do so with as much empathy as I can muster. I call upon the church to stop making same-gender eroticism into some kind of supersin that somehow warrants parents throwing away their children or barring people from the church. I plead with the church to join in efforts to grant full civil rights to gay men and lesbians and to make the church into a safe place, where no preacher will issue denigrating rhetoric or ignorant generalizations to hurt them.

For doing that, I have been subjected to extensive criticism and had some speaking engagements canceled. I am accused of being too sympathetic to homosexual people. One of my friends asked why I was willing to risk my career by preaching for justice for gay men and lesbians. Well, I'll tell you why. I'm trying to make up for a horrendous failure during high school.

ROGER

Roger was gay; we all knew it, and we all made his life miserable. When we passed him in the hall, we called out his name in an effeminate manner. We made crude gestures, and we made Roger the brunt of cheap jokes. He never took showers with us after gym class, because he knew we'd whip him with our wet towels.

I wasn't there the day some of the guys dragged Roger into the shower room and shoved him into the corner. Curled up on the floor, he cried and begged for mercy as five guys urinated all over him.

The reports said that Roger went to bed that night as usual, and that sometime around two in the morning he got up, went down to the basement of his house, and hanged himself.

When I heard about Roger, I realized that I wasn't a Christian. I was a theologically sound evangelical, believed all the points of the Apostles' Creed, and had declared Jesus to be my Savior. But I know now that if the Holy Spirit had actually been in me, I would have stood up for Roger. When the guys came to make fun of him, I would have put one arm around Roger's shoulder, waved the guys off with the other, and told them to leave him alone and not mess with him, because he was my friend.

But I was afraid to be Roger's friend. I knew that if I stood up for a homosexual, people would say cruel things about me too. So I kept my distance. If I had done better, who knows if Roger might be alive today.

I am not asking that Christians gloss over biblical teachings, nor that we justify same-gender eroticism. I am simply reminding Christians that we are supposed to love people—even those we have been socially conditioned to despise. I am calling upon Christians to reach out and show kindness and affection toward their homosexual neighbors—who number at least fifteen million in the United States.

ORIENTATION VERSUS BEHAVIOR

Before we get into any discussion of Christianity and homosexuality, I need to give some definitions and explanations. The first is to differentiate between sexual *orientation* and sexual *behavior*. If a person desires sexual intimacy with another person of the same sex, he or she has a homosexual *orientation*. If a person engages in a sexual act with another person of the same gender, that would be homosexual *behavior*. Sexual orientation refers to what a person *fantasizes* about doing. *Behavior* refers to what a person actually *does*. It should be noted that the Bible talks only about homosexual *behavior*. It does not deal with *orientation*.

Second, we must avoid talking, as many preachers do, about *the* homosexual lifestyle. In reality, there are as many homosexual lifestyles as there are heterosexual lifestyles. For instance, some homosexuals adopt promiscuous lifestyles, and some choose to have monogamous, committed relationships. Still others (and within the Christian community, most) remain celibate.

Most mainline denominations have taken a position that evades condemning a homosexual orientation, but at the same time they refuse to condone any homosexual lifestyle other than celibacy. Hence, they do not condemn people for having the orientation, but they view *practicing* homosexuals as living outside of biblically prescribed behavior.

I personally know many Christians with homosexual orientations who fight against their desires for homosexual behavior through the power of the Holy Spirit. The desire to experience sexual gratification through physical involvement with persons of their own sex is a constant (just as heterosexual desire can be a constant) for many of them, but they are more than conquerors through Christ who strengthens them (Rom. 8:37; Phil. 4:13).

I cannot help but admire these brave saints who endure lives of sexual frustration because of their commitment to what they believe are biblical admonitions against homosexual eroticism. Many such Christians have told me about their long nights of spiritual agony, as they have struggled against the flesh to remain faithful to what they are sure is the will of God. Any who believe that these homosexuals who remain celibate for the sake of Christ are anything less than glorious victors in God's kingdom ought to be ashamed of themselves.

HOMOSEXUALITY: INNATE OR DEVELOPED?

The one thing I do know about homosexuality is that nobody really knows its causes. There are many theories, but there is not enough empirical evidence to give a conclusive explanation as to why some people are oriented to being sexually attracted to others of the same gender.

Some theories propose that the homosexual orientation is inborn. For instance, one inborn theory is a genetic explanation, citing the claim of geneticist Dean Hamer that the Xq28 gene is the cause of homosexual orientation. Others point to the findings of a seldom-cited study suggesting that if a mother is under severe stress in the late stages of pregnancy, the flow of testosterone that imprints the brain of the male fetus is disrupted. This disruption results in a male fetus's failing to be programmed for a heterosexual orientation.

A few years ago, a study done at the Salk Foundation provided further support for an inborn explanation of the homosexual orientation. The study gave evidence that the structure of the brain of the male homosexual, especially the size of the hypothalamus gland that drives sexual behavior, was more akin to a female brain than to a male brain. However, the study is questionable, since the sample of brains studied was limited and confined to gays who had died of AIDS.

On the other hand, some theories suggest that homosexual orientation is not inborn. A more recent psychotherapeutic theory has become very popular in some evangelical Christian circles. This theory is connected with the "reparative therapy" being promoted by both Elizabeth Moberly and Joseph Nicolosi.

The reparative therapy theory puts a different twist on Freud. While in agreement with Freud that relationships with parents lie at the bottom of the problem, Moberly and Nicolosi both go on to claim that when a child has trouble relating to his or her parent of the same sex, homosexuality results. In short, homosexuality occurs because of conflicts and deprivations that occur in a girl's relationship with her mother or a boy's relationship with his father.

Perhaps most common is a proposal that homosexual orientation results from one's being molested or raped in the early years of psychological development. In reality, there is not enough evidence to support *any* theory conclusively. Perhaps John Money, a professor and researcher at Johns Hopkins University, has the best explanation when he suggests a kind of interaction between sociological and biological influences, so that we must disregard any simple single-cause explanation.

We choose our behavior; we do not choose our orientation. Homosexuals decry any suggestion that they have selected their tendencies by asking why anyone would choose an orientation that carries with it so much anguish and alienation.

I must personally admit that I do not know what creates a homosexual orientation. If I had to venture a guess, I would say that probably an array of variable factors interact to produce gay or lesbian orientations. Furthermore, I have a sense that these factors interact differently within different persons, so that no two homosexuals are homosexual for exactly the same reasons or causes. What makes matters even more confusing is that, based on the research that I have done, I believe that what forms the male homosexual orientation may be very different from what forms the female homosexual orientation.

There is one thing of which I am convinced, and that is that homosexuals do not choose their orientation. Whatever the causal factors may be, I am sure that the imprinting of the orientation occurs so early in the biological/social/psychological development of the person that he or she can never recall having made a conscious choice.

CAN ORIENTATION BE CHANGED?

The reason that the debate over the causes of homosexuality is so heated is that if it is the result of social and psychological conditioning in early childhood, or a traumatic event such as being sexually abused in the developmental years of life, then there is the strong possibility that with proper counseling, sexual orientation can be changed. A couple of years ago, *Time* magazine carried a major article reporting on the research of the aforementioned Joseph Nicolosi, a New York psychotherapist. Nicolosi offered specific case studies of one-time homosexuals who claimed that after intensive therapy over a few years, they had changed into persons with heterosexual orientations.

More recently, Robert L. Spitzer, chief of biometrics research and professor of psychiatry at Columbia University, who was primarily responsible for getting the American Psychiatric Association to change its position on homosexuality so that it is no longer defined as a mental disorder, presented a major paper to that same organization, citing evidence he had collected that claimed that homosexuals can change. It should be noted that major flaws in the methodology Spitzer used have raised questions about the validity of his study.

Evangelical Christians generally support the belief that change in sexual orientation is possible. Consequently, they call upon homosexuals to seek the help that they believe is required for transformation into heterosexuals. A whole array of ministries have sprung up that have as their mission to help homosexuals to become straight. Together, these ministries are incorporated into a loosely connected organization called Exodus. Exodus regularly brings to religious gatherings men and women who say they were once homosexuals, but with proper counseling and a lot of prayer, they have changed. These testimonies come across as sincere and convincing; nevertheless, there are questions to be raised about them.

Pro-gay Christian groups regularly give examples of former leaders of Exodus groups who now claim that they said they had changed simply because they were desperate for acceptance in the churches to which they longed to belong. These ex-members of Exodus organizations now say that they were only deluding themselves when they declared themselves "cured," and that they eventually had to give up those claims when they were honest with themselves. Some of the most prominent former Exodus ministry leaders, such as Michael Bussee and Gary Cooper, fall into this category.

There is, of course, the possibility that those who claim to have changed their sexual orientation are really bisexuals who only had to change their behavior. Bisexuals are women or men who are attracted to both males and females. It is possible for them to live comfortably in either a gay or straight lifestyle. Therefore, it is possible for a bisexual who has been living as a homosexual to choose, often out of religious conviction, to live as a heterosexual. When this is the case, the essential sexual orientation does not really change. These people are still bi-sexual, but they have committed themselves to a heterosexual lifestyle as the general population prefers and as is almost always the only way acceptable in evangelical circles.

Alfred Kinsey and his associates did some studies on sexuality in the early 1950s. These studies are no longer highly regarded, and today, both the methodologies that they employed and the results that they garnered from their studies are generally ignored. However, the lasting concept that the Kinsey asso-ciates contributed to our discussion is the proposition that there is a continuum with respect to homosexuality. At one end of the continuum are those who are completely heterosexual in their orientation, and at the other end are those who are completely homosexual in their orientation. According to the Kinsey asso-ciates, few of us can be placed at the extreme ends of this continuum. Most of us fall somewhere along the line. Bisexuals, according to this paradigm, are those persons who fall near the middle of this continuum and, therefore, can choose to live either heterosexually or homosexually.

Personally, I believe that most of those who claim to have been homo-sexuals who have changed into heterosexuals are really bisexuals. Those who have a predominantly homosexual orientation to start with are the ones who tend to revert back eventually to affirming their homosexuality.

POSSIBLE BUT UNLIKELY

It is my own belief that change is possible, but not likely. Because I believe in a God who works miracles, I cannot discount the possibility of change. Furthermore, while there are doubts in my mind about some of the testimonies I have heard from ex-gays, I am not so cynical as to discount all of them. On the other hand, of the hundreds of deeply religious gay males I interviewed while on the faculty of the University of Pennsylvania (1965–1975), I found that all of them had desperately sought change at one time or another. Sadly, all of them had met with only frustration and disillusionment.

I listened to those who had spent a small fortune on reparative therapy with only negative results. Many gay men (I did no studies on lesbians) told me that they had tried everything, from all-night prayer sessions to "being slain in the spirit" at Pentecostal meetings, in vain attempts to become heterosexuals, but in each case the results had proven to be disappointing. Others had submitted to behavior-modification therapy, sometimes even aversion therapy, which included electroshock as punishment for homosexual attractions.

The stories I heard had a heartbreaking sameness to them. They went something like this: "I never remember a time when I was heterosexual. I always knew there was something different about me, but I didn't know what it was. Then, when I was in my early teens, I heard some of my friends telling ugly jokes about 'fags' and 'fairies.' To my horror, I gradually realized that they were talking about people like me, and I hated myself. At church, I heard the minister say that people like me were an abomination to God. So I wanted to change. I tried everything I could think of, but nothing worked. I thought praying and getting deeply involved in the church work would help. When that didn't work, I thought God hated me. Then I gave up on God. After that, I tried to accept myself for who I am."

Some of them said they were much happier having the church and God out of their lives, while others ached for the spiritual connection they no longer had. I found that strict Calvinists had an especially hard time dealing with their homosexuality. Believing in a God who predestines all things, they concluded that He predestined them to be gay and hence to damnation. They cited Paul's writings in Romans 9:19–24:

> You will say to me then, "Why does He still find fault? For who has resisted His will?" But indeed, O man, who are you to reply against God? Will the thing formed say to him who formed it, "Why have you made me like this?" Does not the potter have power over the clay, from the same lump to make one vessel for honor and another for dishonor? What if God, wanting to show His wrath and to make His power known, endured with much longsuffering the vessels of wrath prepared for destruction, and that He might make known the riches of His glory on the vessels of mercy, which He had prepared beforehand for glory, even us whom He called, not of the Jews only, but also of the Gentiles? (NKJV)

Believing that God created them for rejection, many homosexual people reject the God whom they believe has rejected them. The despair that such a theology can create has driven some gays to suicide. I wonder how much such teachings about God are responsible for the large number of teenage suicides each year, making suicide the second major cause of death in the United States. Believing God hates them, some homosexual young people come to hate themselves, and in self-loathing they end their lives.

Another consequence of this kind of theology is for a gay man to say to himself, "Since I'm condemned anyway, I might as well enjoy myself and bed down with as many men as I can find." One of my friends once asked me, "With a theology like that, who needs Satan? Churches that preach that stuff deliver gays to the wolves of the evil one, who wait to devour them."

I contend that change in sexual orientation is possible, but extremely unlikely, and that what we Christians must do is prescribe some alternatives for those who want to remain in the church even as they come out as homosexuals.

DID GOD MAKE PEOPLE GAY?

The reason most evangelicals want to believe that homosexuals can change is because they are usually convinced that to have a homosexual orientation is to be perverted. They contend that a homosexual orientation is contrary to God's intentions in creation. Insensitive preachers, trying to be cute in their sermons, sometimes attempt to elicit a cheap laugh from their congregations by saying, "God created Adam and Eve, not Adam and Steve." Many use remarks like that, which are all too common in evangelical circles, as evidence to claim that evangelicals are homophobic. Nevertheless, the question related to what God intended in creation is a legitimate one and ought not to be dismissed in a cavalier manner. Did God will for some people to be gay?

Some Christians answer this question in the affirmative and go on to declare that gay and lesbian people should celebrate their homosexuality, see it as a God-given blessing to enjoy. This is the belief held by the Metropolitan Community churches that have sprung up all across the nation to minister to those gays and lesbians whom mainline and evangelical churches have rejected. A small but increasing number of churches within each of the mainline denominations also share this conviction. In my own American Baptist denomination, we call them welcoming and affirming churches. These churches welcome gay couples as well as gay singles. Every major denomination has an association of such churches, as well as a significant minority of churches that do not take an official stand on the issue but quietly welcome gay and lesbian singles and couples into safe places where they can be sure that they will not hear anything hurtful from the pulpit.

Recently, I attended a conference of pastors from large churches within a mainline denomination. These pastors were from congregations of more than a thousand members. Each year at this conference a survey is taken, and this particular year, the results indicated that 15 percent of churches represented had an unofficial policy of receiving gay and lesbian couples into their congregations. This was three times what the response had been the previous year. The trend seemed obvious.

Another option is the one held by the recently deceased and well-respected evangelical Lewis Smedes, who served as professor of theology and ethics on the faculty of Fuller Theological Seminary. Smedes believed that we live in a fallen creation and that nothing is completely the way God intended it to be at creation. He saw homosexual orientation as a consequence of the Fall, something God did not intend, but that we, in our existential situation, must handle. He believed that a committed, lifelong, monogamous relationship between homosexuals may be what he would call the "circumstantial will of God."

Given the circumstances in which gays and lesbians find themselves right now, Smedes, in an address given at the 1998 meeting of Evangelicals Concerned, suggested that a committed relationship in which couples establish humanizing love is the best alternative to the life of celibate loneliness that is often the lot for Christian homosexuals. Smedes drew a parallel by pointing out that according to Scripture, God's original intention was that every married couple should have children. When he and his wife were not able to do so, they adopted children. This, he believes, was the best decision they could make, because it enabled him and his wife to live out the "ultimate will of God," which was to be parents who raised children in the nurture and admonition of the Lord.

In a parallel argument, Smedes contended that gay or lesbian marriage is not the original will of God, but it is the circumstantial will of God. This enables the homosexual couple to live out the *ultimate* will of God, which is to have binding relationships that deliver them from loneliness and enhance the humanity and spirituality of the partners.

WHAT ABOUT SCRIPTURE?

Many evangelicals would like to go along with the kinds of monogamous committed relationships Smedes described, but they contend that their allegiance to the infallibility of Scripture does not allow them to do so. They cite various passages from the Bible that prevent them from accepting gay and lesbian marriages. It is important for us to survey those verses and see how pro-gay Christian activists handle them, even if there is objection to their interpretations.

MOSES'S WRITINGS

In Leviticus 18:22, Leviticus 20:13, and Deuteronomy 23:17–18 are harsh prohibitions against what seems to be homosexuality. Yet some scholars contend that these passages do not apply to the modern homosexual argument because these prohibitions are part of the *purity code* of ancient Israel, rather than the *moral code*. The moral code—that is, the Ten Commandments—is binding for all people at all times, whereas the purity code comprises what we commonly call kosher rules for Orthodox Jews. The purity code condemns such practices as eating shellfish, wearing fabric that is made out of more than one kind of thread, having sexual intercourse with a woman while she is menstruating, eating pork, and even touching the skin of a dead pig (which would put the Super Bowl into question!). Most Christians, but by no means all, agree that the purity code or kosher rules do not apply to Christians, who are now obligated to obey only the moral laws of Scripture. What had been declared unclean is no longer viewed as such (Acts 10:9–16; Rom. 14:14).

One rabbi informed me, however, that the measure of how seriously a person should take a purity rule is related to the punishment cited for its violation—in the case of homosexual behavior, death. By this gauge, one cannot easily discard this rule.

Jesus undoubtedly knew about homosexuality, and we can assume that He held to the teachings of the Torah on the subject. But nowhere did He condemn gays and lesbians. In fact, Jesus never mentioned homosexuality. It just wasn't on his Top Ten list of sins. Number one on that list, however, are judgmental religious people who look for sin in the lives of others without dealing with the sin in their own lives (Matt. 23).

It is uncomfortable to note that although Jesus was silent about homosexuality, He did specifically condemn the remarriage of divorced people unless adultery was the cause of the divorce. Nevertheless, most contemporary Christians accept the remarriage of divorced persons regardless of the bases of their divorces. Gays often ask why evangelicals seem willing to accept couples who are divorced and remarried, a sexual relationship that Jesus specifically condemned as adultery, then come down so hard on a sexual relationship that Jesus never mentioned. It's not that gays condemn remarried divorced persons, but only that gays are asking that *they* not be condemned and that the church show as much grace to them.

PAUL'S WRITINGS

Those who make the case against homosexual eroticism usually construct most of their arguments on the writings of the apostle Paul. Citing several passages from Paul's epistles, they contend that they have specific references supporting their point of view. We must give these verses serious consideration.

First of all, there is the passage from 1 Timothy 1:9–10.

> Knowing this, that the law is not made for a righteous man, but for the lawless and disobedient, for the ungodly and for sinners, for unholy and profane, for murderers of fathers and murderers of mothers, for manslayers, for whoremongers, for them that defile themselves with mankind, for menstealers, for liars, for perjured persons, and if there be any other thing that is contrary to sound doctrine.

Those who hold a conservative position on this matter point out that the reference to "them that defile themselves with mankind" is a phrase in the Greek language that specifically alludes to erotic homosexual behavior. On the other hand, there are those with differing opinions about these verses. For instance, some biblical scholars say that in this letter to his protégé, Timothy, Paul was condemning not homosexuality per se, but pederasty—a practice that was accepted in ancient Greece. In those days, a male teacher often took one young boy and personally tutored him. In such a close relationship, it was not uncommon for the teacher to exploit his position of authority by either seducing the boy or coercing him into sexual relations.

And because in Greek culture the youthful boy was its most erotic sexual object, the farther into puberty the boy progressed, the less attractive he became. When the teacher no longer found the student desirable, the teacher usually cast him aside for newer and younger sexual partners. Accepting castration was one technique these psychologically and physically abused young men used to prolong their boyish attractiveness and conceal their oncoming maturity. Evangelical gay activists contend that this practice, which Paul condemned, has nothing to do with the loving, monogamous relationships that they advocate.

In another of Paul's writings, we read, "Know ye not that the unrighteous shall not inherit the kingdom of God? Be not deceived: neither fornicators, nor idolaters, nor adulterers, nor effeminate, nor abusers of themselves with mankind . . ." (1 Cor. 6:9). Yet even here, with what seems to be a clear reference to homosexuals, the case is nonetheless foggy. The Greek word *arsenokoitai*, translated as "homosexual" in the New International Version, has an ambiguous meaning; because the word was seldom used in ancient literature, scholars cannot pin down the meaning with any certainty. We know that it refers to some form of condemned sexual behavior, but we don't know specifically that it condemns homosexual behavior as we understand it.

The text most often cited to support the condemnation of same-gender eroticism is Romans 1:26–27. There we read:

> For this reason God gave them up to vile passions. For even their women exchanged the natural use for what is against nature. Likewise also the men, leaving the natural use of the woman, burned in their lust for one another, men with men committing what is shameful, and receiving in themselves the penalty of their error which was due. (NKJV)

One interpretation of this passage by pro-gay scholars is that Saint Paul did not condemn those born with homosexual orientations, but rather heterosexuals who, by giving unrestrained vent to their lusts, had become debased and decadent. Scholars who conclude this contend that the apostle was condemning heterosexuals who *chose* homosexual behavior as a new, kinky sexual thrill—who participated in homosexual acts as a perversion of their *natural* desires. These scholars premise this interpretation on the fact that Paul wrote his letter to the Romans while in Corinth, a Greek city where the dominant religion was the worship of Aphrodite, a hermaphrodite with both male and female sexual organs. In the worship of this deity, heterosexual men and women acted as members of the opposite sex to experience the sexual side of their deity that differed from their own. According to this interpretation of Romans 1, Paul was railing against idolatry and the obscene sexual practices with which he was familiar in Corinth; he was *not* condemning homosexuality per se.

The only problem with this otherwise convincing biblical interpretation is that Christian tradition has consistently held that Saint Paul specifically condemned all homosexual eroticism. Frankly, it seems a bit arrogant to me to contradict two millennia of church tradition. The church fathers who were closest to

Paul exemplify this (see Cyprian of Carthage, *Letters 1:8*, and John Chrysostom's *Homily on Romans 1:26–27*).

Those who support gay and lesbian partnerships point out that if we yielded to church tradition on *all* points, women would not be allowed to teach Sunday school or serve as missionaries. Unfortunately, there are many who would say "Amen" to that. Furthermore, most of the references in the writings of the church fathers to homosexual behavior do seem to condemn the exploitation of boys rather than homosexual orientation or committed, loving homosexual marriages.

Evangelical homosexuals are torn between their sexual orientations and traditional interpretations of Scripture. It is painful to me that heterosexuals seem unable to comprehend their estrangement and loneliness. Yet I believe that there are some solutions to this dilemma of evangelical homosexuals.

POSSIBLE RESPONSES TO THE DILEMMA

COVENANT

Two Christian homosexual men I know in Chicago solved their problem of loneliness by entering into a covenant wherein they promised to (1) live with each other "'til death do us part," and (2) do so celibately. They chose to live together as lifelong partners "in all love and tenderness" but without the practice of any erotic sexual behavior. These two men claim to be enjoying the humanizing benefits of a genuine love relationship that has given them mutual blessings but does not violate biblical admonitions against homosexual eroticism. I have recently learned of a number of other evangelical and homosexual couples who have adopted similar arrangements.

By the way, I call this a homosexual *covenant* rather than a homosexual *marriage* because of the sexual consummation the latter word implies. *Covenant* connotes a lifelong commitment of mutual obligation, which does not necessitate sexual eroticism. The Church of England affirmed such "wedded friendships" from the Middle Ages right up through the mid–seventeenth century, claims Alan Bray of the University of London, who cites an array of specific cases in which these celibate relationships received church blessings (see *The Tablet*, 4 August 2001, pp. 1108–1109).

Many Christians will disapprove of this arrangement, of course, claiming that the Bible frowns on, if not outright condemns, even romantic feelings between members of the same sex. The Bible tells us to flee temptation, they point out, and such "wedded friendships" obviously put gays and lesbians in very trying situations.

Yet these hard-line critics are hard-pressed to build a solid biblical case for their complaints. If, as they say, lovers cannot live in such a relationship without becoming sexually involved, they are making value judgments about the moral strength and integrity of other Christians—judgments of psychological projection more than anything else. While I do not doubt the honesty of those who have sought an escape from their loneliness in this way, I really think it is unrealistic for the overwhelming majority of homosexuals to live together as intimate couples without getting sexually involved. It is not a solution to the problem I would recommend.

COMMUNITY

Another answer to the loneliness Christian homosexuals face is to live in community. Thousands of Christians across America are finding that it is spiritually and economically beneficial to live together in groups, ranging from three or four to ten or more. Such Christian communities can foster high commitment among the members, which, when it comes to sexuality, means that they more easily can hold sexual behavior in check with others' loving and prayerful support. A Christian community can be a safe place for homosexual persons to be honest about their orientations, so that community members can encourage each other to live lifestyles that glorify Christ.

In such communities, being homosexual or heterosexual would not be a defining issue as to whether or not they are Christians, but *all* members could use their own gifts from God to help others. And who knows but that, in the observation of Christian communities made up of people of all sexual orientations, the evangelical church community would be challenged to realize that "they" are indeed part of "us," and that we are to be mutually responsible and compassionate.

CHURCH SUPPORT

Whatever individuals conclude about the causes or cures of homosexuality, the church should offer more support for gay Christians who want to be celibate members of the Christian community but know that struggling with sexual temptation is more than they can bear in aloneness. It bothers me more than I can tell you that in most churches, gays and lesbians *must* live out their lives secretly, "in the closet," while enduring a daily existence of quiet desperation. One option that I believe churches should consider is to provide support groups for gays and lesbians in which they can be open with each other and encourage each other to remain faithful to their commitments to celibacy. What is needed is some kind of a twelve-step program, so that all of these brothers and sisters in Christ have persons to whom they can turn when they feel themselves weakening. They need fellow Christians who fully understand them, who have been in the same situation, and who know from subjective experience what is happening and how it is possible to overcome such temptations.

I am not suggesting that what I am proposing here will work for every gay or lesbian person, but it could go a long way toward providing the support system that is needed for those homosexual Christians who believe God wants them to be celibate.

My wife, Peggy, contrary to my position, believes that lifelong commitments in gay marriage are a viable option for Christian gays and lesbians. However, she admits that she sometimes meets up with homosexual women and men who believe that celibacy is the only way they can go and still remain faithful to what they believe the Bible requires of them. For these sisters and brothers, I pray that there will be churches that will step forward to start the kind of twelve-step programs I am suggesting.

I long for the day when gays and lesbians can stand up in a testimony meeting at church and say something like this: "I am a homosexual! I have not been physically and erotically intimate with another homosexual for several years, but every day is a struggle. Every day I have to find the spiritual strength to resist the constant temptation in my life. I fight for my soul, one day at a time. And I know that if it were not for the good support group that this church has for me and the prayers of the rest of the church, I would not be able to make it. But thank God for this church, which has provided me with the loving help that I need."

CHRISTIANS' BAD RECORD

Beyond any arguments over what the Bible says or does not say about homosexual behavior is my concern about the meanness and ugly, untrue rhetoric that gay men and lesbians have to endure from many Christians.

It was supposedly a gathering of Christians who had come together to discuss "family issues." But the meeting was specifically about doing something "to defend society from what homosexuals are trying to do to us." The leader of the group said he was determined to "expose the facts about the homosexual agenda and how gays and lesbians are trying to get our children into 'their lifestyle.'" With all the heat and intensity of an evangelist at the highest pitch of his message, he gave to his rapt audience what he claimed were authoritative statistics: "Seventeen percent of all gays ingest human feces, 29 percent of them urinate on their partners, and 37 percent of them engage in sadomasochism."

I had heard those so-called "facts" before. The Christian leader standing up front failed to mention that the "scientific study" from which they were taken is highly suspect among social scientists and was the work of a psychologist whom the American Psychological Association expelled for a breach of ethics that involved lying. The people listening to the speaker were unaware of this omission. They feverishly took notes, and there were gasps of dismay. It was obvious that this man's little speech was influencing them. When he asked group members to respond, one stood and said, "These filthy people are an abomination to God and must be wiped from the face of the earth!"

TROUBLE FROM THE PULPIT

The sad fact is that members of some churches I know about regularly hear this kind of talk from the pulpit. And it is preached not only from pulpits but through the Christian media as well. A mother who asked her ten-year-old boy where he had heard what he was saying—that gays molest little boys—was told, "From the preacher on television."

I am not saying that we in the church have deliberately condoned violence against homosexual people. But there is little doubt in my mind that misguided persons have taken some things that preachers have said in the church, in the name of preaching the gospel, as permission to do terrible and evil things to gay men and lesbians.

Antigay rhetoric has long been a part of what people hear from evangelical pulpits. At a "Jesus festival" that had brought together more than twenty thousand young people, I once had to follow a speaker who created a sensation as he whipped up animosity against homosexuals. He sent shivers of revulsion through the crowd with his vivid descriptions of what he claimed were common homosexual acts. His explicit details of sadomasochistic body mutilations and his generalizations about how homosexuals defecate on each other to get perverted thrills achieved the desired ends. Out of the crowd of young Christians, someone yelled, "Kill the fags!" The evangelist stopped and piously responded, "Oh, no! We should love them! We must hate the sin, but we must love the sinner."

As I stood backstage, waiting to speak, I wondered how that man would explain that he *loved* homosexuals. Was it love to exaggerate the facts and create a frenzy of hate among young people? Was it love to aggrandize his image as a sensational preacher at the expense of the homosexual teenagers who silently suffered as they listened to his tirade? Was it love that stirred some sick kid in the crowd to scream about killing "fags," sending fear into the heart of every gay and lesbian teenager who had to listen to it all in silence? It is so easy to say, "We should love gays and lesbians." After someone stirs a crowd to fear and hate them, they find it harder to put that admonition into practice. One gay man said, "To be told you are loved by somebody like that is like being kissed by somebody with bad breath."

A SHINING—AND SURPRISING—EXAMPLE

When I encounter persons who believe that homosexuals choose their orientations and are perverts whom we should regard as an abomination to God, I want to ask them if they are ready to make those kinds of judgments about Henri Nouwen, one of the great Christians of our time. This man, whose writings have guided and inspired Christians of all persuasions and whose life was a brilliant example of twentieth-century saintliness, was a celebate gay. This brilliant scholar, who resigned a Harvard professorship to serve intellectually challenged and severely disabled people in Jean Vanier's L'Arche community in Toronto, agonized, according to his biographer Michael Ford, over his homosexual orientation. Only after his death, when others went through his personal papers and diaries, did the rest of the world learn of his painful inner battles over his sexual identity. He lived a celebate life at a great price, but he did the right thing.

Henri Nouwen gave up prestige and possible wealth to follow the leading of Christ, to serve as a loving caretaker for people whom the world would throw away as useless. He took upon himself the role of a servant, and his Christlike example shames the rest of us. To be perfectly frank, I think that those who would dare call Henri Nouwen a pervert may well be the ones who really deserve that label.

THE CHURCH NEEDS TO REPENT

The first thing we in the church must do to show our repentance for this kind of hateful talk is to commit ourselves to telling people the truth. For instance, the truth is that there *are* gay and lesbian perverts who threaten little children, but there are also heterosexual perverts who threaten little children. According to the late University of Pennsylvania professor William Kephart, the proportion of homosexuals in this country who molest children in a given year is probably the same, and possibly even a little lower than the proportion of those in the heterosexual community who molest children. Sexually molesting children is a horrendous evil, but to declare from the pulpit that homosexuals are more likely to commit such a hideous crime than are heterosexuals is just an out-and-out lie. The amount of heterosexual molesting and incest that goes on in our society staggers the imagination. And considering the relatively smaller number of homosexuals who ever commit this crime, we ought to recognize that heterosexual offenders should be our primary concern when it comes to protecting our children.

One thing more: in most typical church services, there are probably gay and lesbian persons who have come to worship. In all probability, they are people who live decent lives. They are not into any of the kinds of disgusting orgies described in the demagogic preaching that too often comes from our pulpits. These men and women are likely to be living celibate lives in accord with what they believe Scripture requires of them. Most of them are still "in the closet" and live in fear that their sexual orientations will be discovered. All too often, because they have no one with whom to share their secret, they have to struggle alone against sexual temptation. What they do not need is for some fire-eating preacher to add to their suffering with stupid and mean remarks—all in the name of Jesus.

I sincerely hope that all Christians, regardless of their opinions about causes and possible "cures" for homosexual orientations, will agree on at least this: homosexuals are entitled to the same civil rights that heterosexuals enjoy. We should not allow discrimination in the workplace or residential housing. If employers are willing to provide medical coverage for heterosexual couples living together out of wedlock, then they must be ready to provide the same benefits for homosexual couples. The law should protect all citizens against hate crimes.

Certainly the law must have exceptions so that religious organizations, which have beliefs that prohibit homosexual behavior, are not forced or required to hire those who live contrary to their beliefs. But unless heterosexual Christians are willing to champion calls for justice for gays and lesbians, it will be just about impossible to declare that the church loves them.

STARVED FOR SPIRITUAL CONNECTION

I had a friend who was a pastor in Brooklyn. He was one of the most sensitive and loving men I have ever known. He pastored a church that had seen better days. The community around the church had undergone great change, so that many of the old church members had moved away, and very few new people had come in to take their places. My friend's church was struggling to stay alive.

From time to time, I called this man to find out what was going on in his life. Because he served where he did, all kinds of strange and unusual things happened to him. His experiences have proven to be an invaluable source of illustrations for my books and sermons.

One day as we were talking, I asked him if anything special had happened to him in the past week. He could not think of anything, so I helped him out by getting more specific. "What did you do last Tuesday morning at ten o'clock?" I inquired.

"Oh! That was interesting," he responded. "I got a call that morning from the undertaker who has the place just down the street. He needed somebody to do a funeral, and nobody else he called wanted anything to do with it because the man had died of AIDS. Since he couldn't get anybody else, I told him I'd take the funeral."

"What was it like?" I asked.

"It was strange," he answered. "When I got to the funeral home, I found about twenty-five or thirty homosexual men waiting for me. They were in the room with the casket, just sitting as though they were frozen in their chairs. They looked as though they were statues. Each of them faced straight ahead with glassy, unfocused eyes. Their hands were folded on their laps as though some teacher had ordered them to sit that way. They almost scared me. Several of them wore the kind of clothes that made a blatant statement about who and what they were.

"I did what I was supposed to do," my friend said. "I read some Scripture and said some prayers. I made the kind of remarks that ministers are supposed to make when they really don't know the dead person. After a few minutes, I ended the service, and we prepared to go out to the cemetery. I, along with those men, got into the cars that were to follow the hearse. We rode through the Holland Tunnel to the cemetery, which was located near Hoboken, New Jersey. Then we all got out of the cars and went over to the edge of the grave.

"Not a word was spoken by any of those men, from the beginning of the funeral until I had finished the prayers to commit the remains of the dead man to the earth. They all just stood at the edge of the grave, as motionless as they had been in the funeral home. I said the closing prayer and the benediction and turned to leave. Then I realized that all of those men were still standing in their places, all with blank expressions on their faces. I asked if there was anything more I could do for them. One of them spoke."

"What did he say?" I asked.

"What he said surprised me," my friend answered. "He asked me to read the Twenty-third Psalm. He said, 'When I got up this morning to come to this funeral, I was looking forward to somebody reading the Twenty-third Psalm to me. I really like that psalm, and I figured that they always read it at funerals. You didn't read it.'

"I read the Twenty-third Psalm for those men," my friend said. "When I finished, a second man spoke, and he asked me to read another passage of Scripture. He wanted to hear that part of the Bible where it says there is nothing that can separate us from the love of God. So I read from the eighth chapter of Romans, where Paul tells us that neither death nor life, nor angels, nor principalities, nor powers, nor things present, nor things to come, nor height, nor depth, nor any other creature shall be able to separate us from the love of God which is in Christ Jesus.

"When I read to those men that *nothing* could separate them from the love of God, I saw signs of emotion on their faces for the first time. Then, one after the other, they made special requests for me to read favorite passages of Scripture. I stood there for almost an hour, reading Scripture to those homosexual men, before we went to our cars and headed back to Brooklyn."

When I heard my friend's story, something down deep inside of me hurt. My heart ached with sadness. I realized that the men my friend described were hungry for the Word of God but would probably never set foot inside a church. They wanted to hear the Bible, but they stayed clear of the church, and I think I know why. They feel that church people despise them. And the reason they think that is because—in more cases than I care to mention—church people *do* despise them.

I don't know everything that the church of Jesus Christ should be doing about the complex issue of responding to the needs of our gay brothers and lesbian sisters, but being antigay is not an option. It is a shame and a sin that persons with homosexual orientations usually are forced to discover and use their gifts *outside* the church. Through their struggles, some of our homosexual brothers and sisters have grown in the Lord to the point where they have much that would benefit and bless the straight church.

There *must* be good news for homosexuals. Given the likelihood that their sexual orientations will not change, we must do more than simply bid them to be celibate; we must find ways for them to have fulfilling, loving experiences so that we affirm their humanity and ensure their participation in the body of Christ.

6

Is There a Second Chance for Those Who Die Without Christ?

As a guest on the television show *Crossfire,* I found myself in a face-off with the television preacher Jerry Falwell. Just as time was running out, Rev. Falwell sprang a question that caught me off guard. Out of the blue, he asked whether or not people who did not know Jesus as personal Savior could go to heaven. He demanded an immediate yes or no. Earlier in the program, I had stated that we should simply preach the gospel and leave it up to God to answer these kinds of questions. But that wasn't enough for Falwell. He would settle for nothing less than a clear and emphatic answer.

I suppose I think too much in such settings. My mind immediately went out to all of those parents who had lost babies at childbirth. Would a simple "no" not turn them against God? While I have no biblical support for my belief, I am inwardly convinced that He does not send such infants to hell.

I also thought about all of those who are mentally retarded and not quite capable of grasping the doctrine of the subsitutionary atonement of Christ. Would these people, especially those with Down's syndrome, whom I sometimes find act more Christlike than most of us with normal IQs, be doomed for not saying "yes" to the propositional truths that Falwell deemed essential for salvation?

What about all of those people in Old Testament days before Christ, who might have accepted Christ as Savior but never had the chance? Certainly they would not all be doomed to hell.

I hesitated before I even tried to answer Rev. Falwell. In the opinion of many evangelicals who watched the show, that was more than enough to condemn me. After a few seconds, I feebly tried to respond by saying something about what Paul wrote in Romans 2:14–15: "For when the Gentiles, which have not the law, do by nature the things contained in the law, these, having not the law, are a law unto themselves: which shew the work of the law written in their hearts, their conscience also bearing witness, and their thoughts the mean while accusing or else excusing one another."

Referring to this passage, I began to make the case that God would judge people—including those who had never heard the gospel—on the basis of the light and truth about God that had been available to them. It didn't wash! In the days that followed, I was showered by e-mails, letters, and phone calls condemning my hesitancy and my weak answer. People who had been regular supporters of our missionary enterprises to Third World peoples asked that we take them off our mailing lists. Some canceled speaking engagements, and I went into a depression, wondering whether my days as a speaker on the evangelical circuit were over. Most evangelicals wanted me to state with certainty and confidence that only those who had made clearly understood declarations of Jesus as Savior in this life would escape the fires of hell. I disappointed them, and many of them will never forgive me for that.

MUDDY THINKING

The fact is, evangelical thinking on this topic is muddy. While many, if not most, of us believe in our hearts that innocent babies and the mentally challenged do not go to hell, many of us also declare with certainty that every person who hasn't heard and accepted the gospel is on his or her way to eternal torment—no exceptions. The logic is missing.

I know that some believe in a thing called double predestination. They say that just as God predestined some people for salvation before they were ever born, others He predestined for damnation from "before the foundation of the earth." Going to the Bible, they quote from Romans 9:20–23. They take these verses to mean that though this might seem unjust from our human way of looking at things, God's judgments transcend our concepts of justice, and we must learn to accept them. Again citing Scripture, they point out that His ways are not our ways and that His ways of justice are "past finding out" (Rom. 11:33).

Many people believe this is only further evidence of how important it is for all of us to get out there and tell the gospel story to every living creature on the planet, and that God will hold *us* responsible if we fail to carry out His Great Commission (Mark 16:15). Some point to Ezekiel 3:18, which reads, "When I say unto the wicked, Thou shalt surely die; and thou givest him not warning, nor speakest to warn the wicked from his wicked way, to save his life; the same wicked man shall die in his iniquity; but his blood will I require at thine hand."

On the other side of the argument, there are those who believe that the justice of God requires that He has to make some exceptions. Some feel that theologies that condemn innocents to hell do more damage to the reputation of God than all of the heresies put together. They claim that those who believe in double predestination are imputing to God traits and attitudes we would deem despicable if we found them in any human being.

Regarding this conflict, a faculty member of an evangelical seminary said to me, "I think there are going to be a lot of surprises in heaven. At least that's what Jesus said in Matthew 25. When I read the story of Judgment Day, it seems that a lot of people who thought they were right with God are in for some bad news, and a lot of those who never even knew who Jesus was and is are going to be invited in."

THE GOD OF THE SECOND CHANCE

There is another way of looking at the matter of heaven and hell that I believe deserves our serious consideration. It is in the preaching and writings of the English theologian and novelist George MacDonald. MacDonald is the writer whom C. S. Lewis, as well as the great British essayist G. K. Chesterton, credited with some of his best insights.

MacDonald offered us the possibility that there could be opportunities for those who reject Jesus in this life, or never had the chance to know about Him, to repent and surrender to His transforming love after death. In other words, MacDonald proposed that the possibility for salvation exists even after this life is over. Of course, to many this flies in the face of the verse that states that "it is appointed unto men once to die, but after this the judgment" (Heb. 9:27).

On the other hand, some biblical passages support what MacDonald had to say. Consider that we find in 1 Peter 3:19 and 4:6 clear references to the claim that Jesus goes to preach to those who are imprisoned in a place of death. These are the kinds of passages that MacDonald said upheld his beliefs about the afterlife. In Ephesians 4:9–10 we read, "Now that he ascended, what is it but that he also descended first into the lower parts of the earth? He that descended is the same also that ascended up far above all heavens, that he might fill all things." Is this not a reference to a Jesus who refuses to give up on people, even when they reject Him in this life? Does not this Savior continue His work to save the lost, even beyond the limits of time and space as we know them?

When Jesus called Peter to be the key leader of Christendom, He said, "Thou art Peter, and upon this rock I will build my church; and the gates of hell shall not prevail against it" (Matt. 16:18). Does this verse imply that a church that declares the salvation message will invade hell itself?

THE TROUBLE WITH THEOLOGIANS

According to MacDonald, it is a disservice to God to suggest that God gives up on those who fail to surrender to His love in this life, or that God punishes those who never had the opportunity to trust in Jesus. He contended that God is not as meanspirited as those theologians who would make Him into such a tyrant. "Theologians," he wrote, "have done more to hide the gospel of Christ than any of its adversaries."[1]

MacDonald said that traditional theologians make God into an unfair judge. He claimed that only an unjust tyrant would damn an unfortunate person. MacDonald would not let ill-intentioned theologians try to excuse themselves with their claims that God's justice is totally other than anything that we can comprehend, and that what looks like an injustice to us is ultimately a higher form of justice than we are able to understand. "Not so!" the novelist claimed. We derive our sense of justice from God. We are made in God's image, he asserted, and it is God's justice that is reflected in our hearts as a "natural revelation" (Rom. 2:14–15; John 1:9). God's justice, said MacDonald, does not run counter to what we all know is the essence of justice. The Bible says that "in him is no darkness at all" (1 John 1:5).

MacDonald also said that, given what the Scriptures say about God, theologians have no right to say that He has a dark side. And this, he claimed, is exactly what theologians do when they make God into a deity who metes out punishment to desperate souls in a way that is blatantly unfair. These scholarly professors of theology make it impossible for any reasonable person to believe that a God who could punish "lost" men and women in such a vengeful way is loving. In God there is no darkness, but MacDonald declared that by assigning an evil trait to the good God, some theologians have portrayed God as a dark deity to the minds of many thinking persons.

MacDonald dared to hope that in the end, all men and women will have the opportunity to become sons and daughters of God—if not in this life, then in the next. Given the unequal opportunities to become followers of Jesus that we receive in this life, a just God, he claimed, can offer nothing less than an opportunity for salvation in the life to come.

STILL, SIN IS SERIOUS

No one can accuse George MacDonald of not dealing with sin seriously in his theology. Those who are apart from Christ when this life ends, he said, do experience hell; it is just that he sees the possibility of deliverance from it. His brilliant use of language provides one of the most disturbing and frightening descriptions of hell I have ever read. He describes it as being in "the vast outside," in which the experience of absolute loneliness and the sense of being abandoned go beyond what any deserted or lost child has ever known.

> The ghostly dark beyond the gates of the city of which God is the light—where the evil dogs go ranging, silent as the dark, for there is no sound any more than sight . . . Man wakes from the final struggle of death, in absolute loneliness—such a loneliness as in the most miserable moment of deserted childhood as he never knew . . . All is dark, dark and dumb; no motion—not a breath of wind . . . In such evil case I believe the man would be glad to come in contact with the worst-loathed insect . . . His worst enemy, could he be aware of him, he would be ready to worship.[2]

Given how ugly, despairing, and painful existence apart from God would be, it seems likely that lost souls would readily embrace Jesus, should the Savior come seeking them. But MacDonald pointed out that it would not be that easy. Jesus is the light of God, and those who are in darkness usually shun that light. The Scripture says: "For every one that doeth evil hateth the light, neither cometh to the light, lest his deeds should be reproved" (John 3:20).

HE IS A CONSUMING FIRE

The reason for this reluctance to embrace the light of the Savior's presence is that He is "a consuming fire" (Heb. 12:29). According to MacDonald's reading of Scripture, our loving God destroys everything in us that is unlovable and unholy. Those in "the prison house of death" fear God because they feel that if they are separated from their evil traits, they will no longer be themselves. They know that God is a purifying force who will burn away their unholy traits, even as the Bible says:

> Every man's work shall be made manifest: for the day shall declare it, because it shall be revealed by fire; and the fire shall try every man's work of what sort it is. If any man's work abide which he hath built thereupon, he shall receive a reward. If any man's work shall be burned, he shall suffer loss: but he himself shall be saved; yet so as by fire. (1 Corinthians 3:13–15)

But until we are thus purified, said MacDonald, we will not know or be the persons God meant for us to be when He created us. The identities to which the lost cling so desperately are false identities. The lost will never know their true selves until the lies about themselves are burned away. All that is in them that should be destroyed will be destroyed if only they will surrender to "the consuming fire." They would then become the actualized sons and daughters of God that He predestined them to be (Rom. 8:29–30).

Not just the lost but *Christians* need the purging of the consuming fire. The difference is that Christians *want* to be purged of "the wood, hay, and stubble"— the corruptible traits that keep them from being like Jesus (see 1 Cor. 3:12). Those people who are in Christ press toward this "high calling of God" that the apostle Paul wrote about in Philippians 3:13–14. They long to be in the presence of that one who destroys the spiritual dross in their lives, so that they may experience what is written in 1 John 3:2: "Beloved, now are we the sons of God, and it doth not yet appear what we shall be: but we know that, when he shall appear, we shall be like him; for we shall see him as he is."

As for those who live in hell, MacDonald believed that they will eventually come to a desperate state wherein they will do anything to escape their painful condition of total alienation from God. He asserted that though they endeavor to flee from God's presence, they will learn the hard way that there is no escape from

Him. They will end up saying, "Whither shall I go from thy spirit? or whither shall I flee from thy presence? If I ascend up into heaven, thou art there: if I make my bed in hell, behold, thou art there" (Ps. 139:7–8).

They will learn the truth of Paul's declaration that not even death can separate them from "the love of God, which is in Christ Jesus our Lord" (Rom. 8:39). The unsatiated appetites of the flesh will intensify in the darkness of death until there is such pain from them that, even as much as the lost love those appetites, they, too, eventually will let them go. Then, said MacDonald, the consuming fire will begin to do His work. At that desperate point in the afterlife, not only will the lost yield to the purging, but they will surrender to the One who once said, "If I be lifted up, I will draw all men unto myself" (see John 12:32).

MACDONALD AND ME

I find myself drawn to MacDonald's theology about the destinies of the lost. That sort of thinking appealed to me before I ever read his novels or his sermons. Such ideas were implanted in my mind many years earlier when, as a college sophomore, I read Francis Thompson's classical poem "The Hound of Heaven":

> *I fled Him, down the nights and down the days;*
> *I fled Him down the arches of the years;*
> *I fled Him down the labyrinthine ways*
> *Of my own mind; and in the mist of tears*
> *I hid from Him, and under running laughter.*
> *Up vistaed hopes I sped;*
> *And shot, precipitated,*
> *Adown Titanic glooms of chasmed fears,*
> *From those strong Feet that followed, followed after*
> *But with unhurrying chase,*
> *And unperturbed pace,*
> *Deliberate speed, majestic instancy,*
> *They bear—and a Voice beat*
> *More instant than the Feet—*
> *"All things betray thee, who betrayest Me."*

The poem had a powerful impact on me. The question of how a loving God could punish those who did not believe in Him with unending torture was never one that I could comfortably answer. MacDonald's theology offered the possibility that I wouldn't have to do so.

A RISKY RESPONSE

Some will go ballistic at the notion of possibilities for deliverance from hell, and they will make all kinds of declarations about why an eternal hell is a belief they hold without question. But then they will have to explain why they do not live as though they really believed that. If they did, they would be relentless in warning everyone and anyone they encountered about the hopeless doom that awaits them unless they say "yes" to the message they preach. I find consistency in the fanatic carrying the sandwich board that reads, "Repent! Your doom is near!" and the one who tries to grab every passerby on the street by the coat lapels and asks, "Hey, buddy! Are you saved?" But to say that the billions who have never yet accepted the gospel will burn forever, and then go on about life relatively unconcerned, seems to me evidence of an almost inhuman emotional callousness.

The story is told of the last man in England to be hanged from the gallows. His name was Charlie Peace. On the way to the gallows, the prison chaplain walked behind him, reading from *The Consolations of Religion*, a litany that Anglican priests used for those who were doomed to execution. The priest said: "Those who die without Christ experience Hell—which is the pain of forever dying, without the release which death itself can bring."

Charlie Peace stopped in his tracks. He turned around and asked, "Do you believe that? I mean, do you *really* believe that?"

Stammering, the priest answered, "Well . . . eh . . . yes . . . I suppose I do."

"Well, I don't!" shouted Charlie. "But if I did, I'd get down on my hands and knees and crawl all over Great Britain, even if it was covered with pieces of broken glass, to rescue one person from what you've just described."

It is not for me to say who can resist the Hound of Heaven in the end. Certainly the Bible makes the case that Satan and his angels will resist Jesus everlastingly and therefore have to endure torment everlastingly (Rev. 20:10). As to who else will be there, I cannot even dare to speculate. I leave that judgment to God.

George MacDonald was forced out of the pulpit of Trinity Congregational Church in Arundel, England, in 1853, because the people of his church thought him heretical. Broke, he and his family moved to Manchester, and he tried preaching his theology about God and salvation to any who would listen. Not many did. Then, in the early 1860s, he turned to writing popular novels and used this genre to spread his vision of a God whom he saw as a loving Father, rather than a condemning judge. He did his best to turn people away from what he called "a mean, poverty-stricken faith."[3]

I will not be surprised if many circles of Christian friends drive me away for saying that there is much about MacDonald's beliefs that I find attractive and reasonable—if not orthodox. But there comes a point in life when each of us knows that the time has come to be honest and to speak one's mind. I am not saying that I am convinced that MacDonald is right, but I would be less than forthright if I did not admit that his convictions make sense to me.

THE CASE FOR NONBEING

But I should not be so dismayed over such reactions. John Stott, perhaps one of the foremost preachers and writers on the British scene, caused quite a stir simply by making a case that the suffering of lost sinners might not be eternal. Stott suggested that eternal punishment would be disproportional punishment for sins committed during the limited days in this life. To his way of thinking, there is a hell, but after a time of suffering, the lost will fade into annihilation.

The Seventh-Day Adventists (once treated as a cult, they now are very much bona fide members of the evangelical community), like John Stott, cannot believe that a just and loving God would send those He loves to everlasting punishment. Recognizing that life is a force God imparts and sustains, they argue that being cut off from God is to be cut off from that which maintains existence. To be cut off from God is to cease to exist in any way. They believe, in accord with their reading of Scripture, that "in him we live, and move, and have our being" (Acts 17:28), that without Him there is annihilation of life and the end of self-awareness. Jesus, they say, came to give us life (John 10:10), and therefore, life in any form ceases to exist without Christ. Without Christ, there is only nonbeing.

Those who think that it is impossible to evangelize without posing the threat of hell have to give ground when dealing with the Seventh-Day Adventists, because these fellow Christians are intensely evangelistic and strongly missionary-minded. They work hard at winning converts, and over the years, they have done so with high levels of effectiveness. They win converts by promising life in

Christ for eternity, not by scaring people into the church with the threat of hell. They contend that we are to endeavor to win the world by holding up the beauty of Jesus and His love for us and that this will draw all men and women unto Him.

It is interesting to note that the threat of nonbeing, according to psychologists since Sigmund Freud, ends up being more of a threat than the traditional Christian belief in a hell. Those who examine the human psyche from the perspective of existentialist psychologists contend that the fear of nonexistence is intolerable to most people. Philosophers such as Jean-Paul Sartre and Martin Heidegger view the nothingness that may await us at the end of life as the ultimate threat to meaningful existence. The Pulitzer Prize–winning psychologist Ernest Becker made the case that throughout our lives, we are people who endeavor to evade the reality of our mortality and its concomitant ceasing to be. Neo-Freudians even point to the threat of nonbeing as the cause of the anxieties and neuroses that often plague our existence.

Consequently, preaching annihilation for those who do not yield to life in Christ can elicit an even more intense emotional reaction than the threat of an everlasting torture in the devil's domain. The Seventh-Day Adventists may be on to something that generates more urgency for people to become Christian than all the fire-and-brimstone sermons that have ever been preached.

ANOTHER VIEWPOINT: EVANGELICAL UNIVERSALISTS

Still another response to questions about heaven and hell has come from those Christians whom we would probably label as evangelical universalists. I have been more than surprised of late at the number of prominent evangelical leaders who have admitted in private to believing in some form of universal salvation, even though they would never let their views become public knowledge. Realizing that the vast majority of evangelicals believe in hell and that those who do not give their lives to Christ go there, these writers and preachers keep their opinions to themselves—lest they lose their audiences.

We have to label those who think like this as evangelicals because they hold to the basic belief systems of orthodox Christianity. They believe in the doctrines outlined in the Apostles' Creed. They preach that eternal life comes only by trusting in what Christ accomplished on the cross and in yielding to the resurrected Jesus as Lord, Savior, and God. Most of these evangelical universalists are convinced that the Bible is an infallible message from God. As a matter of fact, it is from the Bible that they derive their doctrines of universalism.

One of the passages that evangelical universalists usually cite is Romans 5:18–19: "Therefore as by the offence of one judgment came upon all men to condemnation; even so by the righteousness of one the free gift came upon all men unto justification of life. For as by one man's disobedience many were made sinners, so by the obedience of one shall many be made righteous." In their reading of this passage, they claim that the word "all" embraces all humanity, whether individuals are Christians or not. They ask if the original sin Adam and Eve committed in Eden doomed all humanity as guilty sinners, isn't it safe to say that through what Christ accomplished on the cross, all men and women are delivered from condemnation and declared righteous?

SALVATION FOR ALL

Evangelical universalists strongly assert that Jesus is the *only* Savior, but they go on to say that His salvation extends beyond those who claim Jesus as Lord and Savior. Using this passage from Romans, they contend that the blood of Christ covers the sins of all men and women everywhere. Their argument is: "If salvation is by grace, isn't it right to believe that there is nothing that anyone has to do to gain it?" (See Eph. 2:8–9.)

They ask how we can turn around and say, "There's something *we* have to do to be saved," just after we have said that salvation is a free gift that we can do nothing to earn. In the Bible, they read that God is "not willing that any should perish" (2 Pet. 3:9), and they say that, eventually, God's will *will* be done. They put great stock in the passage that says that at the end of time and history, every knee shall bow and every tongue shall confess that Jesus Christ is Lord (Phil. 2:10–11). In their minds, *every* means *every*.

In reality, I would love for those evangelical universalists to be right. What loving Christian wants to see nonbelievers tortured forever in hell? Personally, I have wondered how I could enjoy heaven if the non-Christians whom I loved in this life were not there.

The great Swiss-German theologian Karl Barth was moved toward universalism when he tried to be a comforting pastor to those of his parishioners who had lost loved ones who were not believers in Christ. He wanted to give those grieving people hope, and universalism was the only means that he could think of to do that. Barth believed that the grace of God is irresistible, and that when this life is over and the deceased face the reality of Christ in all of His glory, all of those who had not already followed Him would repent and surrender to Him as Lord.

It is very enticing to be a universalist. First of all, universalism delivers Christians from having to answer the question of how a loving God could punish people endlessly for sin that was limited to time and history. Furthermore, the question about the destiny of those who had never heard the gospel and had a chance to become Christians is resolved. The simple answer is that after death they would yield to Christ.

One universalist theologian carried me through his progression of thought with the following argument: "If there is a God, then there is a God, whether people believe it or not. If God is their Creator, that also is true, whether they believe it or not. If the Bible is an infallible message from God, that fact, too, is not dependent on their believing it. So, if Jesus died for their sins and is their Savior, isn't that fact also true, whether they believe it or not?"

THEN WHY EVANGELIZE?

Those who argue against universalism often claim that this doctrine removes the impetus for evangelism. But the universalists' reply to that claim is that evangelism should be a declaration of the good news of what God is doing in this world. Even today, they say, people can, through faith in Christ, find deliverance from the devastating effects of sin and the fear of death. This, to them, is sufficient reason to motivate believers to preach the gospel. People don't have to die to start experiencing the transforming work of God in their lives. We can tell them that it can all start right now. "Behold, *now* is the accepted time; behold, *now* is the day of salvation" (2 Cor. 6:2, emphasis added).

Surrendering to Christ in the here and now enables people to undergo a change of character so that they no longer live according to what the apostle Paul called the "lusts of the flesh." Those who trust and obey Christ enjoy the incredible and wonderful emotional changes that come from life in the Spirit. Paul wrote: "But the fruit of the Spirit is love, joy, peace, longsuffering, gentleness, goodness, faith, meekness, temperance: against such there is no law" (Gal. 5:22–23).

To those who are into humanistic psychology, the evangelist can claim that the salvation experience is essential for anyone who wants to become what Abraham Maslow called "a self-actualized human being." All of us sense that this is a quality of life in which people can enjoy a deep awareness of the glories of existence and realize the inner fulfillment that goes with being "fully alive." This, contend many evangelists, is what Jesus was telling us about when He said, "I am come that they might have life, and that they might have it more abundantly" (John 10:10). They say that to be denied the "abundant life" that comes from being "in Christ" is a terrible loss!

I find much to commend in such explanations as to why evangelism is essential. I like to say that even if there were no heaven or hell, and I believe in both, I would still want to be a Christian, simply because of what Christ does *for* me and *to* me in this life.

A SOCIETY OF WORLD-CHANGERS

Another reason evangelical universalists say we should evangelize is that they see it as a primary means for recruiting men and women into a movement destined to change the world, that is, into the world that ought to be. To become a Christian, they contend, is to become someone through whom God can begin to carry out His social revolution, in which all of the injustices of this present world order are overcome and the kingdom of God is established here on earth. They hold to a conviction that history is going in a purposeful direction. The goal of human history, they believe, is a world transformed into a societal system in which poverty will be no more, wars will cease, all forms of oppression will end, environmental well-being will be restored, and all social institutions, from the family to political/economic systems, will be restructured to show forth justice and love. They see the whole world as being in need of restoration to undo the work of those evil forces that have raised havoc over the face of the earth since Eden.

Evangelical universalists believe that even now, God is at work rescuing this world from all of its suffering, and that God is doing His work through a people who are willing to be saved from sin by the grace of Jesus Christ and energized through the power of the Holy Spirit. They find in Romans 8:19–22 a declaration that this world is waiting for such an army of evangelized and spiritually empowered men and women to take up the challenge of being world-changers:

> For the earnest expectation of the creature waiteth for the manifestation
> of the sons of God. For the creature was made subject to vanity, not willingly, but by reason of him who hath subjected the same in hope,

because the creature itself also shall be delivered from the bondage of corruption into the glorious liberty of the children of God. For we know that the whole creation groaneth and travaileth in pain together until now.

They have no illusions about the limitations of their efforts. Unlike the naive social gospelers of the early years of the twentieth century, they are not liberal theologians whom H. Richard Niebuhr once described as people who preach, "A God without wrath brought men without sin into a kingdom without judgment through the ministrations of a Christ without a cross."[4]

Instead, they believe that the task of changing the world will be completed only with the second coming of Christ. They have what the German theologian Jürgen Moltmann called "a theology of hope." As they struggle to bring "the principalities and powers" (i.e., the institutions and social forces that dominate the present age) into subjection to God's will, they do so with the assurance that Christ will return to join their feeble and failing efforts and carry them to victory. In Philippians 1:6 they find hope in "being confident of this very thing, that he which hath begun a good work in you will perform it until the day of Jesus Christ."

With such an optimistic view of the future, evangelical universalists go to work, trying to win converts into allegiance to Christ. They do so in order to increase the ranks of God's world-changers, and they contend that this alone is sufficient motivation to be radically committed to the task of evangelism.

AM I AN EVANGELICAL UNIVERSALIST?

As you might sense from the tone of my description of the rationale for evangelism that evangelical universalists propose, I find much in what they say to be very attractive. In my own evangelistic efforts, I take that point of view by calling people to Christ, by inviting them to participate with God in the great adventure of changing the world. My message is that of the *first* of "The Four Spiritual Laws," that God loves you and has a wonderful plan for your life. I tell my audiences that God has predestined them to do important work in establishing the kingdom on earth and that He calls them from the mundane activities of a hedonistically driven world to do heroic things in the name of God. In preaching, I declare that God is presently moving in our world, trying to change things, and that each and every listener is created to participate in that work in a special and unique way.

This call to discipleship resonates especially well with young people who are trying to figure out what they should do with their lives. They do not have to read Viktor Frankl's book *Man's Search for Meaning* to realize that, without a purpose for life that is worthy of their humanity, life will be a neurotic experience of boredom and absurdity. They *know* that their lives were made for heroism and not for pleasure. But I am convinced that until they understand their place in God's scheme of things, young men and women will be confused as to how to express their hunger for heroism in ways that make sense.

There is a desire, especially among young people, for a salvation story that not only promises a joyful life after death, but also offers them adventuresome fulfillment in the midst of this life. Yielding to Christ, and allowing Him to direct their lives into becoming a significant part of God's plan for this world, delivers just what they are looking for.

Given my intense affinity for this approach to evangelism, the question can readily be raised as to whether or not I am a universalist. To that question I will have to answer, with a great deal of reluctance, an emphatic "No!"

HELL IS REAL

My primary reason for not being a universalist is that the Bible makes clear references to hell. An array of biblical texts support the doctrine that says that for those who reject the pleas of Christ to love Him and to give themselves to Him, there are dire consequences. These consequences are a direct result of their alienation from God and include complete loneliness, ongoing and intense boredom, being consumed with anger and hatred, torturous guilt, an overwhelming state of anxiety, and intensive, unfulfilled lusts. These are simply a few of the conditions that hint of the abysmal existence that awaits those who have rejected Jesus. Given what alienation from God is really all about, I believe that describing it as endless suffering in flames is only a metaphor for a reality that is far worse.

If you are going to be faithful to the Bible, you cannot avoid what it says in such verses as these:

Marvel not at this: for the hour is coming, in the which all that are in the graves shall hear his voice, and shall come forth; they that have done good, unto the resurrection of life; and they that have done evil, unto the resurrection of damnation. (John 5:28–29)

And I saw the dead, small and great, stand before God; and the books were opened: and another book was opened, which is the book of life: and the dead were judged out of those things which were written in the books, according to their works. And the sea gave up the dead which were in it; and death and hell delivered up the dead which were in them: and they were judged every man according to their works. And death and hell were cast into the lake of fire. This is the second death. And whosoever was not found written in the book of life was cast into the lake of fire. (Revelation 20:12–15)

There are other logical bases for believing in hell, such as the reason cited by the classical Russian novelist Fyodor Dostoevsky in the Pro and Contra section of his *Brothers Karamazov*. In simple language, Dostoevsky has Ivan, one of his major characters, declare that he cannot accept a system wherein hideous injustice goes unpunished. Ivan posits that in the end, all is forgotten and all (i.e., criminals and their victims) are lovingly reconciled without the guilty suffering any dire punishment.

Simply letting bygones be bygones without agonizing repentance is what the German theologian Dietrich Bonhoeffer called "cheap grace." It is unthinkable that the likes of Hitler, after leading humanity into the devastation of a world war and the evils of the Holocaust, might be let off simply with a reprimand followed by a kindly welcome into heaven. Justice requires more, according to Ivan, and he will not accept any theological system that does not deliver it.

NO FREEDOM WITHOUT HELL

Another logical requisite for a belief in hell is that there can be no freedom without it. Freedom always requires alternatives; therefore, there must be alternatives to heaven for freedom to exist. In his book *The Great Divorce*, C. S. Lewis made the case that hell is for people who do not want to be in heaven. He pointed out that those who refuse to relinquish their self-centeredness would find heaven an unbearable place. They would not choose to be there.

Lewis describes egotistical theologians, who crave the status they believe they derive from their intellectual theories about God, as being among those who would reject heaven. Such theologians would not appreciate the realm wherein the most simpleminded would have equal status and, perhaps *because* of their simplicity, a better grasp of the gospel than those who embroider it with sophisticated jargon. Lewis went on to write about a woman who had enjoyed playing the game of life according to the rules a sexist society laid down, and she did not want to be where using her sexual appeal did not gain her attention.

In this cleverly written little book, Lewis gave a variety of other examples of people who would find heaven unacceptable. He proposed that there might be a bus that regularly runs between heaven and hell, so that those who did not like the one place could go to the other. What is important to note in Lewis's writings is that hell is for people who *choose* to be there. If you ask why anybody would choose to live in hell, he suggests that we need only to look around us in the here and now to have an answer. Aren't there many examples among people you know of those who choose to go on living hellish existences in spite of offers of salvation that are readily available? Don't you know people who deliberately turn away from what would be good for them and choose alternatives that they know will lead to tragedy?

If you think that choosing to live in hell is an absurdity, then consider that choosing sin has always been an absurdity. Those who sin usually are well aware of its devastating consequences, yet they go on to commit their sins under the delusion that they can get away with it and that they will be happy in the end. They think they will be able to escape the inevitable and prove false the Scripture that assures them that their sins will catch up with them (Num. 32:23).

LOVE CAN ONLY BE FREELY CHOSEN

Jesus loves us and wants us to love Him in return, but love cannot be forced. It must be freely chosen. Consequently, there must be freedom to reject God, because only with freedom is there the possibility of the uncoerced choice that is necessary for us to love God. This is the kind of logic that Lewis used to make his case. Love requires free will. It is the freedom that God gave Adam and Eve when He created them and placed them in Eden. That first couple chose to turn from God, and people down through the ages have rejected God. The subtitle of the Bible could easily have been *Smart People—Stupid Choices*. Which of us does not look back on the messes that we have made in our lives and ask, "How could I have been that stupid?"

The good news is that God doesn't give up on us when we reject salvation.

God comes after us and pleads with us to repent. God provides for a negation of our rejection through Jesus Christ. For those who come to their senses, as did the prodigal son (Luke 15:11–32), and confess their foolish ways, there is a hopeful alternative to living in hell right now, as well as in the hereafter: "If we confess our sins, he is faithful and just to forgive us our sins, and to cleanse us from all unrighteousness" (1 John 1:9).

What I like about Lewis's approach in talking about hell and heaven is that it delivers us from an image of God that makes God into some kind of transcendental Shylock, demanding His pound of flesh from sinful humanity. If anyone asks how a loving God can send people to hell, Lewis answers that God doesn't. He says that people choose to go there because they do not want to give up the identities that they have forged with their egotism, wealth, power, and prestige. Their refusal to let go of such deceptive means for establishing who they are, and instead establish their personhoods in submissive love to God, is why they are not part of God's kingdom. The self-love that keeps them from loving God is the grounds for their lostness.

Evangelicals, such as Lewis and MacDonald, have worked hard to reconcile the doctrine of a loving and just God with a belief that this God would send to hell people who never had a chance to believe in Jesus Christ as Savior. They are well aware that most evangelicals hold to a theology that prescribes that only those who, in this life, make a profession of faith that agrees with theirs have any hope for eternal life.

Other religions are not so limiting. The Jews are not about to condemn the rest of humanity to everlasting punishment. Even Muslims, who in so many ways are doctrinaire and hard-nosed legalists, do not make their religion the only way to salvation. Followers of Islam strongly affirm that Jews who live according to their understanding of God as revealed in the Hebrew Bible, and Christians who live according to the teachings of Jesus as revealed in the New Testament, also have the promise of heaven.

The belief of most evangelicals that those who have never accepted the gospel message in this life are eternally doomed seems, to more liberal-minded people, to be grossly unfair in light of the fact that most of humanity throughout history never even heard about Jesus and what He accomplished at Calvary. Nonetheless, most evangelicals make a strong biblical argument that such is the case. They stress their belief that God is holy and that a holy God cannot tolerate the presence of sin. Thus, according to mainstream evangelicals, only those who have been "cleansed from sin through the blood of Christ" can come close to God. Sin, they say, cannot be taken lightly or simply dismissed and forgotten. Evangelicals abhor any talk of "cheap grace." Accordingly, they believe that sin must be removed from individuals in order for them to inherit eternal life and that only faith in the salvation of Jesus wrought on the cross can take away that sin.

There is little question that what evangelicals believe about hell and who goes there has given them the reputation of being narrow-minded. To this accusation, most evangelicals, often proudly and sometimes arrogantly, plead guilty. They claim in their defense that truth has always been narrow-minded. Using logic, they say that even as two plus two has always equaled four, so it is that the truth about the way to eternal life is narrowly defined. Evangelicals can quote chapter and verse of Scripture to prove this claim (Matt. 7:14).

It is over and against such an apparent narrowness that a minority of evangelicals, like Lewis and MacDonald, have developed alternatives. Fundamentalist evangelicals howl "heresy" at the very suggestion of such alternatives and gladly accept the scorn of those who contend that their narrowness gives evangelicals a bad reputation. Fundamentalist evangelicals again and again cite Scripture, pointing to the passage that reads, "Woe unto you, when all men shall speak well of you!" (Luke 6:26). "We are not out to win a popularity contest," they say. "We are out to speak the truth, and sometimes truth is hard for some people to hear."

The truth about who goes to heaven and who goes to hell, according to fundamentalist evangelicalism, really is hard for the rest of the world to hear, and whether evangelicalism as a whole will embrace more strongly the fundamentalist message or become more open to other possibilities remains to be seen. Right now, it appears that the fundamentalists are winning this tug of war within the evangelical camp. Whether this will turn off nonbelievers to the gospel or create an urgency that will drive those outside the evangelical community to Christ is a question that is left hanging for now.

7

Are Evangelicals Afraid of Science?

Evangelicalism has usually treated science as a threat and tried to protect believers from research and theories that might undermine their faith. As a boy, I remember seeing the movie *Inherit the Wind,* which depicted the famous Scopes trial where it was debated whether or not the theory of biological evolution could be taught in public schools. The Scopes trial, which pitted Clarence Darrow, the most famous lawyer of the day, against William Jennings Bryan, America's most prestigious fundamentalist, made belief in a literal six-day creation story as told in the Bible seem ridiculous. That movie made a deep impression upon me, and I came away with a sense that science was the enemy of orthodox Christianity and that believers in the Bible should be wary of it.

Times have changed since the Scopes trial, and nowadays Christians have developed the capacity to live quite comfortably with science. We even have learned to use some scientific discoveries to bolster our case for validating what the Bible says.

For many in our postmodern world, Christian apologetics (a rational defense of the gospel) may be quite passé. Trying to integrate the Christian faith with prevailing philosophical thinking and scientific discoveries seems to be an unnecessary and even useless task to those theological deconstructionists who increasingly laugh at these efforts. But for the rest of us, who still think and live in the context of a rational scientific world, apologetics yet has its place. Certainly coming to terms with science has been an important concern for evangelicals.

I feel I need to warn you that what follows in this chapter may seem more than foreign to what is essential for normal faith and practice. Some may even find what I am trying to say pointless and irrelevant to anything meaningful in their lives. Yet what I write here has been a significant part of my own theological thinking, as I have tried to maintain my faith amid the onslaught of questions modern science has raised and the philosophical issues that the contemporary marketplace of ideas has generated. This stuff is really important to me. If what I have written in this chapter seems heavy and you feel overburdened by it all, then you should feel free simply to go on to the next chapter.

However, even as I acknowledge getting into heavy thinking, I have to tell you that many people have told me that the ideas that are to follow in this chapter have proven to be most helpful to them—especially the section on how I use Albert Einstein's concept of time to explore the doctrines of salvation and what happens as we relate to the work of Christ on the cross. If you can stay with me—great!

THEOLOGY CHANGES

Science has defined the mind-set of our modern age, and evangelicals who want to speak meaningfully to our secular society must take science seriously. It prescribes the social context in which Christians think out their beliefs and has a huge impact on the kinds of questions they try to answer and how they go about answering them. Consequently, while the Bible remains the final authority for faith and practice for most Christians, what theologians find in their reading of Scripture and how they relate Scripture to the concerns of the times in which they live do change, especially in reponse to what science tells us. What is going on in the world of science at a particular time greatly impacts theologies. This is true especially when it comes to how theologians answer those questions raised by the prevailing philosophies and science.

Given this reality, it is not surprising that theologies are time-bound, even though the Bible is not. In every age, theologians restructure the Christian faith in an effort to relate the eternal truths of the Bible to the mind-set of the existential situation. They have to recast the theologies of bygone centuries in the prevailing language of the day and the intellectual categories of the present age, which science has largely defined.

The twentieth century was a time wherein cataclysmic upheavals occurred in the thinking of the Western world. Not only did revolutions in transportation and communication create a global village in which we faced alternative religions that challenged the dominance of the Judeo-Christian faith; we also had to come to grips with a whole new understanding of the universe, brought on by the theories of the likes of Albert Einstein. Now, as we enter the twenty-first century, quantum physics will require an even further recasting of how we state the unchanging truths of the gospel story so that thinking people in the emerging new scientific world will understand what we're talking about.

SCIENCE IS NOT A THREAT

What I find most encouraging is that the most recent discoveries and theories of science in our age do not provide threats to basic Christian beliefs, as was the case with the discoveries and intellectual challenges that emerged during the Enlightenment. In reality, the new thought forms and the emerging perspectives of the increasingly evident postmodern world-view actually have created a milieu in which belief in the supernatural becomes relatively easy to hold, and in which there is room for discussion of the kinds of mystical experiences that are so much a part of essential Christianity. It was not always so.

NO LONGER THE CENTER OF THE UNIVERSE

I remember how in the 1950s, Bishop John A. T. Robinson's book *Honest to God* upset the Christian community with redefinitions of basic theological doctrines. Built on the existentialist views of Rudolf Bultmann and Martin Heidegger, Robinson's book declared that the New Testament made sense only against the backdrop of the concept of the three-storied universe of the ancient world. Furthermore, he said that it was impossible to sustain much of what was in the Bible given the modern understanding of cosmology. Robinson contended that in the days of Jesus, the earth was understood as being flat, covered by a dome on which were placed the stars and above which heaven was located. Hell in this three-storied universe was located under the flat earth. Angels ascended and descended from a heaven that was "up there" and the wicked were sent to a hell that was "down there" (see Eph. 4:9).

According to Robinson, once science proved that such a view of the universe was untenable, people would have to abandon much of what the New Testament taught because it was constructed on this ancient understanding of the cosmos.

Bishop Robinson was not the first theologian to recognize that a change in the way people thought about the physical universe would lead to serious challenges to prevailing religious beliefs. The Roman Catholic Church had condemned the teachings of Galileo and put him on trial for heresy. The Roman curia realized that Galileo's ideas posed a threat to its theological traditions. They saw his theories as lending support to the heretical views of mystic Giordano Bruno.

Bruno's vision was one in which the universe was infinite, leaving the earth a comparatively miniscule speck of dust in the vastness of the cosmos. To the church of the Middle Ages, the earth had always been at the center of God's creation, but with this new cosmology, first envisioned by Bruno and then supported by Galileo, there was no center of the universe. Given this new kind of cosmos, the significance of our own world in such a vast setting was incredibly reduced.

The earth, to these Catholic theologians, had always been understood as the main stage on which the great drama of God's creation and salvation was acted out with the human race as primary actors. But given a vast universe as Bruno and Galileo suggested, we would have to see our world as a seemingly insignificant planet circling a moderate-sized star in a rather average-sized galaxy in an infinite universe of billions and billions of galaxies. In such an immense universe, it would be hard to believe that human beings are of ultimate importance.

The Roman Catholic curia readily understood that such an understanding of the cosmos could reduce humanity to insignificance. They were right! In centuries to come, this sense of the inconsequence of human beings would lead to a belief that our lives were meaningless accidents lost in space. This kind of thinking would eventually give birth to nihilistic, existentialist philosophies. Carl Sagan, the popular astronomer, has said as much.

THE PROTESTANT RESPONSE

Negative reactions to changes in the ways that the scientists of the Enlightenment were redefining the universe were also evident among Protestant thinkers. Martin Luther, who evidently affirmed a belief in an inerrant Bible, wrote a tract that was little more than a diatribe against Nicolaus Copernicus. To Luther, Copernicus's claims that the earth orbited the sun, rather than the sun's orbiting the earth, seemed seriously dangerous. Luther argued that in the biblical story of the conquest of the Promised Land, Joshua, hoping to have the day of a crucial battle prolonged so that Israel's enemies would not escape into the night, prayed for the sun to stand still (Josh. 10:12–13). Luther asserted that this passage of Scripture provided evidence that it was the sun that moved, not the earth. The cosmology of Copernicus challenged Luther's reading of Scripture, and that was enough for the great reformer to condemn him.

As we enter the twenty-first century, we are well aware that the authority of the Bible has survived many of the imagined threats that Luther believed were inherent in the theories of Copernicus and that the Roman Catholic Church saw in the theories of Bruno and Galileo. What is even more interesting is that the cosmology that has emerged over the last few decades under the auspices of Einsteinian physics has pushed aside the arguments of Bultmann and Robinson and given grounds for a New Testament world-view. With the new cosmology created under the impact of Albert Einstein's theory of relativity, the concept of an infinite universe, so essential to Bultmann and Robinson's assertions, is itself challenged. Einsteinian cosmology posits a universe that is "unbounded, but limited." This unbounded but limited universe is now being defined as spherical and expanding.

EINSTEIN'S NEW COSMOLOGY

To give some idea about what the universe is like in this new cosmology, imagine it as a gigantic balloon, with all the stars and galaxies placed in the skin of the balloon. If each galaxy is like a dot on the skin of the imaginary balloon, it is easy to picture what will happen as this balloon is blown up. As it expands, the dots (i.e., galaxies) would move away from each other. In the real universe, that is exactly what is happening to the galaxies. Telescopic observations offer evidence that we need to provide validation for Einstein's cosmology and his theories of an expanding universe.

This new cosmology generates all kinds of speculations that intrigue many theologians. For instance, if space and matter are in this curved, expanding universe, we cannot evade the question about the context in which the universe is doing the expanding. To liken the universe to an expanding balloon, with space and matter in the skin of the balloon, we find ourselves inclined to ask, "In *what* is the universe expanding?"

We cannot say that the universe is expanding in empty space, since it is empty space, along with all the galaxies that are "stuck" in it, that is doing the expanding. In other words, we cannot say that the universe is expanding in nothingness, because it is the "nothingness" that we call empty space that is itself expanding.

This new cosmology may seem perplexing, to say the least. But what it does is destroy the arguments of the likes of Bultmann and Robinson, who said that since the universe is infinite, it cannot be transcended and there can be no place beyond the universe that we can call heaven or hell. Arthur Eddington, the astronomer laureate of England, said in his book *The Expanding Universe:* "The super-system of the galaxies is dispersing as a puff of smoke disperses. Sometimes I wonder whether there may be a greater scale of existence of things, in which it *is* no more than a puff of smoke."

We can make all kinds of theological suggestions regarding the context in which the universe is expanding, but the idea of transcending it seems now to be a real possibility. It doesn't take much to recognize the theological implications of this.

Even while we are trying to comprehend something of what Einstein's theories suggest about the shape of the universe, he threw us another curve ball when he told us that the universe is *multidimensional.* Given our categories of apperception (to use the terminology of the philosopher Immanuel Kant), it is beyond our ability to think about anything that has more than three dimensions—yet that is what Einstein expects us to do. In addition to height, width, and depth, he tells us that there is a fourth dimension to the universe. What is even more astounding is that there are scientists and mathematicians since Einstein, such as P. D. Ouspensky, who have calculated up to sixteen dimensions to the universe. The possibilities for what we would consider "miraculous" in such a multidimensional universe are seemingly limitless. What we have thought of as possible or impossible is severely challenged in this multidimensional cosmos.

THE REALITY OF MIRACLES

To help them think outside of the a priori perspectives that come from their having been socialized to see things three-dimensionally, Einstein required his students to read a book entitled *Flatland* by Edwin A. Abbott. In this book, Abbott gets the reader to imagine a man from our three-dimensional universe suddenly showing up in a universe where everything is flat—in other words, in a two-dimensional universe. In this universe, the man from the three-dimensional universe can perform what appear to be miracles to those who are two-dimensional. For instance, he can disappear from the sight of the two-dimensional people simply by jumping up. By taking advantage of a third dimension that is outside their realm of reality, his disappearance appears to be an astonishing feat.

In a two-dimensional universe, a line appears as an insurmountable barrier, but our three-dimensional man can simply step over it. Again, what is nothing exceptional for the three-dimensional man seems to be miraculous to those whose perspective is only two-dimensional.

The point that I want to make here is that those children of the Enlightenment, who would discount the possibility of anything that does not fit in with the empirical perceptions of what they perceive to be a three-dimensional universe, have to be less arrogant about their declarations of what is and what is not possible. The multidimensional universe that is emerging within the framework of modern physics leaves room for a host of possibilities that such skeptical children of the Enlightenment would have ruled out.

C. S. Lewis, in his book *A Case for Christianity*, argued that miracles are not contradictions to the laws of science, but rather phenomena that occur within the parameters of the laws of nature; however, people within our present age have not yet understood these laws of nature. At a future time, stated Lewis, when we have a broader and deeper grasp of the laws of nature, we will treat what once seemed miraculous as both reasonable and possible.

To illustrate this point, Lewis described what a tribe of people in a prescientific society might conclude if, one day, they saw an airplane flying low over their heads. The members of the tribe, seeing that the airplane is made out of metal and believing, according to their limited understanding of science, that metal cannot fly, conclude that they are witnessing a miracle. What they do not know is that there are certain laws of aerodynamics that permit metal to fly, if it is shaped in a particular way and is traveling at a particular speed. The airplane is not contradicting the laws of science; it is simply abiding by laws of nature that are beyond the understanding of the tribal people. So, contended Lewis, what we might think of as miracles are not contradicting the laws of nature, but simply taking advantage of laws of nature that we have not yet discovered.

Following Lewis's explanation, we can argue that, given the possibilities of living in a universe that has more than our perceptible three dimensions and by taking advantage of these other dimensions, things are possible that we would likely consider to be miracles. With modern physics, we are going to have to learn to be more humble about what we say is impossible.

THE UNIVERSE'S BEGINNING—AND END

Still another interesting postulate that comes from this is Einstein's new theory of an expanding universe wherein the universe, as we know it, had a specific beginning and eventually will come to an end. Although scientists once believed that the universe was always there and that there was no event that could be called "creation," this new cosmology forces them to admit that there really was a creation event. Actually, scientists now calculate that the universe was created approximately fifteen billion years ago with the explosion of an unbelievably intense proton (i.e., a unique particle of energy). A good description of what happened way back then can be found in *The Big Bang* by Karen C. Fox. It is one of the more understandable books designed for lay readers like myself.

This astounding description does not fit the theologies of those who preach a six-day creation. It does, however, fit the thinking of those of us who see the opening chapter of Genesis not so much as a literal six-day creation but as a description of the various stages of creation that occurred over years of time. I suppose that one good reason for not believing the Genesis "days" were literal is that God did not create the sun, the rising and setting of which enables us to mark off days, until the fourth day of the creation process. It's hard to imagine having days, as we understand them, without a sun.

Regardless of how secularists may want to evade it, there was a creation event, with all that such an event might suggest about there being a creator. What is more, the universe, as we know it, will definitely come to an end. The second law of thermodynamics is the one pillar that has survived the onslaught of Einsteinian physics. It posits that energy is being dissipated throughout the universe and that eventually all the energy of the universe will be dissipated and the universe will reach what scientists call "maximum entropy." When that happens, the universe will have died. At that point, there will be no more energy, no more motion, and no more time. "Creation" will be no more. As I will note later, time is relative to motion, and since there will be no motion, "there should be time no longer," just as the Bible says (Rev. 10:6).

It is in dealing with the new perspectives on the nature of time and its relationship to motion that modern theologians can gain some rich insights for solving some of the most perplexing problems that have troubled them in recent years. It is to reflections on time and their implications for Christian apologetics that we now turn our attention.

TIME, BIBLICAL AND EARTHLY

Oscar Cullmann, noted for his biblical analysis of how time is regarded in the Bible, contends that time in Scripture is defined as a linear progression reaching from the infinite past, prior to creation, and extending into the infinite future. Historical time, according to Cullmann, is simply a segment out of the linear development that he believes to be an everlasting progression.

On the contrary, Emil Brunner, the Swiss-German theologian, argued that historical time was a created realm within the larger reality of "God's time," which Brunner called "the eternal now." In this eternal now, said Brunner, time as we understand it is transcended, and the concepts of *before* and *after* that go with our linear concept of time become meaningless.

Such arguments about the nature of time, and its relationship to what the Bible defines as eternity, are nothing new to theologians. They have been intrigued by discussions on the subject from as far back as Saint Augustine. It was Augustine who, early on in the life of the church, recognized that a host of theological questions could be resolved if it were possible to figure out how time as we know it is related to God's time. Augustine, centuries before Einstein and somewhat anticipating Einstein's thinking, taught that time was related to creation and that it had a beginning when God spoke the universe into existence. He then raised the paradoxical question as to whether or not there was a time before there was time. As we shall see, an answer to this question is full of theological intrigue.

Surprisingly, Augustine's problems related to theological implications about time might find some resolutions in Einstein's physics. First of all, let us consider what Einstein found out about time. He came up with the amazing discovery that time becomes compressed with increased speed. In other words, the faster we travel, the more time is compressed. While the following figures are not precise, they may help in understanding what this is all about.

- If you were put into a rocket and sent into space, traveling at 170,000 miles per second relative to earth, and then returned in ten years, when you returned you would be ten years older, but all the rest of us would be twenty years older. For those of us who remained on earth, our twenty years would be compressed into ten years of your time.

- If we got you traveling at 180,000 miles per second, our twenty years would be compressed into one day of your time.

- If we could get you traveling at the speed of light—186,000 miles per second—there would be no passage of time at all. If that were possible, all of time would be compressed into one eternal now.

Young people who have watched the television show *Star Trek* have no problem with any of this, because they are used to Captain Kirk and company moving forward in time simply by altering the speed at which the spaceship *Enterprise* travels.

TIME AND "THE NOW"

In reflecting upon how time is relative to motion, I want to declare that I believe God is able to experience time at the speed of light. For God, all of time can be compressed into what the theologian Emil Brunner called "the eternal now." All things happen "now" with God. With God, a thousand years are as a day, and a day is as a thousand years (2 Pet. 3:8). The very name of God implies this reality. God's name is "I AM." God never was, and God never will be. God is always in the "now."

The "nowness" of God lends support to the declaration of theologian Paul Tillich, who contended that God could not be known as an object caught in the time/space continuum in which we live. According to Tillich, God can only be "encountered in the now." We cannot analyze God and then describe God in ways that fit the categories of time-bound logic. God will not yield to positivism (the philosophy that reduces all reality to terms that the five senses can experience) nor be understood in terms of the categories of human logic.

Those philosophers and social scientists who call themselves phenomenologists are most in harmony with the concept of the eternal now. They point out that "now" has no extension in time. They argue that we cannot say that the next minute is now; nor can we even say the next second is now. We cannot even say that the next millionth of a second is now. Now, they contend, is that nonexistent point wherein the past meets the future. Now, in a sense, is not really in time. Yet each of us can say, "I am alive now! Now is where I am!"

Everything that is true about *me* belongs to the past. I can reflect on me—I can take a good look at myself—but everything that I observe about me is in the past. What I can know about me is not who and what *I* am right now. Me is what I used to be. I cannot even tell you what I am thinking now, because in order to do that, I have to stop and consider what I *was* thinking. But again I point out that now is where I am—it is where I exist.

More importantly, God is in the now. For God, all of time and eternity are gathered up in this eternal now. God is the Alpha and Omega, the beginning and the end (Rev. 1:8). Given this assertion about God's being in the now, we can begin to understand why Tillich argued that God cannot be known, as other objects are known, because in the now, there is no objective knowledge. That is because objective knowledge requires reflection, and when we reflect, we can only reflect on what was—never on what is now. If I ask you to reflect on what you are experiencing now, you can only tell me about what you were reflecting upon when I asked you the question.

GOD IN THE NOW

All of this seeming double-talk affirms a basic evangelical truth, and that is that those who would know God must encounter God in the now. Right now, the person who would know God must surrender to God and let God overwhelm and invade his or her mind, body, and soul. A person does not become a Christian simply by gathering objective knowledge about God. In reality, an individual may know all the doctrines about God and have a "sound" theology about what God accomplished in the death and resurrection of Jesus Christ, but he or she still may not *know* God. There is a qualitative difference between knowing all about God and having a sacred encounter with God in the now.

Each morning I try to wake up half an hour before I have to and then lie in bed, experiencing quietude. In the stillness of the morning, I surrender to a possible encounter with God. I wait patiently to feel God's presence. I sense a beckoning, as did the psalmist of old, who heard the admonition, "Be still, and know that I am God" (Ps. 46:10). The "still small voice" of God has no words (1 Kings 19:12), but there comes an inner groaning as I encounter God in the now.

I can talk about this experience with God. I can try to describe it and even theologize about it. But in doing so, I am no longer into the experience. I am only reflecting on the experience that I just had with God. In such occasions of mystical ecstasy, time, in the linear sense, ceases to exist. I am, in such spiritual encounters, beyond time. I am experiencing God in the now. This is the kind of knowledge about God that the apostle Paul was praying to experience when he wrote, "That I may know him, and the power of his resurrection, and the fellowship of his sufferings, being made conformable unto his death" (Phil. 3:10).

Such an encounter with God is one way to experience what we evangelicals call being "born again." It taps into the essence of the conversion experience.

EINSTEIN'S THEORY AND THE CROSS

A great and perhaps most important insight that can come out of the relativity theory is a deeper understanding of what Jesus accomplished for us on the cross. If you believe, as I do, that Jesus is fully God as well as fully human, then you might be ready to accept that there are some existential dimensions of His saving ministry on the cross that Jesus is doing now. As a man, and the only sinless man who ever lived, Jesus lived and died some two thousand years ago. Back there and then on the cross, He took the punishment for our sins. Jesus was the sacrificial Lamb of God—the sacrifice that delivers each of us from the condemnation that is our due because of the dark side of our humanity.

When He died there on that hill outside of Jerusalem, Jesus became the substitute who went through the hell that should have been our lot because of the dirt and ugliness of our sins. That He endured this punishment on our behalf is a historical fact, established in linear time. It is a done deal! There is nothing more to be done to deliver us from the punishment that should be meted out to each of us. We can justifiably talk about the finished work of Jesus. Historically, in time, the perfect sacrifice of His life for ours is an accomplished fact.

SOMETHING MORE

What I have just stated relates to what Jesus did for us back there and then. But there is something more that the would-be Christian should grasp to experience all that Christ's salvation has to offer. In addition to what Jesus did for us, each of us must be ready to surrender to what Jesus wants to do *to* us in the *now*. Because Jesus is not only "fully human" but also "fully God"—even as the Chalcedonian Creed declares—He is able to comprehend time as God. Because He is God, Jesus is able to gather all of time together in His eternal now.

Jesus not only was a man who lived, died, and was resurrected historically; He is also the God for whom all things are in the present moment. That is why He could say to the Pharisees, "Before Abraham was, I am" (John 8:58)! Jesus wasn't using poor grammar when He said that. Instead, He was declaring His divinity. He was saying that the time before there was an Abraham is present tense for Him. Because of His divinity, He experiences all events in time and history as happening for Him in the now.

If you are following all of this, you may be ready to grasp what for me has been one of the most important dimensions of what Christ did and does on the cross. When He hung on Calvary's tree some two thousand years ago, being God, He was—and He is—simultaneously with me here and now. Right now, I am caught up in His eternal now. The centuries that separate me from Jesus's suffering on Golgotha are compressed, as though at the speed of light, so that for Him, He is with me in this instantaneous now. That means that *right now*, in God's divine sense of time, as He hangs on the cross, He is able to empathize with me and, via a kind of spiritual osmosis, absorb into Himself all the sin and darkness of my life.

On the cross two thousand years ago, He took the punishment for my sin, but right now, in His eternal now, He is able to reach out to me from that old rugged cross. Like a magnet, He can draw out of me all the evil that is part of my humanity, as though it were some iron filings.

The Bible says: "For he hath made him to be sin for us, who knew no sin; that we might be made the righteousness of God in him" (2 Cor. 5:21). Here and now, if I surrender to Him, He will purge me and make me pure. If He is in me, and I am in Him in His eternal now, then I become a new creation. Old things pass away, and everything becomes new (2 Cor. 5:17). "Though your sins be as scarlet, they shall be as white as snow; though they be red like crimson, they shall be as wool" (Isa. 1:18).

There is more to salvation than just being delivered from punishment for sin. There is a *cleansing* of the heart, mind, and soul that can occur in the now. It was for this special existential cleansing that King David prayed in Psalm 51. And it is this dimension of Christ's work on the cross that we read about in 1 John 1:9: "If we confess our sins, he is faithful and just to forgive us our sins, and to cleanse us from all unrighteousness."

In this verse, we not only read about the forgiveness of sins that comes from what He did back on Calvary, but we also learn about the *cleansing* that can occur in the here and now. Jesus, being God, can cleanse us today because He is, in the words of the Danish existentialist theologian Sören Kierkegaard, "the eternally crucified." When I preach evangelistic sermons within the church, I usually say, "I know you believe in what Jesus did for you back there and then. But what I want to know is whether or not you are willing to let Jesus do something *to* you *right now.*"

I want to know if you are willing to let Jesus reach out to you from the cross and absorb your sin, making it His own, and at that same instant let His goodness flow into you to take the place of sin. I ask, "Will you let Him impart to you His righteousness? If you will, then on that Day of Judgment, the One who has taken your sin and made it His own in the now will present you to His Father, as it says in the book of Jude, *faultless!*"

MOTIVATION FOR HOLINESS

I do not want to leave the discussion of what goes on with Christ suffering and cleansing us from our sin in His eternal now without pointing out that all of this should provide a great impetus for living the holy life. Every time I sin, at that very instant Jesus groans in agony at Calvary. Even as I sin today, He experiences the agony of ingesting my sin into Himself in His eternal now, as He hangs spread-eagle on the tree back there and then. This is why it says in Hebrews 6:6 that when we sin, we crucify Him anew. In a sense, when we sin, we crucify Him right now.

While spending a few days as the religious-emphasis-week speaker on the campus of a Christian college, I talked with a senior who was quite cavalier about the sins in his life. He told me about having an affair with a married woman. Then he said, "Whenever I commit sin, I remember that Jesus took the punishment for that sin back there on the cross."

In response, I said, "The next time you're in bed having sex with your lover, I hope you can hear the screams of Jesus from the cross; because at that very moment Jesus is reaching across time and absorbing into His own body the very sin that you are committing there and then. The Jesus who hates sin becomes the sinner that you are. The innocent Jesus becomes the adulterer you are, because in His eternal now, He becomes everything about you that He hates."

In the face of the awareness that Jesus takes our sins and suffers for them, even while we are in the act of committing them, we can get a fuller understanding of why the apostle Paul wrote that by His grace our sins will be forgiven, but then added, "What shall we say then? Shall we continue in sin, that grace may abound?

God forbid. How shall we, that are dead to sin, live any longer therein?" (Rom. 6:1–2).

WHAT HAPPENS WHEN WE DIE?

While reflecting on the ministry of Jesus on the cross demands our primary attention, note that this is just the beginning of the theological uses of the time concepts emerging out of relativity theory. I find it fascinating when I consider how many of the perplexing, and at times paradoxical, problems that have haunted the church might somehow be clarified with help from Einstein's theory.

For instance, many Christians are confused about just what happens when they die. Are we immediately delivered to the judgment seat of God, or do we lie buried in the ground to be resurrected at the second coming of Christ? Using time concepts derived from relativity theory, I can suggest some interesting answers to such questions.

SOUL SLEEP

Seventh-Day Adventists, along with many other Christians, have preached that when we are dead and buried, we lie in the ground until the Second Coming. Some have called this the doctrine of "soul sleep." Those who hold to this doctrine have good reasons for believing this way, not the least of which are the explicit words of the apostle Paul:

> For if we believe that Jesus died and rose again, even so them also which sleep in Jesus will God bring with him. For this we say unto you by the word of the Lord, that we which are alive and remain unto the coming of the Lord shall not prevent them which are asleep. For the Lord himself shall descend from heaven with a shout, with the voice of the archangel, and with the trump of God: and the dead in Christ shall rise first. (1 Thessalonians 4:14–16)

> Behold, I shew you a mystery; we shall not all sleep, but we shall all be changed, in a moment, in the twinkling of an eye, at the last trump: for the trumpet shall sound, and the dead shall be raised incorruptible, and we shall be changed. For this corruptible must put on incorruption, and this mortal *must* put on immortality. (1 Corinthians 15:51–53)

Those who believe in soul sleep argue that the Bible does not teach the immortality of the soul apart from the body. They contend that at those funerals where the minister says, "While the body is put into the ground, the soul of the deceased has gone on to be with the Lord," he or she is misleading the listeners. They claim that the idea of the soul being in one place while the body is in another is not what we learn from the New Testament.

What we read in Scripture is that Jesus was *physically* raised from the dead. The Bible is clear about the fact that His tomb was empty on Easter morning. The apostle Paul told us that we also will be physically resurrected, even as Jesus was.

> But someone will say, "How are the dead raised up? And with what body do they come?" Foolish one, what you sow is not made alive unless it dies. And what you sow, you do not sow that body that shall be, but mere grain—perhaps wheat or some other grain. But God gives it a body as He pleases, and to each seed its own body. All flesh is not the same flesh, but there is one kind of flesh of men, another flesh of animals, another of fish, and another of birds. There are also celestial bodies and terrestrial bodies; but the glory of the celestial is one, and the glory of the terrestrial is another . . . It is sown a natural body, it is raised a spiritual body. There is a natural body, and there is a spiritual body. (1 Corinthians 15:35–40, 44 NKJV)

I have had a hard time grasping how all of this is possible, given the fact that over the centuries, almost all of the dead have turned into dust. But then, we are talking about a miracle wrought by God when we talk about our resurrected bodies, and with God, anything is possible. After all, God made us out of dust the first time, so I have come to conclude that a reconstruction job shouldn't be too much of a problem for the Almighty.

The resurrected Jesus had a corporal body that others could recognize and touch (John 20:27). And if we believe the Scriptures, then we will believe that we ourselves will be resurrected in like manner. That means that when the trumpet sounds on that last day, we all will be bodily resurrected. We will have new bodies that, in some ways, will be related to the bodies that we had in this life. But our resurrected bodies will be perfected and transformed, free from any possibility of decay and sickness and death. There is little question that an honest literal reading of the New Testament leads to this conclusion.

INSTANTLY WITH GOD

Standing against the belief about lying in the grave until the Second Coming are most Christians, who believe that at the moment of death, we are instantaneously with God. Those who hold to this doctrine about what happens at death and, at the same time, want to believe in the bodily resurrection of those who "die in Christ" (i.e., the saved) have to do some theological gymnastics to harmonize these two doctrines. They have to cope with the reality that those Christians who are dead and buried are still in the ground, and we can prove that by digging them up. Yet at the same time, they have to explain how these who are "dead in Christ" can instantaneously be physically present with the Lord in heaven.

One way of dealing with the apparent paradox is to posit some kind of "interim bodies" that deceased Christians can use until the Second Coming, when they will exchange them for their resurrected bodies. Dispensationalists often take this route in dealing with the problem.

We can also solve this paradox by suggesting that our souls kind of float around, waiting to be embodied on the day of Christ's coming. This is somewhat easy for those of us who have been raised, albeit unconsciously, under the influence of Greek philosophical thinking. In reality, those of us in the Western world are all heirs to the Hellenistic spirit that has led us to think in categories that have come down to us from the likes of Socrates, Plato, and Aristotle.

It was the Greek world-view that conditioned us to dichotomize the body and spirit in such a way that the one could exist without the other. To the Hebrew mind, such a separation was impossible. According to the ancient Jews, the spirit, or soul, could never exist in a disembodied form, and I believe that it is this Jewish view that we find in the New Testament. But it is the Hellenistic world-view, rather than that of the Jews, that has conditioned our thinking—making it simple for us to believe that a disembodied soul could go to be with God in heaven, even while the body lay buried in the ground.

ONE WORLD AT A TIME

To tell the truth, as a young Christian, I found all of these discussions about what happens at death somewhat preposterous. Like most Christians, I chose not to think about such things, because they only nurtured doubts about the entire system of beliefs, which was my raison d'être. I preferred to think as Confucius did when he said, "One world at a time, please!" In those days, my theology was a coherent system, and to question one part was to call the entire system into question. My beliefs were like a house of cards, and to pull out one of those cards would bring the whole house down. Thus, I just did not want to consider the conflicting beliefs about what happens at death.

To tell the truth, I did not even think about dying back then. Other people died, I thought to myself subconsciously, and like most young people, I was able to drive the idea of my own death out of my mind. But I'm sixty-nine years old now, and the awareness of my impending death, especially after a serious stroke, is inescapable. Consequently, I am now very interested in what will happen to me after I take my last breath.

HELP FROM THE RELATIVITY THEORY

Relativity theory again may come to the rescue to provide some deliverance from the paradoxes that surround our thinking about what happens at death. Personally, I believe that I can make a biblical case for believing that at the moment of death, I will be instantaneously with God in a resurrected body; yet I also believe that my body will remain in the grave until the moment when Christ returns. I can hold both of these beliefs, as paradoxical as that might seem, providing that those *two* moments are one and the *same* moment.

That is exactly what relativity theory makes possible. If I were to die and be buried today and the second coming of Christ were to occur ten years from now, it would seem to those who remained behind that I was enduring "soul sleep" for those ten years. But at the speed of light—God's time—the moment of my death *and* the moment of Christ's second coming would be one and the same. In God's "eternal now," these two moments would be simultaneous.

Given relativity theory, all who died in Christ would be resurrected at the same instant, because no matter when their deaths occurred, they would all be caught up and compressed into one eternal now. There will be no waiting around in heaven for any of my loved ones to arrive. Nor will I have to wait around to get my resurrected body, because at the speed of light (i.e, God's eternal now), the moment of my death will be compressed into the moment when the trumpet sounds and the dead in Christ arise. "In a moment, in the twinkling of an eye, at the last trump: for the trumpet shall sound, and the dead shall be raised incorruptible, and we shall be changed" (1 Cor. 15:52).

WHAT ABOUT PREDESTINATION?

There is another question that Christians don't like to think about, because it leads to endless arguments. It is the question that provides ongoing discussions in the dormitories of Christian colleges and Bible schools. I am referring, of course, to the controversy surrounding the question of whether God predetermines everything or we have a free will to choose our destinies.

Extreme Calvinists, who are committed to believing in predestination, argue strongly in support of believing in a God who determines everything. Usually they leave little, if any, room for the exercising of free will. On the contrary, those who call themselves Arminians argue just as forcefully in favor of their doctrine that people are free to make those decisions that determine what happens in their lives.

When it comes to quoting Scripture, the extreme Calvinists have the upper hand. They contend that if God knows everything—which they affirm without doubt—then it follows that God knows what is going to happen before it happens. And if God knows what is going to happen before it happens, claim the Calvinists, then what God knows *will* happen is destined *to* happen. Foreknowledge, they claim, is tantamount to predestination.

To support their case, the Calvinists readily quote Romans 8:29–30: "For whom he did foreknow, he also did predestinate to be conformed to the image of his Son, that he might be the firstborn among many brethren. Moreover whom he did predestinate, them he also called: and whom he called, them he also justified: and whom he justified, them he also glorified."

The Arminians, on the other hand, assert a belief in free will. They point out that all through Scripture, God gave people the freedom to decide for themselves whether they would obey or disobey Him, and that everyone is responsible for his or her decisions. Did not Joshua call upon the people to choose whom they would serve (Josh. 24:15)? And in the New Testament, do we not read that each moment of each day is fraught with possibilities to make decisions that have eternal significance? Consider Paul's declaration: "For He says: / 'In an acceptable time I have heard you, / And in the day of salvation I have helped you.' / Behold, now is the accepted time; behold, now is the day of salvation" (2 Cor. 6:2 NKJV).

RELATIVITY THEORY TO THE RESCUE

The good news is that relativity theory might resolve the differences between the Calvinists and the Arminians. When asked the question "Does God know what is going to happen before it does?" Einstein's view of time allows us to answer both yes and no. The reason for this seeming double-talk is that, as we have seen, with God there is no "before," nor is there an "after." With God, all things happen now. Given that perspective, God does not know beforehand who is going to be saved or lost, because there is no beforehand with God. Nevertheless, for those of us caught up in the linear progression of time that goes with life as we know it, there *is* a before and an after, so God does know what will happen in *our* before and in *our* after.

Thinking about the realities of existing in this world, we have to affirm with the Calvinists that God knows what is going to happen and who is going to choose salvation from the very beginning of our linear progression of time. That is because God knows the end from the beginning. With God, both the beginning and the end are in the eternal now. On the other hand, given that all things happen *now* with God, God does not know beforehand what will happen. Therefore, with God, we are *not* fatalistically determined, but we can decide right now what we will do and be. In God's economy of time, we are all responsible for our actions. Thus, God's sovereignty is preserved while our freedom is affirmed.

After dealing with the predestination versus free will argument in light of Einstein's theory of relativity, we must again remind ourselves of the question Augustine raised about the "time" before there *was* time. Prior to the big bang, which initiated space and time before the expanding universe got under way, did God have foreknowledge? Since such a "time" is beyond even the categories of Einstein's physics and the calculations of his mathematics, who can say? Might we not, after all, be back in the same quandary of trying to figure out how it is possible to posit free will and simultaneously uphold belief in an all-knowing God?

A WARNING

There is a final warning to consider in our discussion of all of this apologetic material. Before we get too excited about the ways in which Einstein's theories validate biblical Christianity and start employing their positive theological implications, we must be aware that at some future time, it is likely that these presently *new* theories, like all other cosmological theories, will be obsolete. Already, quantum theory, the new theory on the block, is forcing a rethinking of some of the basic ideas relativity theory posed.

For example, physicists are now claiming that electrons can be reduced to vibrating sounds, which would give a lot of support to the biblical ideas that God *spoke* creation into existence and that all of nature sings. Heisenberg's theory of indeterminacy declares that no natural laws govern the motions of electrons around the nuclei of atoms—that there is no known force keeping them in order. Something beyond the domain of known scientific laws holds atoms together. It is easy to relate this to Colossians 1:16–17, where we read: "For by him were all things created, that are in heaven, and that are in earth, visible and invisible, whether they be thrones, or dominions, or principalities, or powers: all things were created by him, and for him: and he is before all things, and by him all things consist."

On the other hand, some might say that to make such a connection is stretching things a lot. Such critics are likely to say that the Bible deals with spiritual matters and is not a textbook on science. That's okay by me, but these people ought to abide by that principle and not try to negate the truths of Scripture with the use of science, as many have done in the past.

Science is more supportive of the Bible today than it was a couple of generations ago. While I believe the Bible is not meant to be a scientific textbook, I do contend that when the Bible connects with science, it does so in a reasonable, compatible manner. I believe that the Bible and the Christian faith it supports are more than able to stand up to the intellectual challenges of our times.

But the primary reason for what I have written here is not so much to prove the Bible to be scientifically true as it is to use science as a tool to address some of the problems that have haunted theologians down through the ages and to try to provide some insights that will help Christians with the essential doctrines of their faith.

WHY *DO* BAD THINGS HAPPEN TO GOOD PEOPLE?

One overarching problem that religious people have to deal with goes beyond anything that can be handled within the categories of science. It is an existential problem with which anyone who gives serious thought to matters of faith has to struggle. I am referring to the problem my friend Rabbi Harold Kushner raised in his book *When Bad Things Happen to Good People*. He wrote the book following the death of his fourteen-year-old son, Aaron, who suffered all his short life with progeria, a condition in which the body ages and dies prematurely.

Kushner contended that eventually we must decide between a God who is infinitely powerful but not loving enough to step in and prevent tragedies like the suffering and death of his son, and a God who is all-loving but limited in power. Kushner chose the all-loving God rather than the all-powerful God.

Theologians have a fancy phrase for labeling this dilemma. They call it "the theodicy problem." We who are not theologians may not give it a name, but we know the problem all too well. Furthermore, sooner or later, each of us must struggle with it as part of our human existence. If you have not confronted this problem yet, the bad news is that you probably will. When that time comes, you will find that the simple, pat answers that we usually give won't do, and you will come close to total despair. You will cry out in the darkness, "Why?"

I am dealing with this problem objectively here and now in the hope that what I have to say might help you when you have to deal with the question existentially—as you surely will. I am also dealing with it for personal reasons, because I know that someday I will have to struggle with it existentially.

EINSTEIN AND GOD

I have chosen to deal with the theodicy problem in this chapter because Einsteinian physics has raised some serious concerns about the way in which we think about God. For instance, in light of Einstein's theory of relativity and the new cosmology that arises out of it, we may have to ask whether it is correct to use such words as *omnipotent, omniscient,* and *omnipresent* when talking about God; and whether or not we use such words has everything to do with how we deal with the theodicy problem. Modern philosophers, such as the logical positivist Ludwig Wittgenstein, have already argued that such words have only poetic value and that there is no basis for empirical validation.

Careful consideration of my handling of the Calvinistic doctrine of predestination in my discussion of Einstein's view of time raises the question of just how much God is in control of what happens in the *future,* since all things happen *now* with God. Put simply, the new perspectives Einstein posed bring to the surface a most troubling and serious existential question that we all tend to suppress: Do we have an infinitely powerful God who is in control of everything that is going on in the universe? Or do we, in freedom, have decision-making power to affect how things go in the world?

People often quote Romans 8:28 when they cannot make sense out of the tragic events of their lives: "And we know that all things work together for good to them that love God, to them who are the called according to *his* purpose" (emphasis added).

This verse does not propose that God is in control of everything that happens or that God is the One who engineered the tragedy. Instead, a correct translation of that verse tells us that in the midst of everything that happens, God is there, and God can bring some good out of it. To erroneously make God the One who sets up the tragedies as part of some great divine plan can make people hate God.

THE FORCES OF DARKNESS

Some years ago, when I was pastoring a small church in New Jersey, there was a man in the congregation whose son died of cancer. During the long time he suffered from this dreaded disease, the child bore his pain heroically. This eight-year-old did all he could to keep his parents from being sad, but his mother and father suffered with him as the cancer ate away at his body.

After his son's death, the father stopped coming to church. When I visited him and tried to convince him to come back to worship with the rest of us, I said, "You can't stop believing in God because of what has happened!"

His response still rings in my ears every time I think of that man. He said, "Oh! I still believe in God. I don't come to church anymore because I hate God."

That father could not reconcile belief in an omnipotent, omniscient, and omnipresent God, who could have saved his son, with belief in a loving God. It is for the sake of that father, and others like him, that I have written what follows. Frankly, I had some serious reservations about including these next few paragraphs; nevertheless, I decided to do so. I decided to go ahead with them because so many people are being turned off to the Christian faith in reaction to the things evangelicals are saying about God that the Bible does not say.

"In him is light," say the Scriptures; "then why," asks George MacDonald, "should we impart darkness to him?" I believe that some of the ways we have defined God have made Him into a dark figure to those who do not know Him.

To make myself perfectly clear, let me say that I do not believe that God is in total control of what goes on in this world. I believe that Satan, along with other demonic forces, is at work in the universe and that God is doing all that can be done to drive back these dark forces and utterly destroy them. However, the forces of darkness do exercise a powerful presence in our world.

THEY ARE ONLY TEMPORARILY IN POWER

God in Christ, say the Scriptures, broke the power of the dark forces on the cross (Col. 2:15), and that means we are dealing now with mortally wounded "principalities and powers." They are nonetheless still alive, powerful, and the enemies of all that is good.

Furthermore, I believe that we have the assurance that because of the resurrection of Christ Jesus from the dead, God's eventual victory over Satan is a foregone conclusion. I do not doubt the truth of the Bible's declaration that there will be a time in the future when Christ shall reign again over all the universe. Then, at His name, every knee shall bow and every tongue shall confess Him as Lord (Phil. 2:10–11). However, between now and that triumphant day, God is at war battling to reclaim this lost creation, which even now is eagerly anticipating its redemption (Rom. 8:19–23).

What I am saying, in nontheological language, is that God lost control of things when humanity and the satanic forces rebelled against Him, giving Satan and Satan's minions the opportunity to work toward making all of creation part of their dark domain. But God so loved the world that He did not give up on it. Instead, God sent His only begotten Son to rescue the world (John 3:16) and to bring it once again under His control.

When Jesus hung on the cross, all the demonic powers in the cosmos were mustered against Him. Satan and his legions thought they had Him just where they wanted Him: God, who was in Christ, seemed to be vulnerable. But three days after the apparent victory of the forces of evil, Christ arose from the dead. He had conquered death!

But His victory over the powers of darkness did not mean that the forces of evil were no more. They are still alive and active in this world, even as God is at work here, driving them toward annihilation. The day will come when that last enemy will be completely subdued, and God will again be Lord over all creation. But that day is yet to come. "Then cometh the end, when he shall have delivered up the kingdom to God, even the Father; when he shall have put down all rule and all authority and power. For he must reign, till he hath put all enemies under his feet" (1 Cor. 15:24–25).

We have historical evidence that the power of God is greater than all the powers of darkness put together and that those dark forces are doomed to lose out in the end. The proof was in the Resurrection. The evil forces of the universe are still alive, but Satan could not keep Jesus in the grave.

Oscar Cullmann, in his book *Christ and Time*, used an analogy from World War II to illustrate this point, as he made a clear distinction between the two definitive days of the war: D-Day and V-Day. D-Day was when the Allied forces landed in Normandy and established a beachhead. The strategizing generals on both sides recognized that the outcome of the war was decided on that fateful day in June 1944. They understood that if the enemy had driven the Allies back into the sea, the Nazis would have won the war. But because the Allied armies prevailed at Normandy, they sealed the doom of the Nazi cause. They guaranteed the eventual obliteration of the Nazi movement at the end of what some have called "the longest day."

What Cullmann wanted us to recognize is that in spite of the triumph on D-Day, the Allies had not yet totally subdued the enemy. Between D-Day and V-Day, there would be many months of suffering and struggle. There would be horrendous battles as the Allied armies, little by little, pushed back the Nazi forces. These ensuing struggles culminated in the V-Day that marked the complete surrender of the enemy and the Allies' liberation of all of Europe.

Cullmann made the point that the Cross and the Resurrection were God's D-Day. In those two events, God in Jesus fought and won the decisive battle. However, God's V-Day has not yet come. God is still at work in this world, driving back the forces of darkness. Satan's power has been broken, and Christ, through the church, is pushing back Satan's control of the cosmos, though the evil one is still alive and free to raise havoc. God's V-Day is not yet here! But because of God's triumph on D-Day, we know how it all will end.

If you ask me if God is Lord over all things right now, my answer is "No! But God will be!" Ephesians 1:18–22 says:

The eyes of your understanding being enlightened; that ye may know what is the hope of his calling, and what the riches of the glory of his inheritance in the saints, and what is the exceeding greatness of his power to us-ward who believe, according to the working of his mighty power, which he wrought in Christ, when he raised him from the dead, and set him at his own right hand in the heavenly places, far above all principality, and power, and might, and dominion, and every name that is named, not only in this world, but also in that which is to come: and hath put all things under his feet, and gave him to be the head over all things to the church.

We are the people of hope who live in anticipation of His reign. We know that "Jesus shall reign where'er the sun does his successive journeys run," just as the beloved hymn declares. But that reign is not yet.

I believe that God is not in control of everything right now because of limitations He put on Himself. God limited Himself in creation in order to grant us freedom. Without freedom, there could be no love. Loving, by definition, requires the freedom to give or withhold love and to choose whom we will love. God did not want puppets who could be manipulated into having to love Him. Instead, He longed for a people who would freely choose to love Him. Hence, God gave us freedom; and in so doing, He relinquished control.

God took a risk in creating us with freedom, and that risk involved His self-limitations. We abused that freedom, and that is why we now live in a fallen universe. But I believe that God is, even now, working to put down all forms of sin and darkness and that His reign over all things is near at hand.

I do not understand how reasonable people can believe that God is in total control of everything right now when there is so much evil and injustice in the world. I grant that this may be a failure on my part, but if I believed that God controlled everything that goes on in the universe these days, I would not know how to explain why innocent children in Africa get AIDS, or why godly people die of cancer, or why there was ever an Auschwitz or a Hiroshima. I would not know what to say about all the disastrous things that go on in the world, day in and day out. I think that those who define God as presently infinite in power and in control of all that happens in this world do God a disservice. They make God responsible for all that is evil and ugly.

To those who ask, "How could a *loving* God allow horrendous diseases to afflict good people, permit insane wars to kill the innocent, and let a man like Hitler create such widespread suffering?" I answer, "God is doing the best He can, and I *know* that God will be victorious over all the evils of the universe on that final day, which theologians call 'the eschaton.'"

We find in Scripture the God who is called "the almighty one"—a God who is greater than all the other forces of the universe put together. We read about a God who, in love, is battling to make the universe into a kingdom over which He *shall* rule. Note that the Bible sets this kingdom in the future. That is why, when we pray the Lord's Prayer, we pray for it to come in the future: "Thy kingdom come, Thy will be done, on earth as it is in heaven."

I find it a welcome relief to believe in an almighty God who is doing all He can to recover the lost creation and to make it into a realm in which His loving-kindness will be evident everywhere and in everything. God says, "I assure you that one day, My love and justice will triumph, and I will reign throughout the universe. Until then, I invite you to join Me in the struggle against the powers of evil and darkness. Go and tell people about My Son and His salvation. Join with those who fight in My cause against the injustices that harm the poor and the oppressed. Participate with Me in My struggle to change the world that is, into the world that ought to be."

Such a God is the God that I find in the Bible, and who has been revealed in Jesus Christ. Such a God is a loving God, and we cannot blame Him for evil. I found it easy to fall in love with this God—and I did. His name is Jesus.

8

Can We Help the Poor Without Making Matters Worse?

It is amazing how much damage has been done by good, well-meaning people who are trying to help the poor. Their hearts are in the right place. They try to carry out the directive of the almost two thousand references in Scripture that admonish us to reach out to the poor with love and sacrificial giving. But in spite of their good intentions, these people often end up doing more harm than good.

The recently deceased Ivan Illich, who for years served as a missiologist for the World Council of Churches, made us aware that Christian generosity, when wrongly expressed, can humiliate and even further impoverish those who are the targets of good-willed intentions. He graphically described in his writings how bright-eyed, enthusiastic, "do-gooder" youth groups from American churches who go on short-term mission trips to poor countries often hurt the very people they want to serve. They do not realize that when they build schools and churches in Third World villages and hamlets, they often are taking construction jobs away from indigenous people who desperately need work.

These short-term mission groups usually arrive with a well-devised plan, the financial resources to buy building materials, and the tools that will enable them to construct a school or a church with a degree of efficiency that appears almost miraculous to those they want to help. The local people are awed but are also left with an increased sense of inferiority. These well-meaning young people may actually have contributed to disempowering the very people they wanted to help by leaving them with a sense that outsiders are the only ones who can meet their needs or solve their problems.

THE LESSON I'VE HAD TO LEARN

Beyond Borders, the mission organization in Haiti with which I have been associated over the last three decades, has taken this problem seriously. At first, we, too, had arranged for church youth groups to do the disabling thing I have just described. But we learned from Illich, and from our own often prayerful reflections on the consequences of the work done by these short-term mission groups, that we needed to restructure our program.

Beyond Borders now offers what we call "transformational travel." This is a program in which our workers take people of all ages to Haiti, not to build anything, but to learn from the Haitian people and to share something of themselves with their hosts. For example, we arrange for mothers from both cultures to get together and talk about their lives, comparing and contrasting the ways in which they raise their children, how their workdays unfold, and the unique difficulties that each of them faces daily. They learn from each other, and the Americans enhance the Haitian women's sense of self-worth as they realize that they have much that is of value to share with their new American friends.

Young people of both cultures play, sing, laugh, and worship together. They share their testimonies, exchange their respective hopes and visions, and examine prejudicial stereotypes.

University students compare ideas and gain further understanding of how the political and economic systems of developed countries, such as the United States, too often serve their own self-interests at the expense of poor nations.

Men sit together drinking coffee, talking about the affairs of government and what can be done to direct Haiti to a brighter future.

These kinds of interactions build mutual respect across cultural lines and help indigenous people believe that God can empower them to change the Haiti in which they live into the Haiti that ought to be. (See the appendix for more information on Beyond Borders.)

Unfortunately, you don't have to go to the Third World to go to the Third World anymore. It exists right here in our own country. It exists in rundown urban neighborhoods as well as in those neglected rural areas where more than half of all the poor of our country live. Many make well-intentioned efforts to help, but unfortunately, too often the problems Illich defined are evident in the results. Among our own economically disinherited citizens, we have a first-hand opportunity to see the way in which attempts to help have done significant harm.

THE DISASTROUS WELFARE SYSTEM

A glaring example of this is obvious in the long-term effects of our own social welfare system. This system was supposed to be a safety net to catch those who had temporarily fallen on hard times or who had been left behind while most Americans enjoyed the benefits of a booming economy. But instead, the welfare system became a humiliating and dehumanizing way of life for millions of our citizens. Over the years, it nurtured a dependence that has destroyed the dignity of people and created resentments among its recipients. These resentments, in turn, generated cheating and deceptions so that eventually hundreds of thousands of people were on the welfare rolls, collecting unjustified handouts, even though they were quite capable of getting jobs and properly supporting themselves and their families. At one point, one out of every six persons in New York City was on welfare, and a large proportion of them were, quite unnecessarily, parasites on hard-working people.

It was only a matter of time before a reaction set in against the exploiters of the system. Angry conservatives justifiably echoed the words of the apostle Paul, who said, "Those who refuse to work ought not to eat" (see 2 Thess. 3:10). The need for change was eventually turned into legislation, and a Democratic president, along with a Republican Congress, passed a reform bill.

That bill would not allow anyone to stay on welfare for more than two years at any one stretch, and it limited the time allowed for any one person to be on welfare to a maximum of five years during his or her lifetime. Many Christians were among those who believed that this bill was too draconian in its proposals, and they pressed for what they believed were essential modifications.

SPECIFIC CONCERNS

For instance, they had concerns over possible cases in which extenuating circumstances might require one to be on welfare more than the allotted five years. Another major concern was that the federal dollars would be handed out to states as bloc grants, with almost no controls over how individual states would spend them. Incredibly, one governor proposed, as would have Ebenezer Scrooge, that his state's allotted federal welfare dollars be used to build prisons!

Furthermore, there were no provisions to ensure that those who had no skills would receive opportunities for training or that adequate day care would be available for those single parents who had to find jobs. Some states already had Workfare, a program that required the unemployed to take jobs that local governments provided. But the new bill made no provisions to set aside time for educational opportunities and for job searches that would enable people to improve their skills and get better employment than the state-mandated jobs. The poor did need help, and many people thought that we had to do better than the welfare reform bill that had just passed.

A NEW VOICE ARISES

At the time, the powerful Christian Coalition was the most successful religious lobbying group in American history. Though it had brought Christians together to address the need for the government to support "traditional family values," as it defined them, it seemed to pass over the concerns of the poor. The voter guides, which the Christian Coalition distributed to millions of Christians through churches, completely ignored the needs of the poor.

Sensing the urgency to provide a Christian voice that would bring together people from across the theological spectrum to speak on behalf of the poor, I, along with like-minded Christians, joined Jim Wallis, the editor of the socially conscious Christian magazine *Sojourners,* to initiate a new political-action organization named Call to Renewal. This is a nationwide effort to establish a voice on behalf of those whom the Bible calls "the least of our brothers and sisters." Already, Call to Renewal is making its influence felt in Washington, and we expect that as it grows in membership, it will do much good by helping the poor in ways that leave them with their dignity intact. (See the appendix for contact information.)

We members of Call to Renewal believe that we must challenge the new tax bills and budgets Congress is passing so that they benefit the poor instead of only serving the interests of the rich. We must question the inequalities in education so evident across America. Call to Renewal is working to make the political and economic institutions both more just and more effective in their responses to the poor, without humiliating them. We want to encourage Christians to avoid paternalism and instead to become partners in a biblically prescribed mission—to be a voice for justice for the oppressed.

Wallis tells the story of going into a Burger King in Washington, D.C., and noticing that the woman behind the counter, in between waiting on customers, ran over to check on three children sitting in the corner of the restaurant. After she had done this several times, he figured out that they were her children and that she had them there to do their homework after school because they had no other safe place to go. I believe, along with Jim Wallis, that as Christians we have to figure out how to help a woman like that. She is someone who wants to work to support her family and, at the same time, be a good and caring mother. She needs a better deal than she's getting, and it is the responsibility of Christians to see that she gets it. That is the work that we formed Call to Renewal to do.

EARLY EFFORTS

In an early effort to draw attention to its intentions, forty founding members of Call to Renewal staged in 1998 a peaceful demonstration in the rotunda of the capitol building in Washington, D.C. When we gently refused to cease and desist, we were arrested. The police actually apologized for what they had to do, complimenting us for being a voice for poor people. National Public Radio interviewed schoolchildren who had witnessed the arrests, and across America the voices of those children expressed their concerns for what was happening to poor people and their support for what we were doing.

Often demonstrations of this sort are full of sound and fury, signifying nothing, but in this case, there were some positive responses from the people in Congress and from President Clinton. Over the next few months, changes were made in the new welfare arrangements so that, while there is still a need for improvements, many of the abuses of the original bill were eliminated. Letting our voices be heard by "the principalities and powers and rulers of this age" made the difference in this case.

RELIEVING POVERTY ON A GLOBAL SCALE

While Call to Renewal continues to address domestic poverty, other Christian groups are organizing to deal with poverty on the global scale. Jubilee 2000 was organized to get Third World debts cancelled. The work of this organization was, and continues to be, absolutely essential if the poor in the Third World ever are going to have a chance to overcome their desperate conditions. Consider the fact that many Third World nations owe so much money to rich countries, to commercial banks, and to paragovernment organizations (i.e., the World Bank and the International Monetary Fund) that while keeping up on their debt payments, these countries have little, if anything, left over for public health programs, education, or funds to develop their own economies. In the African nations, forty cents out of every tax dollar buys none of those things that would improve the lot of the poor. Instead, all of this money is used to pay interest. Making interest payments on the huge amounts that have been borrowed is all that these poor countries can do, leaving them with no means of either reducing their debt or making life better for their own people.

Some argue that these countries never should have gotten themselves into debt in the first place. But we must remember that many of them obtained these loans during the Cold War years, when America and its allies were trying to buy the allegiance of poor nations. In order to gain their support for such things as votes in the United Nations, we and other rich countries lent billions of dollars to financially ill-advised public-works projects that catered to the insatiable appetites of dictators but did little to alleviate the suffering of the masses. In all too many instances, corrupt politicians pocketed money for themselves. Often this loan money was used to build up military machines, which dictators used to oppress their own people. Now those dictators are gone, and poor people are left with having to pay off the debts.

Leading up to the year 2000, Christian organizations in the United Kingdom, such as Christian Aid and SPEAK, organized tens of thousands of young people to pressure government leaders of the G7 nations, the richest and most developed nations in the world, to cancel the debts Third World countries owed. Picking up on the teachings of the Bible as recorded in Leviticus 25, they called politicians to consider that according to this passage of Scripture, every fifty years they should declare a Year of Jubilee in which they cancel the debts of the poor.

President Clinton took the lead in responding to this plea for debt cancellation and proposed that the representatives of G7 nations meeting in Cologne, Germany, set in motion efforts for debt relief. Two years later, when representatives from these same nations met in Birmingham, England, tens of thousands of demonstrators, most of whom the British organization Christian Aid had called together, confronted them. The results were startling! Gordon Brown, keeper of the exchequer, the English equivalent of the secretary of the treasury here in the United States, began to work out the details for the British government to carry out a debt-cancellation program. President Clinton did what he could to effect the same. To date, about 10 percent of Third World debts have been canceled, and while there is still a long way to go, there has been a good beginning. The year 2000, the designated Year of Jubilee, has passed, but the campaign to cancel Third World debts continues.

The first nation to receive significant debt relief was Uganda. But the debts were not simply canceled; instead, those countries to whom Uganda owed money required this nation to use the money that would have gone to service its debts to address the AIDS crisis. Uganda's leaders invested money in AIDS education and in extensive counseling programs. Massive advertising programs were created to warn people against unsafe sex and to provide medical care for those who were afflicted.

The results have been amazing. While in nations across the continent of Africa the incidence of new cases of AIDS has been increasing in a geometric progression that goes off the charts, Uganda has seen a reversal in such trends. The incidence of new cases of AIDS has dropped almost 50 percent in the last few years, while deaths from AIDS have declined 20 percent.

This is a brilliant example of what Christians can accomplish when they organize to let their voices be heard among the decision makers of the political-economic systems that dominate the world. Such efforts are essential as we try to carry out the biblical mandate to help the poor.

G7 POVERTY POLICIES
AND THE THIRD WORLD POOR

Recently, attention increasingly has been focused on the trade relations that rich, powerful nations have with the poor nations of the world. When President Bush visited Pretoria, South Africa, in July of 2003, he ran into angry demonstrators who accused him of pursuing policies that insured massive losses of jobs among the farmers of that nation. They pointed to his multibillion-dollar subsidy for American wheat and cotton farmers. This subsidy left African farmers, who did not have any such subsidies from their government, unable to compete price-wise when they tried to sell their products on the world markets. Farmers and their hired hands shouted at the U.S. president that while Bush's agricultural policies may have shored up his political support among American farmers, they were causing extensive suffering for the farmers of their country.

SPEAK, a strongly evangelical group of university students organized across the United Kingdom, along with other groups such as Tear Fund and World Vision, recognize that if we are to obey the biblical commands to rescue the poor, Christians must become aware of how government policies are increasing poverty in Third World nations and commit ourselves to doing something about it.

Bono, the lead singer for the world-famous rock band U2, has done much to support these efforts to cancel Third World debts and to establish fair trade arrangements, but it's time for preachers to carry out their prophetic obligations and to begin to talk about these issues in their sermons. It's time for evangelical colleges and universities to do what my own Eastern University has done: make sure that their students become aware of how the maintenance of our own affluent lifestyles has raised havoc among the poor of the world.

THE HOPE FROM FAITH-BASED PROGRAMS

Thus far in this chapter, I have focused on those ways of helping the poor that involve changing policies on what sociologists call the macro level. Certainly the policies that govern international trade and economic production need to be monitored, and Christians must do all they can to wrestle against those principalities and powers (Eph. 6:12) so that justice is done. But we also have to make a major commitment to developing programs and ministries on the local level. We must look for ways to alleviate some of the poverty and social pathologies that torment those millions of Americans who have been left behind in the realization of the great American Dream.

I am encouraged these days when I hear about the hundreds of thousands of programs that churches and other Christian organizations have developed that are making a difference on the micro level. Faith-based programs are racking up incredible achievements. Both President Clinton and President Bush recognized this.

Such programs have the best success records of any of the agencies that are designed to help people get off drugs.

- Faith-based after-school programs are reaching out to hundreds of thousands of children across the nation and are providing the tutoring and support system so essential for academic achievement in disadvantaged communities.

- Church-sponsored mentoring programs for those coming out of prison provide some of the best insurance against recidivism.

- Faith-based job-placement programs and entrepreneurship enterprises are now beginning to provide some hope for the hard-core urban unemployed.

- Initiatives from groups such as Habitat for Humanity and the Pittsburgh Project are making decent housing a reality for the first time for tens of thousands of needy families.

The list of all that is going on under the auspices of churches, synagogues, and mosques goes on and on.

During the eight years of the Clinton administration, there was a growing sense that the government ought to get behind these faith-based programs with financial assistance to increase their scope and effectiveness. President Clinton redesigned his pet program, AmeriCorps, so that the young people who served with faith-based programs that provided social services could receive financial assistance from the federal government. The AmeriCorps volunteers with religious organizations such as the Salvation Army could get their living expenses covered, along with a significant contribution to cover their costs for higher education.

A massive rally with wide media coverage in Philadelphia provided the backdrop for General Colin Powell, now the U.S. secretary of state, to call upon Americans to enter a new era of volunteerism and step forward to attack the severe problems poor and oppressed people face. These are the people whom Michael Harrington once called "the other America" in his classic book of the same name.

President George W. Bush continued this call for volunteerism and promised to further help faith-based initiatives. Under his guidance, it has become possible for religious organizations to bid on contracts when the government seeks to hire agencies to render social services.

OPTIMISM EVENTUALLY QUELLED

Everything looked rosy for a while, and the skepticism of many was challenged. President Bush established a new office for faith-based initiatives in the White House. I personally was won over at first and became optimistic about the possibilities of this new alliance between church and state. I saw this cooperation between religious organizations and the government as being crucial for solving the many crises that plague our cities as well as addressing the suffering of the rural poor. But I'm not so optimistic anymore!

At first, I fantasized about the millions of dollars that would be available to those church groups and faith-based community programs that are struggling financially. I thought about how their ministries could expand so that they could help millions more socially and economically disinherited people. Then suddenly, everything seemed to change. There was a reversal in the economy, and seemingly overnight, a $350 billion government surplus became a $350 billion deficit. September 11, 2001, changed America's priorities, and national security became a preoccupation. President Bush initiated the war in Afghanistan, costing America a billion dollars a month. Then came the ongoing war and occupation of Iraq, costing a billion dollars a week. Seemingly overnight, the money for any kind of social programming was extremely limited.

The elderly were crying out for a prescription program that would keep them from having to decide between buying medicine to stay alive or buying enough food to sustain them. More than 44 million Americans, 13 million of them children, still had no medical insurance. The American educational system was in desperate straits. The financial largess that once abounded had disappeared, and with it, the government funding for social programs.

TAX CUTS FAIL TO HELP

President Bush promised deliverance from this recession by initiating tax cuts. The supply-side economic theory behind this policy said that tax cuts would put billions of dollars in the hands of business and industry, and that these sectors of the economy would invest the money in expanding their operations. This expansion, in turn, was supposed to create jobs—thus ending the recession. This strategy had worked during the Kennedy years, but what many of us worried about was that the captains of business and industry would, some forty years later, take this payback money and invest it in moving factories to Third World countries where labor was cheap. Thus, instead of helping the poor and disadvantaged, the result would be that even more Americans would lose jobs while profits for rich corporate interests would increase. Between 2001 and 2003, America lost 3 million jobs—more than at any time since the Great Depression.

After three consecutive tax cuts that largely benefited the rich, we are seeing the accuracy of our predictions, and the poor are still facing economic troubles. There are bad signs for those of us who have been looking to government to help our faith-based programs. Yes, religious organizations are on an equal basis with secular agencies when it comes to bidding for social-service contracts, but our leaders are appropriating less and less money for social services. Faith-based programs have an equal opportunity to get a piece of an ever-shrinking pie. In order to finance the tax cuts that have been enacted, the slots available for workers in the AmeriCorps program have been cut by two-thirds. And this is just the beginning of the hard times for those faith-based programs that, over the past couple of years, have become dependent on government funding.

CUTTING GOD OUT OF THE PICTURE

The worst part of this government's plan to fund faith-based programs, a plan that many of us who worked with such programs did not fully understand, was how much we would have to curtail the sharing of our own faith once we were receiving federal funding. It had always been the impact of God becoming a powerful force in the lives of those we reached through these programs that was the primary reason for their successes.

With Teen Challenge, a faith-based program for drug addicts, it was the conversion of the addict through the work of the Holy Spirit that was the dominant factor that enabled this program to achieve incredible results in helping people overcome their addictions. It was the spiritual dimensions of the programs of faith-based shelters for the homeless that got so many of the homeless off the streets. And it was the solid biblical teachings of so many church-sponsored youth programs that kept many teenagers from destructive behavior. In short, it was the faith dimensions of these programs that made them so successful, and limiting what can be done in the way of propagating faith cuts their effectiveness.

Over the past few years, the government has increased its surveillance of faith-based programs, making sure that they do not spend government dollars in ways that propagate the faith of those who run these organizations. I have seen some of these programs transformed into agencies that are now devoid of any direct religious message. Having expanded with the influx of government dollars, they have had to choose, when push comes to shove, between dollars and the propagating of their beliefs. Far too many of them are choosing the dollars and selling their souls. The government has done some seducing that may have been unintentional, but the effects will be painfully far-reaching.

CRITICIZING BIG BROTHER

Another ugly consequence of the government's support of faith-based programs is that the government now is requiring the recipients of funds to cease and desist from any criticism of their national leaders. The Bush administration has made it official! If you want government dollars, you must not voice opposition to any government policies. Incidentally, the person who gave this directive was an executive in the White House Department for Faith-Based Initiatives who, when he served as an executive for World Vision, a faith-based relief organization that received financial grants during the Clinton years, was highly critical of U.S. policies in North Korea.

What all this means is that those faith-based programs that want the financial benefits that the government offers must give up their prophetic voices. In the end, they will sell themselves, as did Esau of old, for a bowl of pottage. A government program that was supposed to help faith-based organizations is now in a position to silence them. Churches and urban mission programs whose leaders have voiced criticism about policies that are unfair to the poor and oppressed had better learn to shut up if they want any of the crumbs that fall from the government's table. If I seem a bit bitter about all of this, it is because I am.

A REASON FOR HOPE

I am not a fan of the government's faith-based initiatives. I agree with those critics who contend that whenever the government starts giving financial support to religious organizations, the result will be a violation of the constitutional principle of the separation of church and state, unless the religious organizations become secularized. There is good reason to worry that faith-based programs are losing their spiritual edge. A former mayor of Indianapolis graphically expressed this fear: "When you get the government involved with religious programs like this, it's like mixing horse manure with ice cream. It won't do much damage to the horse manure, but it will really mess up the ice cream."

Still, I see a reason for hope. In the midst of all that might be disillusioning about the government's handling of faith-based initiatives, I see growing evidence of heightened conscience within the corporate community. Businesses and industries increasingly are committing themselves to giving money and encouraging their employees to help out in various ministries and agencies that are meeting social needs. In cities across America, more and more companies are recognizing their obligations to the society that has helped make them prosperous, and they are increasingly giving back to their communities in generous ways. I can cite many examples of how the corporate community is teaming up with churches and urban missionary programs to make good things happen, and it would be cynical to say that American companies are doing such things only because it enhances business and will, in the long run, increase their bottom line. It goes far beyond that!

A new breed of corporate executives has appeared throughout the American business establishment, and these men and women have an altruistic streak. Business schools have imbued them with a humanitarian ethic, which is designed to foster what is called "corporate responsibility." The students in these schools are learning that doing good is a win-win arrangement that helps everyone, and that a company contributing to the well-being of a community will generate in the work force a pride that will increase the level of loyalty to the company among its employees. But there is also a growing awareness among corporate executives that their own lives will have a deeper meaning, and that the gratification they get through their business affairs will be brilliantly enhanced, if they can see that in the context of doing business, they are doing good for people who need help.

This commitment to doing good was very evident during the administration of Charles Bluhdorn, who headed up the multinational corporation Gulf and Western in the early 1970s. Responding at first to the negative critiques of its practices in the Dominican Republic by such groups as the Roman Catholic Adrian Sisters and the National Council of Churches, Bluhdorn led his company to invest hundreds of millions of dollars in social and economic programs that would benefit the Dominican poor. Initially, he had to put up with significant opposition from his board members and the stockholders of the company, but Bluhdorn persisted in changing corporate practices in the Dominican Republic, and the result was a change of attitude among Dominicans toward Gulf and Western. Hostility faded and appreciation grew in its place. Today a former top executive of the company, who was once in charge of Gulf and Western operations in the Dominican government, has won a popular election to be vice president of the country.

BEING FAITHFUL IN LITTLE THINGS

When asked how we could feed the billion starving people in the world today, Mother Teresa answered, "One at a time." While it is easy to critique her simple answer and point out that the elimination of world poverty requires major changes in the political and economic systems that dominate the world, we do have to acknowledge some truth in what she said. The way to start taking care of the world is to respond to needs on an individualistic level. When we begin on that level, we will soon find ourselves involved in seeing the need for change on the macro level and understanding the needs to become politically involved. Jesus taught us that when we are faithful in little things, He will make us rulers over great things (Matt. 25:21). I believe that especially applies here.

CHANGING THE WORLD ONE CHILD AT A TIME

A good place to start is by making a commitment to support a child through the sponsorship programs of such organizations as Compassion International and World Vision. For less than a dollar a day, you can feed, clothe, educate, and evangelize a child in a Third World country. Another suggestion is to underwrite some specific development project, such as a literacy program or a job-creation program. In Haiti, the aforementioned organization Beyond Borders has a ministry that establishes literacy programs for children who are virtually slaves. Either these children are orphans, or they come from families so poor that the families cannot feed them, so they are given away. Those who take in these children, called *restavecs* in the Creole language, often exploit and mistreat them. The little schools that Beyond Borders establishes have to hold their classes from late afternoon into the evening, because the children must spend the better part of each day doing slave labor.

The real injustice is not that young children have to do such things as carry water, do laundry, and work in the fields. The real injustice is that there is no letup in their labors. There is no time for play, and if they want to go to school, they may go only after they have completed their daily chores. Nevertheless, these slave children *do* come to school, because they know that if they can learn how to read and write in a country where some 80 percent of the population is illiterate, they will have some hope for the future. (Again, see the appendix for more information on Beyond Borders.)

Still another option for serving the poor in a Third World country is to support an entrepreneurial project through Opportunity International. Over the past couple of decades, this Christian missionary organization has been providing loans that help the poor in developing nations to start up small businesses and cottage industries, which these indigenous people can own and run themselves. To date, Opportunity International has enabled poor people to create more than two million jobs for themselves, family members, and friends. The success of this program has been phenomenal. (See the appendix for more information.)

HELPING THE POOR IN AMERICA

As I have said many times, you don't have to go to the Third World to encounter Third World conditions. People are living in obscenely horrific conditions right here in the United States. One way to help the poor of America is by getting on board as a volunteer with Habitat for Humanity. In addition to its work in countries around the world, this organization, founded by Linda and Millard Fuller and made famous by the involvement of former president Jimmy Carter, builds and rehabilitates houses for poor families all across America. (See the appendix for contact information.) Whatever you decide to do, whether in a grass-roots program such as Habitat for Humanity or on the macro level by joining up with a political action group such as Call to Renewal, you need to make some kind of commitment to helping the poor. The Lord requires this of us all. On that great day when each one of us must give an account of ourselves, we will be asked what we did to feed the hungry or to reach out to help those who were in need or being oppressed. Let's make sure we have a good answer.

9

Is Islam Really an Evil Religion?

Since the horrendous events of September 11, 2001, anti-Muslim attitudes have increased among most Americans. Within the Christian community, prominent spokespersons have used inflammatory remarks to feed negativism toward Islam. One television evangelist has called Islam an "evil religion." Another of America's best-known evangelists has gone on record declaring Islam to be wicked. A prominent fundamentalist leader has called Mohammed a "terrorist," and a former president of the Southern Baptist Convention has suggested that he was a pedophile.

It is easy to imagine how the press plays out such accusations throughout the Islamic world. Muslims take blasphemy far more seriously than do Christians or Jews, and statements that denigrate Islam and its prophet elicit extreme visceral reactions among the billion-plus people of the world who identify themselves as Muslim. Christian missionaries serving in Islamic countries find themselves increasingly threatened by Muslims who react to such accusations by viewing these missionaries as people who despise them. It is no surprise that in some places, Muslim extremists have physically attacked and even killed missionaries.

Hosts on a variety of talk shows on Christian radio have stirred up negative reactions against Islam by citing a verse in the Koran in which Mohammed called for the death of "infidels." The text that they usually cite to justify such violent retaliation is this:

Fight in the cause of Allah those who fight you, but do not transgress limits; for Allah loves not transgressors. And kill them whenever ye catch them, and turn them out from where they have turned you out; for tumult and oppression are worse than slaughter; but fight them not at the Sacred Mosque, unless they (first) fight you there; but if they fight you, kill them. (Al-Baqarah 2:190–194)

When asked about this passage from the Koran, a Muslim scholar contended that this passage must be read in context. Mohammed, he said, wrote this at a time when the non-Muslim tribe of Makkad was attacking and killing Muslims. Those in this non-Muslim tribe were staging regular terrorist attacks on the Muslims in the city of Medina. These verses were not permission for terrorism. Instead, they were a warning against terrorists. While this teaching by Mohammed does not measure up to the teachings of Jesus about loving our enemies and doing good to those who would harm us, it is a far cry from the vitriolic evil that I hear many evangelical critics of Islam say that Mohammed taught.

It is completely unfair to judge Islam by this verse when the overwhelming emphasis of the Koran is to treat Jews and Christians with reverence and respect, to provide freedom for them to worship (but not to proselytize) in accord with their faith and to protect them against harm (Koran 29:46). Consider how we Christians would react if we were judged on the basis of what is written in Deuteronomy 7:1–2, which calls the Jews to practice genocide and "ethnic cleansing." Indeed there *are* passages in Judges wherein God called for the wholesale slaughter of entire tribes of people—even tribes characterized by kindness and gentleness. But we would not want Muslims to think that the God whom we believe was incarnated in Jesus approves of the wholesale destruction of people who live in the area now disputed by Israelis and Palestinians.

Taking certain passages out of the context of the whole biblical message gives a distorted image of the God we believe to be a God of love and justice. To do that is wrong, and it is equally wrong for us to take an isolated passage out of the Koran to demonize Mohammed or to define Allah as a God who wills the annihilation of non-Muslims.

On simply pragmatic grounds, we have to ask what good we accomplish with such inflammatory rhetoric. And we have to ask if those outspoken Christian leaders who claim to be committed to winning Muslims to Christ have given any consideration to the possibility that their accusations might make Muslims even more resistant to the Christian gospel.

GLOBAL IMPACT

The increasingly strained relations between Muslims and Christians have huge implications for the entire world. Samuel P. Huntington, in his book *The Clash of Civilizations and the Remaking of World Order*, sets forth the thesis that conflicts between civilizations (which he defines as religions) and the cultures that they generate will dominate world politics in the twenty-first century. Henry Kissinger called Huntington's book the most important to have emerged since the end of the Cold War. *Foreign Affairs*, the most prestigious journal on international relations, says that Huntington's thesis has generated more discussion than any other in the last sixty years. Zbigniew Brezezinski, one-time national U.S. security advisor, says that this book "will revolutionize our understanding of international affairs."[1]

Assuming that Huntington is right, the years that lie ahead will be marked by armed warfare between followers of the Judeo-Christian religion and followers of Islam. This is already happening. In the Philippines, in Indonesia, in the Sudan, and in Serbia, the battle lines already are drawn between Christian cultures and Islamic cultures. The only question remaining is whether evangelical Christianity will add fuel to the growing fires of this warfare or follow the admonition of Jesus, who called us to be peacemakers. Regardless of how the Muslim world positions itself in relationship to us, ought we not to reach out in love and take upon ourselves a ministry of reconciliation (2 Cor. 5:18)?

Think about how a war between Christian and Muslim civilizations would regenerate the ongoing struggles that have been evident since the Crusades. The bitter battles that marked those religious wars so marred the image of Christianity that missionary efforts to Muslim peoples have been dramatically thwarted even up to our present day. What I see happening, starting with September 11, 2001, and our actions against Iraq, could set back another five hundred years any openness to the gospel in Islamic countries.

At just about every missionary conference I attend, the speakers talk about the need to evangelize those who live within "the 10/40 window." This is a reference to that part of the world between 10 degrees and 40 degrees north of the equator, which covers North Africa, the Middle East, and Asia. The window has in view the areas encompassing most of the world's greatest physical and spiritual needs, most of the world's least-reached peoples, and most of the governments that oppose Christianity.

What evangelicals have to recognize is that the majority of the people who live within that 10/40 window are Muslims. And if we really want to evangelize them, we had better find ways to show love to them rather than wage war against them. To that end, we must critique our rhetoric about Muslims, study who they are and what they believe, and seek out common ground for a creative dialogue in which we can tell them about Jesus and His salvation.

A survey reported in *USA Today* on September 16, 2003, showed frightening declines in favorable attitudes toward the United States in Islamic nations, primarily because of their perception of how we regard Muslim people. In Morocco, the percentage of people holding favorable attitudes toward America dropped from 77 percent in 2001 to 27 percent in 2003. In Jordan, it went from 27 percent to 1 percent; in Indonesia, from 75 percent to 15 percent; and in Turkey, from 52 percent to 15 percent. Americans invented the field of public relations, but it's obvious that we've done a lousy job of it recently, despite the fact that our government spends more than a billion dollars a year on promoting a positive image of America.

CONNECTIONS BETWEEN ISLAM AND CHRISTIANITY

In April of 2002, Peter Gomes, the pastor of Harvard's Memorial Church, invited me to conduct a series of evangelistic meetings for the university's academic community. I did what a Baptist evangelist is expected to do at such meetings: I concluded each sermon by giving an invitation for people to accept Jesus as their personal Savior. The messages emphasized that the resurrected Christ is a spiritual presence who will invade anyone who is willing to surrender to Him.

Among those who responded to the invitation the first evening were two Muslim students. Following the meeting, I talked with them and tried to explain more about Jesus and what it meant to be one of His followers. These young men told me that they knew some things about Jesus from the Koran, but they had not known that He could save them from their sin. As we talked, I realized how little I knew about where they were coming from on this spiritual journey.

My knowledge of Islam was so sketchy and limited that I could not make connections between what they already knew about Jesus and the full truth, which I believe comes through the New Testament. I had taken a graduate course in comparative religions, but I remembered very little that was helpful during that counseling session.

Since that time, I have tried to study and think through what Islam is all about so that I will be able to speak with some understanding of this religion. What I have learned has surprised me, because it has provided me with ways to relate Jesus, as Christians understand Him, to what Muslims believe about the Jesus whom they deem to be one of their greatest prophets. Consider the following verses from the sacred writings of Islam.

- Jesus is the author of creation (Sura #43, Zukhruf: 63).
- Jesus was virgin born (Sura #19, Maryam: 20–21).
- Jesus raised people from the dead (Sura #3, AL-i-Imram: 49).
- Jesus lived a sinless life (Sura #19, Maryam: 17, 19).
- Jesus performed many miracles (Sura #2, Bakara: 87).
- Jesus ascended into heaven (Sura #3, AL-i-Imram: 55).
- Jesus is coming again (Sura #3, AL-i-Imram: 45).

Needless to say, regardless of any points of similarity between the Christian view of Jesus and that held by Muslims, there are marked differences. First and foremost, Christians believe that Jesus is God incarnate. We believe in the Trinity. Most important, we believe that salvation from sin and the gift of eternal life come from what Jesus accomplished for us on the cross. These are doctrines that Muslims do not accept. On the other hand, what Muslims do believe provides a good place to begin the dialogue that could win Muslims to Christ. For instance, we could ask, "If Jesus is not God, then how can the Koran declare Him to be the Author of creation?"

ONCE HARMONIOUS

We must not consider normative the incredibly strained relations that presently mark any interaction between Christians and Muslims. For the past thousand years, relations between Christians and Muslims have been comparatively harmonious.

In Toledo, Spain, these two religions coexisted in relative peace for seven hundred years. Needless to say, war tends to bring out the worst in people, and the Crusades were no exception to that reality. During the Crusades, both sides committed slaughters and atrocities, but an objective evaluation will lead to the conclusion that Christians, by far, were responsible for the worst of it.

More recently, the struggle between Israel and the Palestinians has contributed to growing contention between Christians and Muslims. Certain Christian fundamentalists have lent uncritical support to the Zionist movement because, either consciously or unconsciously, they buy into the eschatology of John Darby, the founder of the Plymouth Brethren Movement, who taught that the return of Christ was contingent upon the Jews returning to their homeland and rebuilding the temple in Jerusalem. Palestinians, as well as their Muslim brothers and sisters around the world, have, quite understandably, strenuously resisted the Zionist movement.

The Muslims contend that delegates from the various countries that make up the United Nations had no right to partition what was then Palestine and, by so doing, declare the land that Arab peoples had occupied for hundreds of years no longer theirs but henceforth the new state of Israel. In the wars that have followed, hundreds of thousands of Arab people have lost their homes and now live in refugee camps.

Most evangelicals support what the Zionists are doing, believing that they are acting out the will of God for the restoration of Israel. They see this as a prerequisite for the second coming of Christ. To this end, they have lent financial support to the armies of Israel and have pressured Congress, through various lobbying groups, to finance the state of Israel. Right now, one-third of all the foreign aid that the United States gives away in any given year goes to the state of Israel, and most of it is used for building up the military. The displaced Arabs and the countries bordering on Israel are no match for the U.S.–financed Israeli military machine. Consequently, Arab peoples in particular, and Muslim people in general, regard Christians as being allied with their enemies.

Mohammed never meant for Christians and Muslims to be at such odds with each other. He saw Islam as building upon the revelations of God that were inherent in Jesus. He taught that all Muslims should protect the Christians who lived among them as "people of the book." By that, he meant that the teachings of Jesus, as recorded in the Gospels, came from God. Furthermore, Mohammed taught that the salvation of Christians would be dependent upon how fully they had lived up to the teachings of Jesus. Islam is a salvation-by-good-works religion and teaches that the righteous Christians who live out the teachings of Jesus will be saved.

SHARING THE BLAME

None of these conciliatory comments about Islam are meant to conceal the reality that Muslim governments ruling in the name of Allah are committing some serious wrongs. It has been said that evil is never perpetrated with such enthusiasm as when it is done in the name of God. And much that goes on today in the name of Allah is contrary to what Mohammed and the Koran teach. The terrorism that occurs under the guise of Islam, the persecution of Christians in places like the Sudan, and the calling for a militaristic jihad against Western nations all run contrary to what was inherent in the teachings of Mohammed.

For example, Mohammed transformed the concept of jihad into a war against the sin and decadence that exist within the Muslim community itself. It was only in the earliest days of Islam that jihad had the militaristic dimensions some contemporary leaders of Islamic nations now assume.

When the idol-worshiping tribes of Mecca threatened Muslims, who were under the direction of Mohammed, with genocide, jihad was a holy war of survival. After realizing victory over those threatening armies, Mohammed turned jihad into a war against the materialism and the lusts of the flesh among his own people. This is a far cry from what it has become on the world scene today.

LOOKING FOR THE GOOD IN EVERYTHING

When judging another religion, we should always endeavor to see the best that it offers, rather than the worst. Too many Christians find it all too tempting to look at some of the extreme fundamentalistic tactics and practices of Islam and judge the whole of the religion by what they see in its distortions. But what about the Christian fundamentalists who make ugly statements, promote forms of oppression, and behave in a variety of ways that are contrary to the ways of Jesus? I would hate for non-Christians to evaluate who and what we are by pointing to the prosperity theology that televangelists commonly preach.

Those who claim that God is on our side as we go to war embarrass me. It upsets me that some of America's most prominent evangelical leaders contend that God is on our side in the war. If we do not want Christianity judged on the basis of those that distort it, then we ought not to judge Islam that way.

Both Christianity and Islam are missionary religions. We feel Jesus calls us to convert Muslims to Christianity, and Muslims believe Mohammed commands them to convert all Christians to Islam. This inevitably results in conflict between their religious community and ours. But the competition for converts would be much less contentious if there were a sense of fairness on both sides.

WHAT'S NEEDED: IMAGE IMPROVEMENT

The Muslim community could do a lot to enhance its image among us if it made some important changes. For instance, while a Muslim country such as Malaysia grants to Christians the right to worship according to their own faith, it has severe penalties (in some cases, death) for any Christian who tries to convert a Muslim to Christianity. At the same time, there are no restrictions on Muslims who try to convert Christians to their faith. Muslims demand the privilege to proselytize in Western countries, but they deny the same right to Christians in most societies where Muslims are in political control.

Fair is fair, and if Muslims want to improve their image in Western countries, they ought to offer something akin to the separation of church and state that exists in the United States. Freedom of religion should include the right to win converts. Muslims will say that such freedom is contrary to the Islamic understanding of what a Muslim government should allow. To that, I still say, "Change, if you want the kind of respect for which you plead."

ASSUMPTIONS AND MISUNDERSTANDINGS

Christian critics of Islam love to point out that Muslims are opposed to modernity; that they are trying to turn their backs on progress; and that they take their people back to an earlier time, shunning the "benefits" of Western culture. We act as though our Western society is superior to their ancient ways and love to talk about the backwardness of the Muslim way of life. We point to the status of women under the Taliban in Afghanistan as evidence, and we consider the head coverings many Muslim women wear as evidence of the male chauvinism that dominates their society.

Before we make our criticisms too loud, we need to take a good look at ourselves and ask if our Western culture is not just what some Muslims accuse it of being: *decadent!* Have you been to the movies lately? Have you watched TV in recent years? Have you paid any attention to the words of the rap music that sells far and wide among our youth?

Can you find anything good to say about the collapse of sexual morality, the epidemic of drug use, and the rise of alcoholism in America? Consider the breakdown of family life, the insolence of children, and the pervasiveness of vulgar language. Think about how often people profane the name of Jesus and the way in which ridicule of the sacred in the media has become commonplace.

Most of all, look at how materialism has become the dominant religion in America. Ponder all of these ugly matters and a host of others I've not even mentioned; then ask whether the word *decadent* is or is not a fair designation of modern Western culture. At the very least, consideration of these things will help us to understand why those in Muslim cultures want to reject our way of life and hold on to their traditional values.

LOOKING DEEPER

I once hosted a radio show about religion on which I had a Muslim woman as a guest. I asked her why she wore the Muslim covering called the chador and whether or not she saw wearing it as antifeminist. This bright young woman let me know in no uncertain terms that wearing the chador was not required at her mosque and that she wore it by choice. She went on to remind me that feminists in the West often complain about being treated as sex objects, then added, "If they don't want to be *treated* like sex objects, they shouldn't *dress* like sex objects. They put on clothes which expose parts of their bodies in suggestive ways, they make themselves up to be seductive, and then they get bent out of shape because some man takes the bait and makes moves on them. When I wear the chador, people are required to look into my face and relate to me as a person. It is out of modesty [Remember the word?] that I cover the rest of my body in ways that enhance my dignity."

I had little to say in response to her, although I still have real problems with a religion that, in many ways, I perceive as oppressing women. But then, I have to remind myself that there are Christian groups in the West that also articulate the ideology of male chauvinism and readily promote sexism as an accepted value. All in all, we would be wise to take seriously the admonition of Jesus to get rid of the beam in our own eyes before we go looking for the splinters in the eyes of our Muslim friends.

EXAMINING AN UGLY RUMOR

Recently, I was rather taken aback by the declaration that Mohammed at the age of fifty married a six-year-old girl and consummated that marriage when she was just nine. Were that true, then the accusation that Mohammed was guilty of child abuse would be valid, and the claim that Islam condoned the exploitation of women would have to be taken seriously. I have traced the sources for this statement and found the most widely employed authority to be the book *Unveiling Islam*, which was written by a couple of ex-Muslims who I believe were out to do a hatchet job on their former religion.

While looking into this matter, I was referred to Yahiya Emerick, an American convert to Islam, who has authored fourteen books and published a host of articles on interfaith issues, including articles in the *Journal for Religion and Education*. This Muslim scholar contended that the bride in question was A'ishah, the daughter of Mohammed's friend Abu Bakr. Emerick, along with a host of other Islamic scholars, claimed that A'ishah was *not* six years old when she was married. He says she was twelve years old when she was betrothed for marriage and that the actual marriage did not take place until she was sixteen.

I leave it to you to decide who is right about this. Maybe the truth is somewhere in the middle. But before we go pointing the finger at Mohammed too quickly, consider that Oxford scholar Karen Armstrong has claimed that Mary was about twelve years old when the announcement came that she was to give birth to Jesus. In the ancient world, people were betrothed and married much younger than is the case today.

BOTH SIDES AT FAULT

I could go on endeavoring to explain how misunderstandings have aggravated relationships between Christians and Muslims over the years and pointing out the way in which each side has demonized the other. Christians can refer to the Muslims' kidnapping of seven Trappist monks in the Atlas Mountains. The Muslims held the monks hostage in order to force the French government to release several Algerian terrorists from prison. When the French refused, these radical Muslims slit the monks' throats, to the horror of the rest of the world. Muslims can point to the rapes and slaughter of thousands of Muslims by so-called Christians in Serbia that are still fresh in our memories.

There is no doubt that each side has dealt out cruelty and death since the days of the Crusades. Which side comes off looking the worst depends on which side is telling the story. In 1997, the Central Mosque in Woking, Surrey, England, was firebombed. In London, graffiti saying "Jesus Christ is Lord" desecrates the walls of Muslim worship centers. But then, we Christians can point out how Muslims have burned down churches in Pakistan. But what good do all such accusations and counteraccusations do? What we really need are some examples of ministries of reconciliation. Thankfully, such stories are readily available.

MODELS OF RECONCILIATION

FRANCIS AND THE SULTAN

In the autumn of A.D. 1219, in the midst of the Fifth Crusade, Francis of Assisi did a most Christlike thing. Traveling to Egypt with soldiers bent on destroying the Muslim armies and reclaiming the Holy Land for Christianity, Francis left the Christian camp, crossed the battle line, and entered the camp of the Muslims. His avowed task was to share the salvation and love of Jesus with the great sultan Al Kamil, the leader of the Muslim armies.

Francis had already preached to the army of the Crusaders and had so influenced many of them with the peace message of Jesus that a number of knights had lain down their arms and joined the Franciscan movement. But Francis would not be content until he also preached the gospel to those whom Christians considered the enemies of Christ.

Both Arabic and English sources tell us that Francis won the heart of the sultan. Some even suggest that the sultan accepted Christ as Savior. There is no doubt that what happened changed the lives of both men forever. Francis stayed for an extended time in the Muslim camp, and Kamil gave him and the Franciscans permission to preach the gospel in Muslim lands. It is said that Kamil once declared, "Oh, Francis, if I ever meet another Christian like you, I will become Christian."

What we seldom consider is how this meeting changed Francis. Instead of encountering a barbaric pagan, as he had been led to expect, Francis met a highly cultured man whose deep sensitivity for spiritual things created an immediate basis for common ground. It is certain that after their time together, Francis no longer regarded Muslims as a pagan enemy under the reign of Satan or as the embodiment of the Antichrist. He found something of Jesus alive and well in his new friend, so much so that they were able to pray together. What happened to Francis gave him a compassion and understanding toward Muslims that we Protestants would do well to study and emulate.

LOUIS MASSIGNON

In more recent times, we can find a model for reconciliation with the Muslim community in Louis Massignon, a highly recognized academic and a political officer in the High French Commission for the occupied territories in Palestine and Syria. While in Baghdad, Iraq, Massignon fell seriously ill, and if not for the loving care a Muslim family gave him, he would have died. At one point, when near death, he had a spiritual experience that he called "a meeting with the stranger." Most say that "the stranger" was Jesus. Others contend it was a loving Muslim. One thing is certain: Massignon's perception of Muslims was changed forever because of this vision. For him, the Arab world would henceforth mean sacred hospitality, deep friendships, and an enriched spiritual life.

Massignon went on to live among Muslims in France, establishing a community of prayer, visiting prisoners, teaching Algerian immigrants, and upholding the way of nonviolent resistance against the injustices of French colonial rule. He taught Christians to remember that the Arab race also descended from Abraham and was the result of Hagar's tears. From the Bible, he pointed out that before Isaac, the father of the nation of Israel, was born to Sarah, her husband, Abraham, had fathered another son named Ishmael with his servant Hagar. Sarah's jealousy forced Abraham to drive Hagar and Ishmael away, but Abraham prayed at Beersheba, "Oh, that Ishmael may live in Your presence!" and God replied, "As for Ishmael, I have heard you. Behold, I will bless him and make him fruitful and multiply him exceedingly. He shall be the father of twelve princes, and I will make him a great nation" (see Gen. 17:18–20).

Massignon taught that because the Arab race started with Hagar's tears (Gen. 21:16–18), as recorded in the Bible, Christians should therefore show respect for Muslims and express loving tolerance toward them, even when they do not return such love and tolerance. His greatest fear was that Jews, Christians, and Muslims, all of whom in one way or another came from the seeds of Abraham, would fail to live peaceably together and that wars between them would result in such destruction that the gospel's message would be set back another thousand years, even while people of goodwill were trying to undo the impact of the Crusades.

MYSTICISM PROVIDES COMMON GROUND

Beyond these models of reconciliation, a theology of mysticism provides some hope for common ground between Christianity and Islam. Both religions have within their histories examples of ecstatic union with God, which seem at odds with their own spiritual traditions but have much in common with each other. I do not know what to make of the Muslim mystics, especially those who have come to be known as the Sufis. What do they experience in their mystical experiences? Could they have encountered the same God we do in our Christian mysticism?

The founder of this movement was Hasan Al Basri (A.D. 642–728). Basri reacted against the corruption of Islam in Iraq and the ways in which Islam had slipped into materialism and the abuse of its political power. His attempt to bring about religious reform very much paralleled the path of Francis, both in style and in spiritual direction. Both men sensed a sacred presence in everything and claimed to have experienced a mystical union with God. The Sufis even had a dimension of spirituality that included "speaking in tongues," which could be compared to what goes on in present-day Pentecostalism.

One of the Muslim mystics, Ibn Al Arabi, put a great emphasis on Christ and spoke of Jesus as "the Word," "the Spirit," and "God's tongue." He said of Christians, "In my youth I denied the others' belief and made them my enemy. Now my religion is the religion of love." He said of Jesus:

He is the living being, without beginning, without end.
He is the word, discriminating and integrating.
He is to the world the ringstone of the ring.
The plane of inscription
The sign by which the king deals his coffer
He is called vice-regent then
Since the transcendent guards him through his creation
So he made him his vice-regent charged with the safeguarding of his property
And the world is preserved as long as the complete human being remains in it.
Don't you see that if he were no more . . .
The entire order would vanish into the afterworld
Where he would be the eternal seal on the treasure chest
That is the afterworld

Such a statement is closer to what evangelicals say about Jesus than the sort of things I hear coming from theologically liberal Christians.

One Sufi Muslim was so into Jesus that he was accused of having secretly become a Christian. Al Hallaj talked about experiencing the presence of God in other people, and in the end, he so identified with Jesus that he told his friends, "On the supreme example of the Cross, I intend to die." Great Christian leaders such as Duns Scofus, Roger Bacon, and St. John of the Cross readily acknowledged how reading the Sufi philosophers such as Al Hallaj enhanced their own understanding of their faith.

ONE WAY TO GOD

I am *not* suggesting that we are all in the same God camp. We are not. The differences between even the most spiritual of the Sufi Muslims and the evangelical Christians cannot be ignored. But to define Islam as an evil religion is irresponsible. To say that Muslims are wrong is one thing, but to call their founder "wicked" and to generalize about them in a demonizing way is unjustified. Any possibility of the evangelization of Muslims requires that we go to them as friends. Right now a great deal of damage has been done to that possibility.

A student at Princeton Theological Seminary once asked the Protestant theologian Karl Barth, "Do you think that other religions can be valid avenues to God and His salvation?" Barth answered, "No! No religion can provide a valid avenue to God and His salvation. Not even the Christian religion. Only Jesus Christ can serve as a mediator to God."

Barth was right on target with that statement. A personal relationship with Jesus is the only means of being intimate with God. But we will never know in this life who has this mystical involvement with the resurrected Jesus through the power of the Holy Spirit, and who does not. On that day when we all must stand before the judgment seat of God, there will be a lot of surprises. Jesus said as much, and He may turn away some who said all the right things theologically by declaring, "I never knew you" (Matt. 7:23).

It also may be the case that many who never would have called themselves Christians were truly possessed by Christ and will be invited into the eternal kingdom.

A leading evangelist told me about an encounter he had with a non-Christian during a trip through China that raised that possibility. While there, he visited the monastery, and as he entered the walled-in gardens of the place, he noticed one of the monks in deep meditation. At the prompting of the Spirit, he went over to talk to the man, and with his translator, he explained the story of Jesus. He opened the New Testament and showed him what the Bible taught about salvation. As he spoke, he noticed that the monk was visibly moved. Actually, there were tears in the monk's eyes. My friend, the evangelist, then asked, "Won't you accept this Jesus into your heart and let Him be your personal Savior?"

The monk answered with surprise, "Accept Him? How can I accept Him into my life when He is already there? All the time you were telling me about Him, His Spirit within me was affirming the truth of what you were saying. Constantly I heard His Spirit say, 'He is talking of Me! He is talking of Me!' I do not need to accept Him. He is already in me, affirming the message of your Bible. I have known Him for a long, long time."

My friend asked me, "Was this man possessed by Jesus before I ever arrived? Was he a Christian before he knew the name of Jesus? And, if I had not come with the gospel message, would God accept him on the Day of Judgment?"

I don't know how to answer the questions my friend posed, but I do know this: we should preach the gospel to every living creature and let the judgment of who is saved and who is lost fall into the hands of the Judge of the universe.

10

Are Evangelicals Too Militaristic?

Patriotism can become idolatry if a people pledge ultimate allegiance to their nation and view God as the legitimater of their society's values. If people do not heed the warning that the apostle Paul gave us in Romans 1:18–23, they can easily turn "the glory of the uncorruptible God" into "an image made like to corruptible man" and end up worshiping themselves, rather than the Creator.

George Bernard Shaw once said, "God created us in His image, and we decided to return the favor." Too often those of us in the American evangelical community have had a tendency to do just that.

An outside observer, visiting our churches and listening to what we have to say about God, could easily conclude that we have taken the Jesus of Scripture and transformed Him into an American. Instead of allowing Jesus to be an incarnation of Yahweh, we have made Him into an incarnation of our own traits and values. Many of us American evangelicals not only make Jesus into an American, but also view Him as a deity who provides sanctification for our affluent, consumeristic lifestyle. We have created a Jesus who will fight to preserve America and all that our nation stands for. Such tendencies are increasingly obvious in evangelical Christianity, but I want to emphasize that they are only tendencies. Obviously there is much that transcends this hypernationalism, but all too often we have turned patriotism into idolatry.

In recent times, especially since the second war in Iraq, the tendency to identify the American cause with the cause of Christ has become increasingly evident. Shortly after 9/11, I was traveling by automobile across the state of Alabama, and within a stretch of two miles I passed three different churches, each displaying a wooden cross with the American flag draped over it. Such a merger of the symbol of our nation and the symbol of the Christian faith has dangerous implications. It is evidence of the kind of patriotism that I call idolatry.

Any attempt to cloak nationalism with religious legitimation is bound to lead to militarism in a nation that is a superpower. It then becomes easy to view the armies of that nation as an instrument through which God exercises righteous judgment upon the earth. People who hold this opinion view those who oppose the ideals of the nation as enemies of God who must be held in check, if not destroyed. More than a little bit of this kind of thinking has crept into evangelical rhetoric and our perception of the recent war with Iraq. It is not surprising that many who are outside the evangelical community view it as being allied with "get tough" militarism. When we go off to war, too many of us are convinced that Jesus is on our side. Why shouldn't He be? We have made Him into one of us.

In reality, this picture of all evangelicals as militant patriots is somewhat of an exaggeration, because a significant portion of our community, especially among groups like the Mennonites and the Church of the Brethren, opposes war on biblical grounds. Also, there is a significant minority within the mainstream of the evangelical community who, even though they believe that there is such a thing as a just war, have not been convinced that the invasion of Iraq fits into the "just war" category. Nevertheless, the image of evangelicals as nationalistic militarists who believe that God's blessing is upon the actions of American troops, regardless of where they go and what they do, is the image the mass media portrays. It does not help that some popular television evangelists have made the war in Iraq into a moral crusade.

Politicians demonstrate how well they understand the temperament of evangelicalism when they come looking for support for America's military ventures. No doubt, President Bush was well aware of the positive reception he would get when, in 2003, he spoke to the National Religious Broadcasters. He told those at the convention that "America has always been a religious nation—perhaps never more than now." He got a standing ovation on the convention floor when he declared the war in Iraq to be a cause defined by the religious absolutes of "good versus evil, right versus wrong, human dignity and freedom versus tyranny and oppression." In that speech, the president went on to say that our nation sought no selfish gain in this war and that we were "on the side of God." I believe that the president was wholly sincere—and that's what scares me.

In no way do I wish to convey that patriotism is a bad thing. Love of nation is a good thing, but Christians must never succumb to the tendency to say, "My country right or wrong—but right or wrong, my country!" Having an allegiance to a God who transcends the nation and claiming an ultimate citizenship in the kingdom of God, the Christian should be saying something like, "My country—may she always be right. And when she is not right, may I do my best to call my country to repentance."

A TROUBLED PACIFIST

Before I go any further, I have to confess that I am what could be called "a troubled pacifist." I say that I am troubled about my position because I don't have an easy answer for those who ask me whether or not there are times when a nation must oppose tyranny with violence. Yet I find that what can easily be called "simplistic applications of the teachings of Jesus" necessitates for me a pacifist posture.

When I read the Sermon on the Mount, in which Jesus called upon His followers to return good for evil and referred to peacemakers as "the children of God," I find support for the pacifist position. When I hear Him say, "Those who live by the sword, die by the sword," I am inclined to take such a statement as a call to abandon any form of militarism. As I read on in the New Testament and come to the teachings of the apostle Paul in Romans 12:14–21, I find further support for a pacifist approach. In those verses we read:

> Bless them which persecute you: bless, and curse not. Rejoice with them that do rejoice, and weep with them that weep. Be of the same mind one toward another. Mind not high things, but condescend to men of low estate. Be not wise in your own conceits. Recompense to no man evil for evil. Provide things honest in the sight of all men. If it be possible, as much as lieth in you, live peaceably with all men. Dearly beloved, avenge not yourselves, but rather give place unto wrath: for it is written, Vengeance is mine; I will repay, saith the Lord. Therefore if thine enemy hunger, feed him; if he thirst, give him drink: for in so doing thou shalt heap coals of fire on his head. Be not overcome of evil, but overcome evil with good.

Some will argue that the Hebrew Bible reveals many instances when God called upon His people to do battle. Any reading of the history of Israel in the

Old Testament will reveal a God who led people into battle and blessed them with victory. Whenever someone cites such passages, I have to remind myself that in the Sermon on the Mount, Jesus laid out a morality that transcended that which Moses prescribed in the Old Testament. Jesus said that He had a *new* commandment. When I contend that Jesus called it a "new commandment," I believe He meant exactly that, and that it *is* a *new* commandment. Consider His words in Matthew 5:38–39: "Ye have heard that it hath been said, An eye for an eye, and a tooth for a tooth: but I say unto you, that ye resist not evil: but whosoever shall smite thee on thy right cheek, turn to him the other also."

Also consider the words of Jesus in verses 43–45 in that same chapter.

> Ye have heard that it hath been said, Thou shalt love thy neighbour, and hate thine enemy. But I say unto you, Love your enemies, bless them that curse you, do good to them that hate you, and pray for them which despitefully use you, and persecute you; that ye may be the children of your Father which is in heaven: for he maketh his sun to rise on the evil and on the good, and sendeth rain on the just and on the unjust.

Church historians will readily agree that the early church assumed a pacifist position. Most agree that it wasn't until Constantine replaced the Roman eagle with a cross, as he marched his troops into battle, and thus embraced Christianity as the religion of the state, that the church abandoned its pacifist stand. Constantine marched his troops into the waters and baptized them, but they were instructed to hold the arm that bore the sword above the water level so that the warring part of their bodies would not be sanctified.

THE JUST WAR THEORY

Saint Augustine gave theological legitimation to certain forms of militarism when, in the fourth century, he articulated the concept of a just war. Later, Protestants would look to John Calvin for a reaffirmation of that concept, and today most Protestants embrace what can be called "the just war theory."

But I raise a very serious question: do evangelicals who embrace the just war theory affirm its principles in contemporary America? This question is especially pertinent when dealing with America's most recent military exercises in Iraq.

It would be useful to evaluate our participation in that war using the just war principles.

A primary principle of the just war theory is that the war be the only means for the nation to protect itself. The justification for America's invasion of Iraq was that Iraq posed an imminent threat to our security. Our leaders contended that Saddam Hussein had at his disposal weapons of mass destruction, which he could unleash to attack us and other nations within minutes of deployment. We had good reason to believe that; as Jesse Jackson said on British television, "We know they have weapons of mass destruction—because we have the receipts."

Of course, Jesse Jackson was right. Not wanting the Shi'ite revolution in Iran to spread over into Iraq, our government not only provided the means for chemical warfare so that Saddam Hussein could hold back the Shi'ites in the south and the Kurds in the north, but we actually provided logistical support so that his armies could use those weapons effectively. President Clinton points to his predecessors as having provided that support for chemical warfare. Of course, we must question whether or not additional support for Saddam Hussein was provided during the Clinton years.

We now know that the justification for invading Iraq was built on false premises. There is a general consensus that there was a time when Saddam Hussein had weapons of mass destruction, but whether he had them at the time we invaded Iraq is another question. The American people were misinformed by the president, who now says that he was misinformed by the CIA. The CIA, on the other hand, contends that it never told the president there was any degree of certainty that Iraq had the weapons we were led to believe they had at the time we invaded them. There may have been strong suspicions, but are suspicions justifiable grounds for war? Those who hold to a just war theory would have a difficult time saying yes to that proposition.

When former president Jimmy Carter, in an Op-Ed column in the *New York Times,* argued against the thesis that the invasion of Iraq qualified as a just war, he was severely criticized. It was Carter's contention that Iraq posed no military threat to the United States. In response, the Christian media came down hard on the born-again Carter, contending that it was inappropriate for a former president to comment on matters of foreign policy at a time when the present administration was dealing with a crisis.

It has become difficult for Christians to make decisions about whether or not a war is just in an age in which national security often requires the government to keep secrets. When Secretary of State Colin Powell was asked about the sources of the proof that Saddam Hussein had weapons of mass destruction and that Iraq posed a threat to America, he said that he could not reveal his sources without compromising those who worked in the intelligence community. We now know that such proof did not exist.

Indeed, there are risks when we have openness in government, but it may be that a closed government is even more dangerous. If we are going to have a just war, don't we, as a democratic people, really need to know what is going on?

There are risks that go with open government, but I do not want to see our country give up being a democratic society even in the interest of improving national security. Benjamin Franklin once said, "When a nation makes its security more precious than its freedoms, it will end up with neither." As Christians who enter into the decision-making process of whether or not a war is just, should not we be requiring more information from our government than we are getting?

DID WE TRY EVERYTHING
BEFORE WE DECLARED WAR?

The second consideration for determining whether a war is justified is the necessity of being relatively certain that all alternatives to war have been exhausted. Before the war in Iraq, we should have asked whether this war could have been avoided if we had created more of an international consensus to oppose Saddam Hussein. Did we exhaust the possibilities of dealing with this crisis through the United Nations? We know that Arab nations would have been willing to join in an effort to end the threat that our leaders had led us to believe Saddam Hussein posed. Unfortunately, evangelicals have offered little support for the United Nations. Many of our preachers actually have suggested that the United Nations may be the instrument used by the Antichrist to impose his evil control over the world. Even now, any regular listening to Christian radio will reveal cynicism and scorn toward that international body.

I do not hold such a negative view of the United Nations. I believe that, in spite of all of its failings and shortcomings, it still can be a major instrument for facilitating peace and that God can use it to accomplish much good. Furthermore, I believe that if we are to abide by the principles of a just war, we must exhaust all the potentialities of the United Nations. In the case of the U.S. war in Iraq, we dismissed the pleas of other nations to continue negotiations with Iraq and to give the UN weapons inspectors more time to search for weapons of mass destruction. In my estimation, America went to war too hastily.

Jim Wallis, the aforementioned editor of *Sojourners* magazine and founder of the political action group Call to Renewal, was promoting a viable alternative before the United States declared war on Iraq the second time. Key to this plan was that the International Court of Justice indict Saddam Hussein for war crimes and crimes against humanity. This would have delegitimatized his government and provided a legal basis for kidnapping him and bringing him to trial in the Netherlands. Such a plan had already proved viable in bringing about regime changes in Serbia and Rwanda. Wallis's plan won the attention and support of some highly placed members of the British government, but the White House had already made the decision to go to war before the plan got the attention it deserved. We now have a report from the former secretary of the treasury asserting that plans to go to war with Iraq were being formulated from the first meeting of President Bush's cabinet and that the decision to go to war was made without any consideration of what the just war theory requires. This may explain why the White House was not willing to give the Wallis plan a hearing.

DID THE GAINS OUTWEIGH THE LOSSES?

None of what I have said should be taken to mean that I do not agree with those who claim that Saddam Hussein should have been removed from power. Not even the strongest antiwar activists could say anything positive about Saddam Hussein. This was a leader who had utilized the worst kinds of torture to maintain his rule and promoted atrocities that resulted in the deaths of thousands of people who had raised little more than their voices in opposition to his rule. Among the credible reports that leaked out of Iraq was one stating that on more than one occasion, he had infant children tortured in front of their mothers in order to elicit confessions. Saddam Hussein was an evil ruler, and we can all agree that removing him from power was a good thing.

A former student of mine, presently serving with one of the inner-city ministries that I helped establish, took a sabbatical a few years ago to study Iraq first-hand. He toured the country, interviewed both Christians and non-Christians, and came back saying that reports of the evil regime of Saddam Hussein were, for the most part, true. This young man also reported that he had found widespread resentment of the regime.

Nevertheless, we still must ask whether or not we carefully considered if the good this war accomplished outweighed the harm it did to innocent people. I do not think America sufficiently reflected on that question before attacking Iraq, and such consideration is required according to the just war theory.

Of course, the long-term effects of this war are difficult to ascertain right now. On the one hand, many of the people in Iraq seem to be relieved that Saddam Hussein is gone. But on the other hand, the people of Iraq do not seem to accept us as liberators. Much to the surprise of many, Iraqis are calling the very armies that did so much to free them of a tyrant "armies of occupation." Cries of "Yankee, go home!" echo up and down the streets of Baghdad, and we wonder if the Iraqi people are duly grateful for the sacrifices our men and women in uniform made in order to give them a new lease on life.

Recently, while in New Zealand, I read on the front page of that country's main newspaper that twenty-two American soldiers in Iraq had committed suicide, and more than six hundred of them had been returned home because of severe psychiatric trauma. According to the newspaper, the navy reported that up to 20 percent of the American soldiers who had served in Iraq would require psychiatric care when they returned to the States. When I returned to America, I tried to find out if that report had appeared in the newspapers in our country. No one could remember seeing such a report, and I began to wonder why the foreign press was reporting on important things that were happening to our service personnel in Iraq, while Americans did not seem to be informed as to what was going on.

Even more important is that we consider the lives lost in this war. These days, it usually does not appear on page 1 or even page 2 or 3 of our newspapers when American soldiers are killed in Iraq. And what of the many Iraqi citizens and soldiers who have been killed in the conflict?

While most observers will agree that, given the enormity of this war, our forces kept civilian casualties at as low a level as possible, I do not believe America has shown sufficient remorse for the Iraqi men, women, and children who have died. I am haunted by the words of one of my former students, a committed Christian pacifist, who chose to be in Baghdad when the bombing began. He witnessed massive destruction as bombs fell on that capital city. Working in a Baghdad hospital, he cared for some of the many wounded civilian casualties of the bombings. His comments to me about the war reflected his agreement that Saddam Hussein was a very evil man who had to be removed, but he went on to say, "If a man is abusing his wife and children, you do not stop him by burning down his house with his wife and children inside it with him."

SOME FAR-REACHING CONSEQUENCES

As just war theorists make their case, some of the long-term consequences of this war warrant second thoughts on our part. Most of the billion people of the Muslim world perceived the attack on Iraq as a renewal of the Crusades, in which the conquering armies of the Judeo-Christian nations of the world set out to impose their culture, and specifically their religion, upon the world. Many Muslims view our war on Iraq, and our overwhelming and unbalanced support of Israel against the Palestinians, as the beginnings of a holy war that will pick up where the Crusades left off. The ramifications of this kind of thinking for Christian missionaries who had hoped to evangelize the Muslim world are all too obvious.

Another negative consequence of the war that we must consider is our loss of moral authority. America has hitherto contended that preemptive attacks, such as the attack of the Japanese on Pearl Harbor, are unjustified. Now, after what we did in Iraq, we have lost the right to make such moral judgments. If some nation such as North Korea stages a preemptive strike on another nation (e.g., South Korea), it will be hard for us to do any condemning. Should the attacking nation contend that its own security was dependent upon such military action, that nation would be making the same case the United States made to justify this second Gulf War.

Today, America appears hypocritical to the member states of the United Nations. We condemned Iraq for not complying with UN Resolution 1441, which required that Iraq fully cooperate with weapons inspectors, and used this as our basis for going to war. But then we ignored the will of the United Nations when we invaded Iraq. This kind of duplicity seems to mark us as those whom James 1:8 called "double minded."

This second Gulf War also caused us to lose the incredible goodwill we had enjoyed following the terrorist attacks on September 11, 2001. I was in Argentina on that terrible day, and four days later I witnessed a crowd of a half-million people gathered in the center of Buenos Aires for a prayer vigil, during which they prayed for the people of the United States. From other cities around the world came an outpouring of affection and support for our country. The world was behind us then, but now we have become one of the most resented countries on the planet, largely because of what the rest of the world viewed as an arrogant act of power when we invaded Iraq.

The just war theory says that the good that any war achieves must outdo the evil. I am not convinced that this is the case with this second war with Iraq. Is the world really safer today than it was before the war? Is America more secure?

There is no evidence that al Qaeda was in Iraq prior to our invasion. The private papers of Saddam Hussein, recovered after his capture, give ample evidence that he had instructed his people to have no contact with al Qaeda or other outside terrorists, lest such contacts be used as a pretext for an American invasion.

Al Qaeda was not in Iraq prior to the war, but its members are certainly in Iraq today, spreading terror and creating conditions that could lead to a civil war. Some can argue that the war in Iraq, instead of diminishing the threat of terrorism, as the president claims, actually may have generated more terrorism. Our behavior as a nation has caused many Iraqis, along with other Arabs, now to view terrorism as their only means of striking back at a superpower they cannot resist in any other way. It seems that there is a major terroristic attack almost daily in Iraq, and I fear that in the days that lie ahead, such terrorist acts will not be confined to that part of the world.

THE SUFFERING SERVANT
VERSUS THE GOD OF VENGEANCE

How we view the war in Iraq, and whether or not we consider it a just war, has a great deal to do with what we believe about God. One evening, just before the second war in Iraq began, I was watching *Larry King Live* on television. Four clergymen were discussing whether or not the war in Iraq was justified. As the program unfolded, it became increasingly clear that while each of these men talked about Jesus and quoted Scripture in making his case, the four had little in common. What emerged for me was the realization that while all of them believed in God, they did not believe in the same God.

Two of the men, a Methodist bishop and a Catholic priest, presented a Jesus who can best be described as "the suffering servant." They talked about a Jesus who they believed was taken from the Gospels, especially from the Sermon on the Mount. They emphasized that Jesus called us to be "peacemakers," and they thought this meant that we should strive to "overcome evil with good." Their Jesus was one who did not talk of retribution but told His followers to turn the other cheek in their confrontations with evil. These men made a major point that the Jesus of the Gospels requires His followers to love their enemies and do good to those who would do them harm. For them, the ethic of Jesus was meant not only for personal relationships, but also for our interactions on the societal level. Theirs was a Jesus defined only in terms of sacrificial love.

Arguing against the bishop and priest were two well-known television evangelists. This pair, representing evangelicalism, emphasized the God of the Old Testament, who ordered armies into battle to utterly destroy the enemies of Israel. Theirs was a God who willed the annihilation of the morally impure people in those wicked cities whose abominable sins offended God's holiness. The God they presented to the listening audience was the "man of war" described in Exodus 15:3, who destroyed all that was not pure and righteous. The biblical support for their description of God also came from parts of the New Testament, especially from the book of Revelation, where John described Jesus as the conquering Lord of history—the Lion of Judah (Rev. 5:5). The Jesus they preached was an avenging God who rained down judgment on the evil people of the earth. They quoted Romans 13:4, where Paul declared that the government "does not bear the sword in vain" (NKJV).

This God, who through violence purges evil from the earth, has certainly been part of the American consciousness over the years. He is the warring deity described in the "Battle Hymn of the Republic." Consider these lines from that hymn, which was Abraham Lincoln's favorite:

> Mine eyes have seen the glory of the coming of the Lord,
> He is trampling out the vintage where the grapes of wrath are stored,
> He has loosed the fateful lightning of his terrible swift sword,
> His truth is marching on.

I am sure that many biblical scholars and theologians have little difficulty reconciling these two conflicting images of God, but on that television show, the two images seemed dramatically opposed. For the most part, the evangelical community has embraced the God who is the vengeful warlord and has downplayed the image of God as the suffering servant.

ARMAGEDDON ABOUT TO BE REALIZED?

The God those television evangelists described was the One who seemingly had ordained America to destroy the evil government of Iraq. Those two men stated in no uncertain terms that what was about to happen in Iraq was a fulfillment of biblical prophecy, and the evangelical community widely circulated their opinion. In the book of Revelation, we read about the Battle of Armageddon (Rev. 16) in which, in anticipation of Christ's rule over the world, the armies of God defeat the armies of Satan. Books supporting the belief that the coming war in Iraq was this battle appeared in Christian bookstores, and a rash of radio preachers upheld the same message.

Do not for one moment think such interpretations of prophecies are of no consequence. They are often taken seriously, even by people in places as high as the White House. People proclaimed alarmist messages such as the one that Saddam Hussein should be considered the Antichrist. When their predictions proved unfounded, these "prophets" of doom just went on as though they had never said anything about such matters in the first place. Yet the consequences of their reckless talk can be serious. I ask, ought they not at least admit their mistakes and say, "We're sorry"?

We must note that religious leaders, such as the pope and key executives of all mainline denominations, opposed such apocalyptic prophecies and made public declarations that our government had not explored all alternative avenues of resolving the problems of Saddam Hussein's regime. They made pleas to the U.S. government to hold off on the war until those other avenues could be tried. Only the church leaders of the Southern Baptist Convention, the largest Protestant denomination in America, voted overwhelmingly to lend support to the war effort and to fully endorse the policies of the Bush administration as having met the criteria of a just war.

MY OWN STRUGGLES WITH THE DIFFERING IMAGES OF GOD

To be honest, I have had trouble for a long time accepting the Old Testament God who orders the death of every man, woman, and child who stands in the way of His chosen people taking over the Promised Land. What has really troubled me is that I find it very difficult to believe that this genocide came at the direction of the same loving God revealed in the New Testament. I am not the only one who has difficulty with these seemingly opposed images. One of the earliest heresies in Christendom claimed that the God of the Old Testament was not the same God we find in Jesus Christ. I do not, for one moment, entertain the idea that the God of the Old Testament is other than the God revealed in Jesus, but I do have problems making everything fit together into one unified image. Inevitably, each of us must struggle to resolve this dilemma, because there is little question that the way in which we define God has everything to do with how we view war.

I once heard a lecture given by the pacifist Mennonite theologian John Howard Yoder, in which he defined God entirely as one who is bringing in His kingdom as the suffering servant, who, in Christ, rejects violence as the means. Afterward, a minister with an opposing view entered into a heated dispute with him. When the argument had reached an impasse, the minister said, "Well, John, in the end, we both worship the same God."

After a poignant pause, Yoder answered, "No . . . I don't think we do."

It appeared to me that the religious leaders who appeared on *Larry King Live* also had two different Gods. One was a warlord, and the other was a prince of peace. Therein lay the basis of their differences.

NO NATION CAN CALL ITSELF GOD'S INSTRUMENT

While different beliefs about God have far-reaching consequences insofar as we view the war with Iraq, I must declare loud and clear that no nation should ever view itself as the God-ordained instrument of His will. We must guard against ever letting politicians play up such a theme, as they so often are tempted to do. William Shakespeare gave expression to such cynical use of God and Scripture in his play *Richard III* when he wrote: "But then I sigh, with a piece of scripture / Tell them that God bids us to do evil for good; / And thus I clothe my naked villainy with odd ends stol'n forth of Holy Writ; / And seem a saint when most I play the devil."

We must be on guard against politicians, however sincere they may be, who give to our nation a messianic designation. Such was the case when, in the face of the Spanish-American War, Senator Albert J. Beveridge of Indiana addressed the U.S. Senate and said: "Almighty God . . . has marked the American people as the chosen nation to finally lead in the regeneration of the world. This is the divine mission of America . . . We are the trustees of the world's progress, guardians of the righteous peace." He went on to quote Matthew 25:21, where Jesus said, "Thou hast been faithful over a few things, I will make thee ruler over many things."

It's easy to see how leaders with such convictions could take a nation into war, believing that God was on their side. Abraham Lincoln sounded the corrective note against that tune when he proposed that we should be asking if we are on God's side.

QUESTIONS THAT BEG FOR ANSWERS

What if our country had followed the admonition of Scripture and, instead of maintaining an embargo on Iraq for more than a decade, applied the directives of the apostle Paul, who said, "If thine enemy hunger, feed him; if he thirst, give him drink: for in so doing thou shalt heap coals of fire on his head" (Rom. 12:20)?

According to UN statistics, the embargo the United States imposed on Iraq following the first Gulf War was responsible for the deaths of at least half a million children. They died from either the consequences of malnutrition or a lack of medicine. The purpose of this embargo had been to make the people of Iraq angry with Saddam Hussein so that they would rise up and overthrow his government. Instead, it got them to hate America, the country that they viewed as having caused them so much suffering.

If, instead, America had fed their hungry, cared for their sick, and blessed their people, might the Iraqis not have been more supportive of our aim to rid their country of weapons of mass destruction? Might not the goodwill thus engendered among the Iraqi people have been more effective than the embargo in undermining the regime of Saddam Hussein?

At the outbreak of the second Gulf War, some students from Eastern University, where I have served as a faculty member for thirty-five years, went to Iraq as part of a Christian peacemaking team. Jonathan and Leah Wilson-Hartgrove were among them. They flew to Jordan, then made the perilous fifteen-hour journey to Baghdad by car, arriving at night just before the U.S. forces started their aerial bombing. Leah reported to the press, "We are not naive. There is little possibility that our presence will stop the war. However, we believe that our being there makes a big difference in the Iraqis' lives and in our own lives . . . We offer a presence of peace to those in Iraq who are facing tremendous danger and are terribly afraid."

One of the colleagues of these brave young Christians sent an e-mail saying, in essence, that somewhere in recent years, Christians had set aside the necessity of having congruence between what they believe and what they do. He went on to make clear his belief that what American Christians did when they supported this war was a departure from Jesus, who taught us to love our neighbors—regardless of who they are.

The early Christians did not view themselves primarily as citizens of the Roman Empire, but rather as citizens of the kingdom of God. They saw themselves as ambassadors of the kingdom, which already was becoming a reality in "this present age." The name they gave to themselves was "sojourners." These men and women lived by an ethic that was alien to the nation in which they dwelt, and they paid a heavy price for doing so. Were they wrong to take the teachings of Jesus so literally as to deem all wars unjust? Would they have acted the same way in the face of Hitler or Saddam Hussein?

OUR ATTENTION AND INPUT ARE ESSENTIAL

Regardless of how we answer these questions, we all must recognize that indifference is not an option when it comes to the wars in the world around us, or to the decisions that our leaders make about going to war. While we are not to be "of" this world, we are still to be "in" it (John 15:19; 17:11). We are called to speak to those in power with prophetic justice, and also with love. For America's leaders and for its military establishment, we must provide a new prayer of serenity. Perhaps the one written by Roland S. Homet Jr. in his book *The Wisdom of Serpents: Reflections on Religion and Foreign Policy* will do. It reads: "God grant us the serenity to tolerate conduct that does not threaten us, to focus on the real threats as priorities for response, and to understand what motivates other people." Such a prayer might lead our nation to believe that the way to peace is not simply by destroying our enemies but by addressing the poverty and oppression that breed terrorists; it is repenting of the materialistic self-interest that too often marks our policies and decision making in the face of war.

I still do not know if we can avoid war, but I am committed to working for peace because Jesus requires that of all who would be children of God. Furthermore, I believe that we Christians must recognize that our ultimate allegiance belongs to the kingdom of God and that we are primarily ambassadors of that kingdom to the nation in which we live (2 Cor. 5:20). Understanding this will free us to speak of the values of the kingdom of God to our present age, regardless of how radical and countercultural this makes us appear.

Critiquing the society according to biblical imperatives is not unpatriotic. Calling the nation to the judgment of God does not represent disloyalty. I believe that the time has come to give the radical Christianity in the Sermon on the Mount a chance to be lived out in the face of war. G. K. Chesterton once said, "It is not that Christianity has been tried and found wanting. It is that it has never been tried."

11

Do We Understand Why So Many People Throughout the World Hate America?

People like Ann Coutler, the TV political pundit, often say that people like me who raise criticisms about America and our way of life really hate this country. Quite the opposite. I love America! I love it enough to want it to live up to its highest ideals. I love it enough to want it to be "the city on the hill": an example to the world of what a nation can be, where freedom and justice enable people to make for themselves those decisions that determine their personal and national destinies. I love this country so much that I do not want to see it fall from its pinnacle of well-being into a state of disarray—which it surely will, unless it changes its ways. That's why I choose to critique America from what I believe to be a biblical perspective.

Ours is a pluralistic society, and I have no intention of joining those who would make our country into a nation that gives official primacy to the Christian faith. On the other hand, I am convinced that our nation can move toward actualizing the ideals of love and justice that we find in the teachings of Jesus in such a way that people of other nations, and even people with no religion, will applaud. That is why I join the loyal opposition that will settle for nothing less than an America that is always striving to be its best. Such an America must be sensitive to its shortcomings, and often we can perceive those faults most clearly when we see ourselves as others see us.

Since the catastrophes of September 11, 2001, Americans have come to the shocked awareness that people out there in the rest of the world hate us more than we possibly could have imagined. To our amazement, we have discovered that some in foreign lands actually celebrated what happened at the World Trade Center in New York City and at the Pentagon in northern Virginia on that fateful day. We could not understand such reactions. We asked, "Have we not been the most generous nation on the face of the earth, feeding the hungry, rescuing those who were victims of natural disasters, sending some of our finest and best to fight and die for freedom?" Did those people who were expressing contempt for America have no appreciation for the sacrifices that we Americans made on the beaches of Normandy and on the islands in the Pacific, with no desire at all to establish an American empire?

We liberated conquered and oppressed peoples and gave away billions of dollars to rebuild devastated nations, and we did so without thought of reward. After such generosity, we asked, "Why does the rest of the world not show us more appreciation?"

AMERICA'S BUM RAP

Before we try to answer such questions, I have to say that often America gets a bum rap from some of our foreign critics. They blame us for what really isn't our fault at all. For instance, Thomas L. Friedman, in his book *The Lexus and the Olive Tree*, points out that the emerging nations of the Third World usually want the benefits of modern technology (the technology they so often borrow from us) but then blame us for the negative social consequences that are the side aspects of that technology.

There is no doubt that technological changes bring with them massive social changes, in everything from family life to religion. Tractors and other innovations in farm machinery eliminate jobs in agricultural communities, with the consequence of people being pushed out of rural communities and into burgeoning cities. Within those cities, the traditional values of the extended families, which once existed in small-village life and in the open countryside, break down and even disappear. The rationalistic approach to life that goes with living in an industrialized urban society tends to diminish the importance of religion and make former beliefs seem like foolish superstitions. People under the spell of the moral relativism that usually goes with dwelling in a diverse mass society cast aside the folkways and mores that once gave order to life in bygone days.

Unfortunately, most people of the world do not understand that technology is an independent force that devastates *all* cultures, including our own. They embrace scientific technology with all of its benefits (i.e., modern medicine, modes of production and transportation, and instruments of communication) but grow angry at many of the social changes technology brings about. They blame those changes on what they call "Americanization." What they usually fail to recognize is what Jacques Ellul described so well in his book *The Technological Society:* that technology has a life of its own and exercises the same effects on every societal system regardless of where it comes from or where it is applied.

They do not understand that if they want to maintain the traditional ways of life they have enjoyed in their preindustrialized societies, they should shun the technological innovations that are destined to destroy that way of life. They can't have it both ways. When they say they want our technology but not our culture, they fail to recognize that our culture is largely a creation of our technology, and if they accept our technology, their ways of living will also change. They should stop blaming America for the consequences of a technology that they desperately want to embrace.

TECHNOLOGY AND MORALITY
ARE IRREVOCABLY TIED

On the other hand, much that we send to developing countries along with technology is excess baggage. Perhaps the most obvious example of this is in the content of the television shows and motion pictures that we export to the rest of the world. It is possible, and certainly desirable, for people in other lands to have the kinds of television sets that we have without being fed a regular diet of the sexual seductiveness of the likes of Britney Spears or the pornographic denigration of people that takes place on programs like *The Jerry Springer Show.* There is much to support the claims of the ayatollahs in Iraq or the complaints of Buddhist priests in Tibet that America is exploiting decadence. Television has already become a worldwide phenomena, but the content of our television shows is too often an expression of all that is wrong with America. As young people in foreign lands imitate so much of what they see on our television shows, we should not be surprised that their elders despise us for what we send their way.

Some years ago, I was in Santo Domingo during the week that followed New Year's Day. Student radicals at the state university had rallied to protest the

Americanization of their country via the mass media. To express their hostility, they burned in effigy a life-sized, stuffed replica of Santa Claus. Their protest sent the message, loud and clear, that they were fed up with the indoctrination of Dominican children through movies and television shows depicting the American version of Christmas. These university students were calling for a recommitment to the old Latin American custom of having children believe that their holiday gifts came on the visit of Magi, a celebration that occurred on the fifth and sixth of January, rather than from Santa Claus on Christmas Day.

Burning Santa in effigy was symbolic. These young people were rejecting the content of the American messages about Christmas that were bombarding their country through the mass media. They were not rejecting the *instruments* of the media, such as movies and television. Instead, they were claiming that the media and the messages coming over the media were two separate entities, and they believed that they could embrace the one without the other. Sociologists such as Marshall McLuhan, who has expertise in the study of the impact of the media on society, are not so sure that the two can be separated.

PROBLEMS MULTINATIONAL CORPORATIONS CREATE

Many, especially those with leftist leanings, believe that much of the havoc, privation, and suffering that goes on in Third World countries is directly related to the practices of the huge, multinational corporations that dominate the world economy. They blame America for unfair trade arrangements, the robbery of national resources, unjust labor practices, and the manipulations of the currencies of other countries, because so many of the corporations that are responsible for such practices were founded in America and still have their corporate headquarters here.

The latter fact is becoming less and less true, as many multinational corporations are locating their headquarters and financial operations "offshore" in order to get away from paying the taxes that go with registering profits made on U.S. soil. What most people in other countries usually fail to recognize is that these U.S. corporations seldom have loyalties to any particular nation, even their own.

Instead they often exist as independent entities that serve only their own self-interests and the interests of their stockholders. Do companies like Nike really care about what happens to American workers when they export their manufacturing to Asian nations? How many corporations really think about the image of

America they are exporting when they exploit workers in the Third World with low wages and use child labor?

SWEATSHOP AGENDAS

Social activists like myself have made much of what goes on in the sweatshops that American-based companies often establish in Third World countries. It should be noted, however, that in most cases, the workers in these sweatshops are being paid exactly what the market price for labor in these countries can bear, and in many cases, these workers are receiving more than the going rates. The people who have the jobs usually are grateful for the work, living as they do in places where unemployment can run as high as 50 percent. The executives of the companies justify the low hourly wages they pay by pointing out such things.

The executives of Nike make no apologies for the fact that in a given year, the entire group of employees who produce Nike shoes in Southeast Asia are paid less than the basketball player Michael Jordan was paid for the brief advertisement he made to market those shoes. Without such ads, contend those corporate executives, there would be no market for Nike products, and the poor who work in their factories would be out of work.

All of these arguments are valid, but the profits from these companies are usually enormous, and a fair sharing of those profits with those who work in their factories is what the Bible requires. Consider what James wrote in his epistle:

> Go to now, ye rich men, weep and howl for your miseries that shall come upon you. Your riches are corrupted, and your garments are motheaten. Your gold and silver is cankered; and the rust of them shall be a witness against you, and shall eat your flesh as it were fire. Ye have heaped treasure together for the last days. Behold, the hire of the labourers who have reaped down your fields, which is of you kept back by fraud, crieth: and the cries of them which have reaped are entered into the ears of the Lord of sabaoth. (James 5:1–4)

Employers should pay workers, according to the Bible, what is fair and what is necessary for them to have good lives, insofar as that is possible. They should do this, regardless of how little the market will bear in the way of wages.

Do not be surprised that there is resentment against America, which many perceive to be the mother of such multinational corporations. These exploited people are smart enough to know that they are in a nonnegotiable position, and while they realize that they are being exploited, they also know that they can do nothing about it—except to hate America.

FIRST, DO NO HARM

Those of us Christians who are opposed to the exploitation of workers in the Third World must be very careful about what we do, lest we cause more harm than good. As a case in point, the Disney Corporation was producing T-shirts in Haiti with the likenesses of Mickey, Minnie, and the other characters of the Disney menagerie. The factory owners employing these workers paid them a pittance compared to the profits that Disney was making when it sold the shirts here in the United States. So, across the country, many Christians, like myself, voiced our opposition to Disney's exploitive wages.

Unfortunately, the company reacted by completely shutting down its Haitian operations, and hundreds of Haitians lost their livelihood. This was a case where we Christian do-gooders caused hundreds of Haitians to suffer. Those jobs were actually paying more than what was then the going hourly wage in Haiti, and now that source of employment is lost.

We Christians must find ways of bringing about justice that are not only effective, but also wise and beneficial to the poor and oppressed.

OUR GOVERNMENT'S CONTRIBUTION

I don't want to give the impression that big corporations are the only agents of oppression of the poor. Our government's covert operations are a special cause of outrage. But here at home, we Americans usually are indifferent to what the CIA has done, and continues to do, in interfering with and even controlling the governments of other countries for America's self-interests.

We all know what happened on September 11, 2001. But how many of us have any awareness of what happened on September 11, 1973? On that earlier date, the CIA staged a coup on the democratically elected government of Chile. The president of Chile, according to the CIA, committed suicide—even though the autopsy revealed that he had been shot in the back. In place of the democratically elected president, Salvador Allende, the CIA imposed upon the country the military dictatorship of General Augusto Pinochet. The atrocities Pinochet committed against his own people are notorious and well documented.

In Iran, the CIA again struck with violent effectiveness when it ousted the democratically elected government of Prime Minister Mohammad Mosaddeq and installed Mohammed Reza Pahlavi as the shah. In the wake of the overthrow of the Iranian government, the two sons of Ayatollah Ruhollah Khomeini were captured, tortured, and killed. Might such facts help us to understand better the hatred of America by Ayatollah Khomeini in particular and by the Iranian people in general? People from other countries are amazed at how little Americans know about what is going on in the rest of the world and how indifferent we seem to be about the actions of our government. If you travel overseas, you will be surprised at how much more the newspapers of other countries cover world events when compared with our newspapers.

In Nicaragua, our government financed a bloody uprising against a legally elected government. The hero of the evangelical right, Oliver North, played a key role in supplying the arms for that revolution while keeping his activities a secret from President Ronald Reagan. What is more upsetting is that certain American television evangelists raised money on behalf of American-supported revolutionaries, the Contras, who carried out this ugly war. We did much the same thing in El Salvador, with CIA airplanes bombing villages. Covertly, illegally, and without the support of Congress, our government did all it could to destabilize the government that the people of El Salvador had elected.

Equally evil, on the other hand, is the fact that our government has spent billions of dollars to prop up tyrannical dictators throughout the Third World. All over Africa, we have kept despots in power with economic aid and by supplying them with arms, usually to the painful detriment of the well-being of indigenous peoples. Perhaps the most notable recent example is our supporting of the corrupt regime in Saudi Arabia, where we know there has been much support for al Qaeda.

As I've mentioned, we invaded Iraq in response to the September 11 attacks, even though we suspected all along that the money trail led back to Saudi Arabia, and that seventeen of the nineteen hijackers who flew those planes into the World Trade Center buildings and the Pentagon were from Saudi Arabia, the others being from Egypt. Many hold the opinion that our desire for Saudi oil has determined our policies toward the Saudi government. I have heard it said that if the major export of Iraq had been mushrooms instead of oil, we would never have invaded.

Students in our public school system never learn much, if anything, about such things, because increasingly America is indoctrinating students rather than educating them. Most high-school students cannot even locate Saudi Arabia on the map, let alone gain any kind of objective perspective on U.S. foreign policy. Most of them still believe that we actually did discover weapons of mass destruction in Iraq.

AMERICAN CHRISTIANITY AT FAULT

Not even American Christianity can escape blame for the hatred that other nations direct toward our country. One of our most notable television evangelists invested in the diamond and gold industries in Africa. Later he pleaded with Christians across America to support a collapsing tyrant in Liberia because, as he said, that president was a "born-again Christian." This evangelist probably would deny that his real concern was that his multimillion-dollar investments in Liberia would be threatened if that government fell.

Evangelicalism and America are so interwoven in the minds of many in the Third World that hatred of American policies often turns into hatred of the indigenous Christians who are their neighbors. In the thinking of many, Christianity is an American religion. Consequently, throughout the world, indigenous Christians have endured persecution because they are unable to get their fellow nationals to see that faith in Christ is not necessarily an American thing.

Also, Third World nations often view our missionaries as agents who are out to subvert other nations and to foster American imperialism. Unfortunately, there have been isolated cases wherein returning missionaries have participated in debriefings by the CIA in the hopes of helping those countries in which they had served. But such debriefings have hurt the image of all of our missionaries. Unless we Christians speak out against the injustices and oppressive practices that are American in origin, Christianity will continue to appear simply as another manifestation of our national interests, and our missionary efforts will be increasingly hampered.

EVANGELICALS' ROLE

We evangelicals are part of the reason the rest of the world often sees a duplicity and a double standard in America's dealings with them. For instance, we argue against separation of church and state here in America, and some of us even claim that the founders of our country deemed America a Christian nation. We decry the fact that often the Supreme Court has ruled that signs of the Judeo-Christian faith be removed from the public arena, and we argue that the First Amendment of our Constitution has been distorted so as to make religion an orphan in the American society. We want *our* Bible read in public schools, and we want public functions to be opened with prayer to *our* God, and we are angry when our courts say otherwise. In short, we want our Judeo-Christian religion to be part of public life.

Yet, even as we want *our* religion to be present in government and schools here at home, evangelical Christians are calling upon the powers in Washington to make sure that the governments of other nations are completely secular so that Christianity can have full freedom of expression. We know that if the Iraqi people are given free choice, a Shi'ite Islamic government will be established there, because that is the religion of the majority. This would severely curtail the evangelistic efforts of Christians.

OUR APPARENT ARROGANCE

W. I. Thomas, the noteworthy sociologist, once said, "If things are real in the imagination, they are real in their consequences." We can argue as to whether or not Americans really are arrogant, but we have to deal with the reality that a great proportion of the world's population thinks we are. This negative judgment is all too easy to understand, especially given the pronouncements coming out of Washington since the horrors of September 11, 2001. When the Security Council of the United Nations voted down the U.S. request for an invasion of Iraq, with Germany and France voicing the strongest opposition, U.S. Secretary of Defense Donald Rumsfeld simply dismissed these two countries as "the old Europe." Secretary Rumsfeld then referred to former Eastern Bloc nations, such as Bulgaria and Poland, which, though not members of the security council, were supportive of America's position, as "the new Europe." Dismissing longstanding allies who had put up money and sent in troops to support our efforts in Afghanistan in such a cavalier fashion incurred severe negative reactions around the world.

When President Bush taunted fanatical terrorists in Afghanistan and Iraq with his words "Bring them on!" it did not help our image. I believe that the president did not mean those words as most people took them, but to the rest of the world they lent credence to the image that our detractors love to create, namely, that we Americans are swaggering cowboys who are all too anxious to show off our military might and macho prowess.

We ignored the wishes of the United Nations and invaded Iraq without a consensus of international support. It was as though we were saying, "Who needs you? We're America, and nobody tells us what to do and what not to do." Of course, we may be required to eat humble pie, because as our campaign in Iraq bogs down and the cost of the war soars, we realize that we may have bitten off more than we can chew.

Our leaders are now going back to "the old Europe" to ask for help in bearing the expenses of rebuilding war-torn Iraq. But even in our pleas for help, the rest of the world perceives us as being arrogant. We want their money, and we are asking that they send troops to relieve our American soldiers of some of the burden of maintaining security. At the same time, we declare that we are unwilling to share control of Iraq.

AMERICA'S MIXED MOTIVES

"Why don't you want to share the burden of governing Iraq?" asks the rest of the world. "The only thing you'll have to give up is total control of Iraqi oil!"

As I've mentioned, the overwhelming opinion of the rest of the world is that our whole Iraqi operation was primarily a selfish grab for Middle East oil. They contend that we do not care that the entire Islamic world has been agitated to the point where many Muslims now quietly applaud terrorists and that the possibilities for world peace have been severely crippled, as long as we get what we want. After all, 10 percent of the world's oil is in Iraq, and another 10 percent is in Uzbekistan. The problem with the oil in Uzbekistan is that the best way to get it out would be with a pipeline through Afghanistan—another country over which we just seized control with our military power.

I am not arguing over whether or not there is truth in such opinions. I am simply saying that these opinions extensively exist. As a matter of fact, I think you would have to be a complete cynic to believe that our government would create all of the present havoc and suffering in Iraq, and send so many American soldiers to their deaths, just to serve the interests of American oil companies. I cannot believe that.

Remember that the invasion of Iraq had bipartisan support and that even former President Bill Clinton agreed with President Bush that Saddam Hussein had to go. However, it would have diminished criticism if Halliburton, the company over which Vice President Dick Cheney once presided as chief executive officer, and which continues to provide him with big checks for "back pay," had not been given exclusive rights for rebuilding the Iraqi oil industry just one week into the war. You will have to admit that, given the cynicism about America in much of the world, that was a bad public relations move.

One British critic remarked that "to give Cheney's company those oil rights shows that your government doesn't care what the rest of us think of America. So don't be surprised if we don't think well of you. Furthermore, why weren't the Iraqi people given the job of rebuilding their oil industry? They were the ones who built it in the first place. They have the know-how to rebuild those oil refineries. You Americans think that you are the only ones who have the scientists and engineers who can handle that job."

The British critic has a point. That President Bush gave the job of rebuilding Baghdad to the Bechtel Corporation, one of the biggest contributors to his campaign fund, lends support to the widespread opinion that our invasion was not as altruistic as we might want others to believe. The people of Iraq built Baghdad in the first place, so why don't they get to rebuild it now, especially when the people of Baghdad need the employment opportunities that such rebuilding would involve? When World War II ended, we sent those devastated European countries the money they needed to rebuild, but we didn't assign the job to American companies. Are we saying that we do not think the Iraqi people are competent enough to rebuild their own country?

THE GOOD EVANGELICALS HAVE DONE

We evangelicals have to shoulder some of the responsibility for recent negative reactions to America, given that (as I mentioned in chapter 9) some of our leading spokespersons have made disparaging remarks about Islam that have been widely reported throughout the Muslim world. I heard one prominent preacher say that Islam was a major threat to anything good in the world. That kind of talk does not foster positive relations with Islamic people in other countries.

But having taken us to task for the ways in which we have contributed to, and even generated, hatred toward America, I believe it is important also to note that over the years, we evangelicals have done much to earn positive points for our country in the eyes of the world. American missionaries have established schools and hospitals in those far corners of the world where they were desperately needed.

Evangelicals have been brilliant in addressing the economic needs of the poor. The programs that groups such as Compassion International and World Vision promote have fed, clothed, and educated millions of children through child sponsorship.

In a particularly heroic move, World Vision established child-sponsorship programs in several Muslim countries. I say it was a heroic move because in so doing, World Vision opened itself up to significant criticism from some evangelicals. Those critics complain that in most Muslim countries, the children who are receiving the material help that they so desperately need do not hear the gospel. Of course that is the case, because in such Muslim countries as Niger, Senegal, and Mali, the government forbids sharing the gospel by foreign missionary organizations.

Thank God that in such places, World Vision goes ahead with its efforts to feed the hungry, clothe the naked, and care for the sick anyway. They know that while Scripture tells us we are supposed to give special attention to those who are either Christians themselves, or open to becoming Christians, it also tells us that we are supposed to "do good unto *all*" men and women (Gal. 6:10, emphasis added). While World Vision's ministries to the poor in Muslim countries have great potential for making people in those places open to the gospel sometime in the future, the bottom line right now is that World Vision does what it does because it is the right thing to do.

SPONSORSHIP PROGRAMS CREATE OPENNESS

Several years ago, I went to Senegal with some World Vision workers in order to make a motion picture for use on university campuses. The plan was to give American students some idea of the ways in which people were suffering due to the drought that was then ravaging the Sahel region of Africa. We hoped that students seeing this suffering would respond by raising funds to help the victims of the drought.

One blistering hot day, I was visiting a desert village in the north of the country, near the border of Mauritania. World Vision had established a child-sponsorship program there that had been a major means for sustaining the people through this very difficult time. The gratitude of the people was obvious as they welcomed us to talk with the village chief and with the Muslim imam (a teacher of Islam).

Several hundred village people gathered around and listened in on our discussion. After exchanging the expected courtesies and pleasantries, I asked the imam what Mohammed might have to say about the sufferings that his people were enduring. After he answered my question at length, as best he could, he asked me, knowing that I was a Christian, what Jesus might have to say about the same thing. Because the imam was the one who had raised the question, I knew that it would be both proper and legal, even in this Muslim country, for me to respond—and I did. It gave me a great opportunity to talk about the ways in which we Christians believe that the resurrected and spiritually present Jesus is ever present in times of trouble, and how He gives to those who call upon Him the strength to endure such hardships. Upon further questioning by the imam, I was able to lay out the essentials of the salvation story, not only to him and the chief of the tribe, but to all the villagers who were standing around us, listening.

In this village, it was World Vision's loving help that had created this openness to the gospel message. But I have to add that even when we sense that such wonderful opportunities to preach the gospel might never be available, Christians are still to feed the hungry, clothe the naked, minister to the sick, and stand up for the oppressed. We do that because God loves us unconditionally, and He calls us to extend that love to others unconditionally. This is why World Vision is helping children in Muslim countries.

THE EFFECTS OF MISSIONARIES ON THE WORLD

The work of Christian missionaries has earned accolades for America from many poor nations, because the United States sends out more missionaries than any other country in the world today, according to the United States Center for World Mission in Pasadena, California. And it is certainly the primary source of funding for many of the international social welfare and social justice programs that offer the only hope for many of the poor and oppressed in desperate situations.

But there are those who put down American missionary work, claiming that in reality, missionaries are exporting American cultural values rather than biblical Christianity. Some historical novels, such as *Hawaii* by James Michener, describe how missionaries ridiculed and helped to destroy indigenous cultures and were agents of those colonial nations that had brought native peoples into subjugation. While there is some truth in such accusations, I assure you that a careful survey of what evangelical missionaries have done over the years, by way of meeting the social and physical needs of indigenous people, will reveal that their overall impact has been overwhelmingly positive. The good work has reflected on America in ways that should make us all proud. Also, in recent years missionaries have learned more and more about how to contextualize the gospel so that it is freed from American cultural trappings.

A recent study of the national leaders in Third World countries reveals that most of them were educated in missionary schools. Most of the leadership elite in all sectors of the Third World owe a debt of gratitude for what they learned in such schools. It is these missionary-trained leaders who give us hope for the social and economic development of the Third World.

Yes, there is evidence that at times, evangelical missionaries have presented a Jesus dressed in American garb, and perhaps unconsciously, they have made Christianity into their own cultural religion. And probably more often than we would like to admit, the churches they have planted overseas have incarnated our American values instead of expressing a Christian faith that transcends all ethnic identities and cultures. But after all is said and done, most American missionaries have so expressed the love of Christ around the world that those peoples who see Christianity and America inexorably linked have seen the best of what America has to offer.

A SPECIAL OPPORTUNITY

At this particular point in the history of the world, we Christians have an opportunity to use our influence to help America improve its image. The magnitude of the AIDS crisis in both Africa and Asia is so horrific as to be almost beyond our comprehension. If we can lobby our government to address this crisis with the vast resources at its disposal, not only will we do great good, but our efforts will go a long way toward helping others redefine our country in very positive terms.

Of the180 million people who live in Africa south of the Sahara desert, some 40 million of them have AIDS. This disease has orphaned 13 million children in that region. I personally have visited villages in Zimbabwe and South Africa where the oldest persons were teenagers because all of the adults had died.

Bono, the lead singer of U2—the most famous rock music group in the world today—has committed himself to addressing the AIDS crisis and is using his celebrity status to organize support for a monumental effort by America to turn things around. In a conversation I had with Bono, he said, "I know that celebrity status is a foolish and temporary thing, and I have chosen to spend my currency on Africa." Bono has influenced President Bush dramatically, and the president has made a major step in the right direction by committing America to spend $18 billion on the AIDS crisis in the Dark Continent.

Massive campaigns to educate people about the preventive measures they can take to avoid contracting the disease, along with the provision of treatment programs and drugs for people infected with the HIV virus, are very expensive, but they have already made an incredible difference. I mentioned in chapter 8 that in Uganda, the one country in Africa where such programs have been implemented, the results have been phenomenal. Largely as a result of lobbying by Christian social action groups, such as Christian Aid in Britain, the debts that Uganda owed to the World Bank and the International Monetary Fund were canceled, with the stipulation that the monies that would otherwise have been spent on its debts be used to address the AIDS crisis by implementing such programs. The positive results in Uganda should spur us to like efforts in the other countries devastated by HIV/AIDS.

If we use our vast resources to rescue the suffering and care for the victims of HIV/AIDS in Africa, I believe we can make friends of many people around the world who do not think well of us now. This kind of commitment will enhance our survival as a nation, because the survival of America is more dependent on the friends we make than on the armies we deploy. Bono may be right on the mark when he says that this is the moment when America must prove its greatness. Future generations will judge us, he claims, by whether or not we worked to eliminate from the earth the real weapon of mass destruction—AIDS.

Jesus says that God expects much of those who have received much (Luke 12:48) and that one day He will judge the nations (Matt. 25:31–32). Let us so live and give that when He weighs us in the balance, we will not be found wanting. This is America's hour. Let the Christians of this country rise up and ensure that this time does not pass without those who live in it doing what Christ has called us to do.

WAKE UP, AMERICA!

The rest of the world does not think well of us right now; it envies us. When asked what country on the face of the earth they hate most, the answer most often given, especially in the Third World, is *"America!"* When these same people were asked, "Where would you most like to live?" the answer was usually the same: *"America!"*

But the rest of the world also sees our flaws more clearly than we do. I recently was privileged to be in on an interview with a journalist from Indonesia. An

American asked him the same question that you and I are asking: "Why do so many people around the world hate America?" The journalist answered, "Because you have so disappointed us. We expected better of you than you have demonstrated over the past few years. We used to think that America was the ideal nation. Yours was a country in which there was justice for all and your people showed us a generous spirit. That no longer seems to be the case. Whether it is true or not, the world now sees America as an arrogant bully using its power to impose its will on other nations.

"We have seen this in the Middle East. The inferior consideration America has given to the Palestinians as compared to the overwhelming support your nation has given to the Israelis, despite their sometimes oppressive tactics, makes it impossible to believe that you deal with others evenhandedly and with justice.

"The way America has imprisoned Arabs—holding them without trials, keeping their friends and families from knowing where they are, denying them lawyers or any of the due processes of law that we thought you made available to everyone—has left us disillusioned. America is holding prisoners who have not even been charged with crimes, and we hear that you plan to try them in secret military courts. This seems fascist to the rest of the world.

"The nationalistic self-interest which America has demonstrated in its trade policies, and the ways in which you have treated debt-ridden countries, is evidence to the rest of the world of a selfishness that disillusions us. It is not that you are worse than the rest of the nations of the world that there is so much hatred toward you. It is because we thought you were better than the other countries that we are disappointed. And now, we hate you for that."

LOSE THE DOUBLE STANDARD

It is time for America to live up to the belief that as a nation, we *are* humanity's best hope. This is the hour for America to demonstrate justice and benevolence, which I believe are still inherent in our national character, to the rest of the world. I've mentioned the fact that the world sees us living by a double standard. To them, we appear to demand of other nations what we do not expect from ourselves or our close allies. For instance, we are filled with righteous indignation when countries such as North Korea or Iran develop nuclear weapons, but we think that it's okay for our country to maintain a huge nuclear arsenal. Furthermore, we say nothing about the two hundred nuclear weapons presently in the hands of the

Israelis, but demand that its enemies not be allowed to develop such weapons. We know that Israel has these weapons because Mordechai Vanunu, the Israeli nuclear technician and whistle-blower, revealed that fact as a humanitarian gesture.

In another example of our double standard, we expect the rest of the world to abide by international law, yet when 139 nations signed the treaty that established the International Criminal Court, the United States compelled the European Union to grant it immunity. It was as though we were saying that we could do what we wanted and that we would not submit to the judgment of the world when it came to things like the activities of our CIA agents. Clare Short, the former secretary of state for international development in the United Kingdom, said that when we show so much compassion for children of the world, but then refuse to join in the UN Conference on Children because we would not agree to abolish capital punishment for anyone under eighteen years of age, she has a hard time understanding us. Incidentally, only one other country— Somalia—has failed to sign on to the conference.

We justly condemned Saddam Hussein for not submitting to the will of the United Nations and abiding by international law, but then we ignored the will of the United Nations and flaunted international law by invading Iraq. Our double standards are obvious to those around us. We must change!

The greatness of a nation is marked by its willingness to face up to its flaws, to admit them, and then to repent and correct what is wrong. Arrogance, coupled with the power to sustain that arrogance, is not worthy of the great legacy of our founders and can lead only to our downfall. May God deliver us from that and teach us humility.

President Bush has told us that there are those in the world who hate us out of envy, because there is so much good in America that they wish they had. That is true, but it is only part of the story. Some of that hatred we deserve, because it stems from our failure to live up to our own ideals.

God promises to restore such a man—or nation.

A CALL TO REPENTANCE

The Bible calls us to let judgment begin with the household of God. That is to say, we Christians had better begin holding each other accountable for what we are doing in the world, so that our consistent commitment to justice validates our testimonies for Christ.

Beyond that, we have to begin going to school board meetings and asking questions about what our children are learning about both American history and the present policies of our government. Our interest in our children's education must go beyond the usual concern about the teaching of secular humanism in public schools. In Japan, children are learning a distorted view of World War II that, incredibly, holds America responsible for the war. Let us make sure that this kind of distortion of history does not go on in our own schools. When we do not teach our children the mistakes that we as a nation have made in the past, we doom our sons and daughters to repeat them.

During our bicentennial celebration, we evangelicals often cited a Bible verse that we offered as a call to all Americans. It reads: "If my people, which are called by my name, shall humble themselves, and pray, and seek my face, and turn from their wicked ways; then will I hear from heaven, and will forgive their sin, and will heal their land" (2 Chron. 7:14). I believe it would be a good thing if we heeded this call and repented, not only of the sexual promiscuity and consumeristic materialism that have become the hallmarks of our times, but of our failure to pay attention to what we have done collectively to poor and weak peoples around the world. Such repentance might be the start of undoing the hatred so much of the world aims at us. We need to repent and teach our children to repent of the sins of neglecting those who are in need, while pursuing lifestyles that are dependent upon the exploitation of weak nations. We must repent for not paying attention to those things our government has done that are contrary to the will of God.

I was criticized for comparing our nation to the ancient city of Sodom when I preached to President Bill Clinton and other leaders of our government at the official prayer service that was part of his second inauguration in January 1997. I quoted from Ezekiel 16:49, which reads: "Behold, this was the iniquity of thy sister Sodom, pride, fulness of bread, and abundance of idleness was in her and in her daughters, neither did she strengthen the hand of the poor and needy." I really do believe not only that this verse describes the Sodom of old, but that we can justifiably apply it to the America of today. And I also believe that national repentance is required.

12

Are Evangelicals Right About America Being in a Moral Decline?

It seems as though we Americans have always been ambivalent about ourselves. On the one hand, we are ready to nod our heads in agreement with those prophets of doom who predict dire consequences stemming from the perversities of our people. On the other hand, we are willing to affirm the optimism about the future that Social Darwinism, the dominant philosophy during the first part of the twentieth century, so well expressed.

We Americans act as though God owes Sodom and Gomorrah a note of apology if He does not punish America with fire and brimstone, but then we turn around and applaud those politicians who declare us to be the most virtuous, fair, idealistic, and just people on the face of the earth. It just may be that this apparent ambivalence is a proper and correct reaction to the realities of our times. It is an ambivalence that derives from what Jesus taught us to expect as history unfolds. In His parable of the wheat and tares, He taught us to expect good and evil to grow up and be evident alongside each other.

Another parable put he forth unto them, saying, The kingdom of heaven is likened unto a man which sowed good seed in his field: but while men slept, his enemy came and sowed tares among the wheat, and went his way. But when the blade was sprung up, and brought forth fruit, then appeared the tares also. So the servants of the householder came and said unto him, Sir, didst not thou sow good seed in thy field?

from whence then hath it tares? He said unto them, An enemy hath done this. The servants said unto him, Wilt thou then that we go and gather them up? But he said, Nay; lest while ye gather up the tares, ye root up also the wheat with them. Let both grow together until the harvest: and in the time of harvest I will say to the reapers, Gather ye together first the tares, and bind them in bundles to burn them: but gather the wheat into my barn. (Matthew 13:24–30)

America can justifiably be regarded as a mixture of both wheat and tares: the positive and the negative—filled with virtue and, at the same time, marked by sin. So much of what we see and hear seems to indicate that America is going in the wrong direction. There is ample evidence of the growing encroachment of evil both in our institutions and in our personal lives. Yet, at the same time, there is also much evidence that things are getting better and that Americans are experiencing a growing sense that God is at work in the land.

AUGUSTINE: A CONTEMPORARY APPLICATION

Perhaps Saint Augustine, that early church father, can help us understand what is going on. Augustine expressed the same kind of ambivalence about what was happening in his world. In his classic work *The City of God,* Augustine saw the same two opposing forces at work within the Roman Empire as we see working within America today. On the one hand, he saw the society in which he lived as decadent and caught in a downward spiral that would lead to its destruction. Augustine realized that the barbarians were at the gates of Rome and that it was only a matter of time before those uncouth hordes waiting at Rome's borders would come rushing in to overrun the Eternal City. Weakened by the excesses of an affluent, sensate lifestyle that had made them soft and corrupted by a lapse in moral values, Rome's citizens were devoid of the fortitude essential to standing up to the challenges that Augustine knew were imminent. Consequently, he wrung his hands in despair.

Yet Augustine also saw that within the Roman Empire was a special group of people who offered hope. These were the Christians, who embraced a set of countercultural values that came from being part of what Augustine called "the city of God." The city of God was the church that was set in the midst of the empire. Augustine saw the church as the salt that served to preserve the empire and keep it from total collapse. He believed that even if the empire were to fall, the church, the city of God, would survive. From the ashes, it would rise up and grow. It would be what he called "the bride of Christ."

This bride would be glorified as she moved toward that final day when Christ would return. Augustine believed, and I follow his beliefs, that the wheat (i.e., the city of God) and the tares (this world with all of its evils) would grow up alongside each other until that day when, as Jesus said, the wheat and tares would be separated. On that day, contended Augustine, the wheat (the church) would be gathered up, together with all the people of God throughout history, into a glorious harvest. Augustine believed that between the present and that time when Christ returns to set up His kingdom here on earth, the church (the city of God) would serve the empire by exercising within it a powerful influence for good.

Jesus likened the church to salt when He called His disciples to be a preserving presence for good in society. Augustine contended that the church should live out its calling from God by being the agent of God, pervading society with the righteousness that would improve society's moral climate and keep it from degradation.

In answer to the question as to whether or not our society today is in moral decline, Augustine would probably answer, "It all depends on the church!" Are we the salt of the earth, as Jesus called us to be? Are we a church that is vibrant and expressing God's love and justice in our nation? Are we maintaining a quality of life that is contagious, spreading righteousness to those around us?

SIGNS OF HOPE

I see encouraging signs of spiritual vitality emerging in American Christianity, especially within its evangelical congregations. Therein, I believe, lies the hope for our nation. America is not the city of God, but we who are the church can permeate our country with a spiritual revival that can keep our nation alive and well.

A friend of mine attended a patriotic ceremony at his daughter's school following the September 11 tragedy. As part of the evening's program, students recited inspiring statements by America's historic founders. After each recitation, the entire fourth-grade class shouted out, "America will live forever!"

To such statements, Augustine would say, "No way." To talk that way is idolatry. We dare not treat our nation with any sense of ultimacy. The kingdoms of this world will pass away, but the kingdom of our Lord will live forever, and the mission of the citizens of the city of God is to be the salt that preserves our society and the light that guides it. How well we live out this calling will determine the immediate future of America, but no kingdom, save the kingdom of God, lives forever.

That being the case, let us consider what is happening in our nation and try to determine whether or not the church is being the salt and light that Jesus called it to be.

WHAT IN THE WORLD IS THE CHURCH DOING?

THE STATE OF THE UNION

Those who think that evil is growing in America are absolutely right. If you pick up any newspaper on any given day, you will find enough newsprint to validate that conviction. You will see stories of crime and corruption from the lowest levels to the highest levels of our society.

Degradation is evident, not only in the political arena, where it has long been a part of the American scene, but now also within the church. Scandals have wreaked havoc in the Roman Catholic Church, as we have learned of the far-reaching extent of the pedophilia among its clergy. What has made matters worse is the bishops' cover-up of the priests' horrendous wrongdoings. Protestants had best not be piously smug, however, in the face of the problems of their Catholic brothers and sisters; they have had their own array of ugly scandals with which to deal. Along with our own sexual scandals, Protestants must consider the embezzlement of funds by some of the prominent officers of mainline denominations and the misuse of money by certain television evangelists.

In business, we have seen more and more evidence of deception by corporate managers. Their crimes have led to the losses of billions of dollars for elderly people living on retirement pensions, and their manipulations of prices have brought hardships to hundreds of thousands of working people who have consequently lost their jobs. White-collar criminals in Enron, Arthur Andersen, World Com, and other huge, multinational corporations have staggered our imaginations with their evildoings.

When we evaluate the mass media, it is easy to discern that the standards of decency are falling. Pornography is increasingly evident on our newsstands, and even on television. In the words of the old hymn "Abide with Me," we hear, "Change and decay in all around I see . . ."

It is easy to conclude from all this bad news that the tares (the weeds representing evil) are growing up and taking over. If you want to be pessimistic about what's happening, you can find much to support your case. But you would be getting only half the story. While evil is strong and getting stronger, if you take another look, you also will find a lot of good out there. As the parable suggests, the wheat (representing the good things of the kingdom of God) also is evident and growing. Jesus told us in this parable that along with the evil, the good works that glorify His Father will continue to increase until the harvest, when Christ will return and establish His perfect kingdom of justice, love, and well-being for all of us.

THE STATE OF CHRISTENDOM

It doesn't make the headlines, but all kinds of wonderful things are happening in our world, in spite of all that is evil and demonic. Across America, churches are being born and reaching out to huge numbers of previously unchurched people. A revitalized commitment to the poor and the oppressed is emerging among American Christians. This concern is part of the deeper understanding of a holistic gospel that is springing up in a church that is both evangelistic and oriented to social action.

While I have already pointed out that mainline denominational churches are in decline, with fewer and fewer people in attendance weekly, I have also noted new, independent churches with names like Family Life Center, Vineyard Congregation, and Christian Life Center popping up in both rural communities and urban neighborhoods all across the country. These new congregations express a vitality and a joyful excitement that attract many whom traditional churches have alienated.

Megachurches are no longer a rarity in America. They are accessible to most Americans in communities everywhere. While highly evangelical, most of these new megachurches seem to have escaped those legalistic traits of the fundamentalist subculture so often stereotyped and ridiculed by such ditties as "We don't dance, and we don't chew, and we don't go with girls who do."

These new megachurches are usually well balanced in their ministries, challenging people both to social ministries and to a personal spirituality marked by theological depth and growing Christian maturity.

One of the best examples of how balanced and effective these megachurches can be is the now famous Willow Creek Community Church in South Barrington, Illinois. Pastored by its founder, Bill Hybels, this church has grown in just a couple of decades into a congregation of more than twenty thousand. In addition to ministering to those within its own church family, Willow Creek has more than four thousand members engaged in some form of social outreach ministry during the week. These men and women serve in soup kitchens, shelters for battered women, tutoring programs for at-risk children, and activities for senior citizens—the list goes on and on. One of Willow Creek's more innovative ministries has church members who are mechanics fix up secondhand automobiles, then make them available at no cost to poor people who need them to get to their places of employment.

REVIVAL IS ASTIR

I believe that revival is in the air and that it is changing the behavior patterns of Americans in noticeable ways. All across America there are evangelistic efforts that are bringing hundreds of thousands into a deep faith in Christ. On university and college campuses, movements like Campus Crusade for Christ and Intervarsity Christian Fellowship continue to thrive, even when they elicit negative reactions from those who criticize their sometimes aggressive styles of evangelism.

It is not just young people who are experiencing this revived enthusiasm for the Christian faith. Among middle-age Christians, the popularity of mass gatherings to hear gospel music defies everyone's expectations. The annual Praise Gathering that Bill and Gloria Gaither sponsor is a good example of this. More than fifteen thousand participants go to Indianapolis for this event each fall. During the rest of the year, the Gaithers sell out auditoriums and arenas across the country, bringing together huge crowds who find both blessing and entertainment in listening to and singing a mixture of old hymns, newer songs, and southern gospel music. The Gaither *Homecoming* videos, which appear on television across the country, have sold millions.

Evangelists such as Benny Hinn, Luis Palau, and T. D. Jakes speak to full stadiums night after night, and Billy Graham can still fill a football stadium anytime he chooses to hold one of his crusades. Something wonderful is happening out there, and you have to be blind not to see it.

EVIDENCE OF CHANGING SEXUAL BEHAVIOR

If you want more evidence that good things are happening in our midst, consider the changes taking place in the sexual behavior of Americans. Despite a lot of preachers' rhetoric to the contrary, America is *not* going down the sexually promiscuous tubes. Saying it is may give some pulpiteers a prophetic tone, but it is just not true that America is into a wholesale moral decline when it comes to "family values."

Some of these prophets of gloom point to things like the fact that abortion is now legal in America and tell us that women practice it with shocking regularity. But such doomsayers are not facing up to all the facts. Back in 1950, an extensive study on abortion indicated that 30 percent of women over the age of thirty had had one. That year, there were more than a million abortions in America. Given that the population of the country in 1950 was less than 200 million, those figures are evidence that long before the Supreme Court's *Roe v. Wade* decision, abortion was just as common as it is today. What is more important to note is that the numbers and percentages of women having abortions presently are down significantly from what they were just over ten years ago. Going by statistics alone, one might conclude that the liberalization of abortion laws has not influenced things as much as we originally may have thought.

This trend away from the high incidence of abortion may be due in part to pro-life advocates who promote their message about the sacredness of all life. Also, women are turning away from using abortion as a form of birth control. This progress owes little thanks to the courts and the law, but instead, it has come about through moral persuasion. The church may not have done all it could do to convince people that abortion is not the best solution to unwanted pregnancies, but it has done far more than many people think.

The sexual revolution of the 1960s is over, and statistics bear that out. When it comes to premarital pregnancies, the facts are very encouraging. There has been a dramatic drop in premarital pregnancies since 1990, and again, moralists have much to cheer about. We cannot be sure of why this is so. Some of us make the case that this drop in the incidence of premarital pregnancies is due to the fact that young people are increasingly remaining celibate prior to marriage. We argue that programs such as True Love Waits, which the Southern Baptist Convention promotes, have gotten hundreds of thousands of teenagers to take a pledge not to have sexual intercourse until after marriage. Those with a more cynical bent say that the specter of herpes and AIDS scares young people and makes them increasingly reluctant to have sex outside of the safety of marriage between virgins.

Others believe that the decline in the incidence of premarital pregnancies may be due to young people having more access to condoms, because programs make them available through schools. That is possible. Whatever the answer is, it has important implications as we deal with the question of whether or not America is in moral decline.

Older people, as well as young people, give evidence of becoming more and more morally responsible. Whatever may be our conclusions about the motivations of young people when it comes to changes in their sexual behavior, there is evidence that adults are not the libertines that we have been led to believe they are.

The most recent comprehensive study on American sexual behavior coming out of the University of Chicago tells us some fascinating things that fly in the face of the claim that America is just one big Peyton Place. That study, which allowed respondents to answer anonymously, belies the impressions about America's morality that come across via television soap operas, music videos, and so many of our motion pictures. Among the findings of the University of Chicago researchers are the following:

- Americans are largely monogamous. Eighty-three percent have one or zero sexual partners in any given year.

- Most Americans do not go for the kinky stuff. When asked to rank their favorite sex act, almost everybody (96 percent) found normal vaginal sex the most appealing. In second place was an activity that many may not have even considered a sexual activity—watching their partner undress. This is hardly the wildly decadent behavior that we have been led to believe is prevalent among Americans.

- Adultery, this study found, is relatively rare. Nearly 75 percent of married men and 85 percent of married women say they have always been faithful. When adultery does occur, it is a relatively rare occurrence. Consider the fact that 94 percent of Americans were sexually faithful to their partners during the past year.

When these statistical findings, garnered from the research team of Edward Laumann, Stuart Michaels, and Robert Michael, were published, those popular writers who like to shock us with their questionable "pop" surveys went ballistic. Bob Guccione of *Penthouse* magazine yelled, "Positively outrageously stupid and unbelievable." *Cosmopolitan* editor Helen Gurley Brown cynically said,

"Two partners? I mean, come on!" Jackie Collins, who wrote the book *The Bitch, The Stud,* responded by asking, "Where are the deviants? Where are the flashers? Where are the sex maniacs I see every day on television?"[1]

None of these doubters is ready to admit that the sexual revolution of the sixties is over, that marriage is again a stable institution, and that fidelity is increasingly a part of the American way of life.

ARE WE BLIND TO THE GOOD THINGS?

Recently I joined Bob Jones, the president of the well-known Bob Jones University, on the *Larry King Live* television show. The topic of discussion centered around the very question I am addressing in this chapter: is America in moral decline? Bob Jones was adamant that America is definitely in decline and that this moral failure was to be expected given what he believed the Bible said. Such a decline, he contended, was one of the conditions of society that would be evident preceding Christ's return to earth.

As I reflected upon Bob Jones's dire predictions, I had to wonder how he reconciled this belief with his convictions about prayer. I know that he believes in the efficacy of prayer, and I know that he is aware that all across our land, millions of people persistently and earnestly pray for a spiritual and moral revival in America. Why does he find it difficult to believe that God is answering these prayers and that a spiritual and moral revival really is beginning to break loose among us?

Politicians recognize that something in the way of a religious revival is under way. They know that born-again Christians are becoming so numerous that to ignore their concerns is political suicide. Politicians know that it is almost impossible to turn the dials of radios and television sets without coming across religious programming. Religion is definitely in the air.

It may be that Bob Jones is being victimized by his own theology so that he just cannot see what so many of us say is everywhere evident—namely, that God's people are alive and well in America and that they are impacting our nation for good.

Perhaps Bob Jones would say that while there is some evidence in America of revival, it is a revival that is not touching the majority of Americans; and while there is what he would call a remnant of true Christians in America, most churches have compromised their testimonies by embracing the values of the world and departing from true biblical teachings. I have a sense that Bob Jones would lament what he would call an upsurge in "apostate religion" and say that true Christianity, according to his understanding, is struggling hard to survive in what he sees as an increasingly corrupt nation. He would probably say that while there might be some temporary reversals of an overall downward trend toward perdition, we should not be deluded into thinking things really are getting better.

IT DEPENDS ON WHO YOU TALK TO

When it comes to judging whether or not America is in moral decline, the answer will be determined on the basis of who is making the judgments. If you are asking white, middle-class, Anglo-Saxon Protestants, you are likely to hear that America is morally disintegrating. Some of them might even say that this country is well on its way to the kind of fall that ended the Roman Empire.

On the other hand, those whom racism and sexism have victimized over the years would probably contend that America is getting better, even becoming more moral than ever before. African-Americans, for instance, have no desire to see any kind of return to the days of yesteryear when they had to endure the humiliations and injustices of a Jim Crow society. If racial discrimination is regarded as sin (and I believe it should be), there is certainly less of it today than there was a half-century ago.

Racist attitudes are still rampant in America, but racial discrimination has declined. African-Americans no longer have to sit in the back of buses, drink water from separate drinking fountains, swim at segregated beaches, use separate toilet facilities, and put up with having their faces absent from the mass media. The dehumanization that accompanied the humiliations they endured in the past two hundred years has diminished dramatically. The discrimination that once kept them out of the best universities and barred them from a vast array of employment opportunities has been challenged and significantly lessened. As far as African-Americans are concerned, things may not be what they should be, but they certainly are not what they once were. The dream of equality, which Martin Luther King Jr. so brilliantly articulated on the steps of the Lincoln Memorial, though not yet fully actualized, is well on its way.

The Hispanic community also is gaining power, particularly as its numbers grow. Hispanic people are increasingly finding their voices in the political arena, and politicians are working hard to get their votes by ensuring them of all the benefits that go with being treated with justice. Little by little, they are gaining the same rights and privileges that other immigrants enjoy. For them, America is getting better.

Certainly women can point to an improvement of their lot within American society. They are demanding and increasingly seeing an end to the sexist values that once were so evident in the public sphere.

If sexism is viewed as an evil—and I believe it should be—there is less of it in America today than there was fifty years ago. The glass ceiling that kept women from upward mobility in the professions and in the business world is being shattered. More and more, in the world of sports, women are gaining equal opportunities. Rape victims often used to be treated as the guilty parties in court cases, but this is not allowed today. Increasingly, women are gaining protection from domestic violence.

According to Betty Friedan, most women agree that the sexism that for too long diminished their dignity, denied them political power, penalized them economically, and regularly prevented the actualization of their potential is being overcome. This is moral improvement. Today, my granddaughters have the prospects of opportunities my wife never dreamed of when she was their ages.

POVERTY: WERE THE "GOOD OLD DAYS" REALLY GOOD?

There has been more hope for the poor during the last twenty-five years than ever before in the history of our country. We too easily forget the incredibly immoral neglect of the needy that was so evident in the early part of the twentieth century. As a case in point, nothing in the history books that our children read in school describes the tens of thousands of homeless, orphaned children on city streets during the first three decades of the 1900s.

So severe was the problem of homeless children that at one point, the Society of Friends (Quakers) chartered trains to take them out to the farm belt for adoption. The trains stopped at rural railroad stations where the children disembarked and lined up for inspection. Then farmers picked out and adopted any of the children they thought would be good farm workers. In retrospect, this sounds like a shocking practice, but given the conditions of the time, it was probably one of the more humane options available. We forget what America was like during the Gilded Age. It was an immoral time characterized by the story of some millionaires who mocked the poor by literally lighting their cigars with dollar bills. Less than a mile away from where they did this, people were on the verge of starving to death.

When we claim we were more moral in the "good old days," we ignore what it was like when none of the poor had any medical coverage. I saw a dentist only once during my growing-up years, and in the first sixteen years of my life, I visited a doctor's office only when my head was split open after an ugly fall in a schoolyard. Our family had no medical coverage and lacked the means for regular medical care during those early years of my life. Nevertheless, some people look back on those years in which society largely ignored the needs of the poor as a time when America was highly moral. It wasn't. Neglecting the poor is sin, and the poor were neglected more in the past than they are right now.

MY MOTHER'S STORY

Allow me to tell you my mother's story, because it will give you some idea of how sinfully neglectful of the poor America was in the early years of the twentieth century. Then, you judge whether or not, in terms of morals, those really were the "good old days." Listen to the story of my mother's childhood, and then determine whether or not America was a kinder, gentler nation back there and then.

My grandmother came from Italy and married shortly after arriving here in America. She had three children and did her best to raise them in spite of her family's very limited income. When her oldest child, my mother, was only nine years old, my grandfather was killed in a trolley car accident. With no money for basic sustenance, my grandmother sought help, but none was available.

There was no government welfare system back then. There was no safety net for decent people who fell on hard times. My grandmother feared that her children would starve. She begged from every charity she could, but to no avail. The only possibility for saving her children was to put them into an orphanage, and for this to be possible, the children had to be without *both* parents.

My grandmother made a fateful decision. She decided that she would leave her children, either by committing suicide or pretending to do so. Then, she figured, the orphanage would have to take them. She wrote out a suicide note, gave it to my mother, and instructed her to wait awhile, then take the note to the nearby police station.

My grandmother hugged my mother and her brother and sister good-bye, sure that was the last time she would ever see them. Then she left her frightened children in the small basement room where they lived and started down Federal Street in Philadelphia toward the Delaware River, crying hysterically.

Whether she was really going to commit suicide, or simply disappear from the neighborhood forever, was something my grandmother would never tell me. What I do know is that, crying and mumbling, she caught the attention of W. Everett Griffiths, a student at Eastern Baptist Theological Seminary in Philadelphia. It was this young man, serving in a Baptist mission among the Italians in South Philadelphia, who saved my grandmother's family. He found out what the trouble was, took my grandmother home, gave her some money for food, and figured out how they could survive. He got my nine-year-old mother a job polishing jewelry for the owners of some stores on that block in Philadelphia known as Jewelers' Row. With what my mother earned each week, the family eked out a bare-subsistence lifestyle.

Because of the kindness and efforts of that young seminary student, my family became Baptist. The whole family joined the little Baptist settlement house where W. Everett Griffiths served as pastor.

Throughout her life, my mother suffered from ailments that could be traced back to the malnutrition that marked her life during her childhood years. Those who would glamorize the past as a golden age of morality seem to forget that America did little to fulfill any moral obligations to poor and oppressed people, such as my mother's family, during those years.

DEFINING TERMS

When we address the question as to whether or not America was better then and is now experiencing a moral decline, we have to determine exactly what we are talking about. If we make superficial judgments from our casual observations of what is on television and what we hear in the music that pervades the youth culture, we could easily conclude that America is going the way of Sodom and Gomorrah. On the other hand, if we focus on what has happened with regard to the treatment of African-Americans, Hispanic and Asian people, women, and especially the poor, we would have to say that things have gotten better. It might be an oversimplification, but it seems to me that when it comes to personal morality, America may have suffered a significant decline, but when it comes to matters of social justice, much has improved.

Political conservatives tend to see personal morality as what is most important, while political liberals tend to give primary attention to whether or not equality and justice are evident in society. Consequently, it is easy to figure out why conservatives regarded Bill Clinton as a decadent man, while liberals view George W. Bush as an evil influence in America. The sexual dalliances of Clinton appalled conservatives, while liberals looked askance at Bush's record on the environment, affirmative-action policies for minority racial groups, the rights of women, benefits for the poor, and his use of the military. Given those differences, it is easy to understand why, when answering the question as to whether or not America is in a moral decline, liberals are more likely to say that America is a better society than it was fifty years ago, while conservatives will probably conclude that America is on a slippery slope, sliding to perdition.

EVANGELICALS: PERSONAL *AND* PUBLIC MORALITY

I am convinced that most evangelicals today believe that the Bible requires righteousness on both the societal level *and* the personal level. Most of us see the need to join together to work for justice in the political and economic sectors of our society. We regard saving the environment from the degradation of polluters as a moral imperative. We are convinced that establishing fair trade policies with Third World countries is an ethical responsibility.

We evangelicals, regardless of whether or not we believe that the poor will be with us always, have a strong desire for America to live out the biblical requisites to care for the poor. We are willing to work hard to provide the poor with medical care, decent housing, and adequate diets. When we read the Bible and learn of a God who will judge our nation according to how well we have provided for the needs of those whom Jesus called "the least of these" (Matt. 25:45), we realize that caring for the poor is an obligation we cannot ignore.

At the same time, we recognize that if America is to live up to its call to greatness, we must, as individuals, live in such a way that purity and righteousness mark our private lives. We must call upon our churches to encourage people to be faithful in marriage and to avoid any kind of lascivious living. We agree that we must resist the materialism that marks America's increasingly consumeristic way of life. In short, we accept a biblically prescribed morality that applies to both our social policies and our personal relationships.

Therefore, we evangelicals want to couple our commitment to social justice with a high level of personal morality in the lives of all our citizens, Christian and non-Christian alike. There is a hunger among us for "both/and." We will not settle for "either/or." Even as our country shows signs of realizing the virtues embodied in Martin Luther King Jr.'s dream for equality and well-being for all of our citizens, we will not say that we are improving as a nation until we see individuals repenting of the sins that mark their hearts and minds.

Our goal is a holistic righteousness that will crown our personal good with a just and equitable brotherhood and sisterhood, from sea to shining sea.

13

Is Evangelicalism
Headed for a Split?

Until recently, evangelicals have gotten along fairly well together. As a struggling minority within Christendom, they could not afford the luxury of squabbles and divisions. Of course, there were extreme fundamentalists who found even Billy Graham to be too ecumenical and "liberal" for their liking. And there have always been fringe groups that stood apart from mainstream evangelicalism, staging sporadic attacks on those evangelicals whom they felt had compromised with "the world." Nevertheless, evangelicals have generally avoided sibling rivalry. They even were able to bond well enough to form the National Association of Evangelicals, an organization that now exercises more political clout than the National Council of Churches of the mainline denominations.

However, in the face of explosive growth, a variety of political and theological differences that hitherto have been overlooked seriously threaten that peaceful coexistence. The first crack in the evangelical community has become evident in the ways in which its members react to political issues. In their early days, evangelicals were nonpolitical. During the 1960s, they seemed indifferent to the dramatic issues that were shaking the nation. Their leaders said very little during the traumatic days of the civil-rights movement. As a matter of fact, many evangelical leaders viewed Martin Luther King Jr. with suspicion, and some of them believed that King's movement was some kind of Communist plot. Consequently, the secular media began to see evangelicals as being, for the most part, politically conservative Republicans.

Over the past couple of decades, however, there has been, among evangelicals, a growing uneasiness with this alliance with conservative politics. Many of them had a sense of guilt about their relative indifference to the moral issues raised over civil rights and, later, over the war in Vietnam. Groups such as Evangelicals for Social Action, led by Ron Sider, and the Sojourners Community headed up by Jim Wallis, began to call for evangelicals to develop a strong commitment to social justice. In November of 1973, a group of socially concerned evangelical leaders assembled in Chicago and drew up what has come to be known as the Chicago Declaration. Some of those who signed this declaration were the beginning of what might be called "the evangelical left."

At first, most evangelicals ignored the rumblings of their socially liberal brothers and sisters and their call to address the "structural evils" of society. Many politically conservative evangelicals did not have much of an idea as to what "structural evils" were. For them, evil was something that was inherent in individuals, and the idea that evil could exist in the ways in which economic systems and political institutions were structured was beyond their understanding.

TWO ISSUES GALVANIZE EVANGELICAL POLITICAL POWER

The evangelical right's indifference to political and economic structures was destined to be shattered, however, by two highly charged social issues: abortion rights and homosexual rights. When the Supreme Court ruled on *Roe v. Wade*, making abortion legal, evangelicals had a political issue that rallied them into crusading mode. Then, as gays and lesbians began to demand laws that would protect them from what they perceived to be discriminatory practices, many conservative evangelicals were even further stirred to political involvement.

This new political activism by the evangelical right was to coalesce around what it would call "family values." I mentioned earlier in the book that Jerry Falwell organized a movement that he named the Moral Majority. With his extensive television and radio outreach, Falwell was able to mobilize evangelicals to support the Republican Party, which in turn put planks in the party platform to support the Moral Majority's "family values." Falwell can justifiably claim that the election of Ronald Reagan was due in part to his efforts to make a host of evangelicals into politically active Republicans.

Following an unsuccessful run for president in 1992, another television evangelist, Pat Robertson, organized an even more effective political action group called the Christian Coalition. Utilizing the vast network of campaign workers who had assisted him in his bid for the presidency and putting them under the organizational control of the one-time president of the Young Republicans, Ralph Reed, Robertson soon set the Christian Coalition on its way to becoming one of the most powerful forces in American history.

This sudden flexing of political muscle by the religious right caught those on the evangelical left off guard. They were, for the most part, in agreement with their conservative brothers' and sisters' views on abortion and homosexuality, but the evangelical left differed greatly with those on the right when it came to other social issues. Politically liberal evangelicals were shocked when the Christian Coalition issued voter guides through churches, telling Christians how they should vote in coming elections. The voter guides sided with the National Rifle Association on gun control, opposed the agenda of environmentalists, and worst of all to people on the evangelical left, ignored the needs of the poor.

Those who differed with the agenda of the Christian Coalition and the other groups on the religious right were poorly organized, and what was even more of a problem for these politically liberal evangelicals was that they lacked any media outlets that could match what the religious right had at its disposal. Over the previous decades, politically conservative evangelicals had created thousands of radio and television stations. They even had their own TV networks. In short, the religious right controlled the airwaves and was able to communicate its views to tens of millions of Americans daily. The religious right had the microphone, and the evangelical left was relegated to media irrelevancy. So thorough were the communications skills of the religious right that it became difficult in many evangelical circles to call oneself a Christian if you were not committed to the Republican Party.

THE WAR SEPARATES RIGHT FROM LEFT

I believe that the conservative politics of the religious right will hold sway in the evangelical community into the foreseeable future. Howeyer, there is a growing awareness that a significant minority within this community does not go along with the conservative political agenda. Recently the presence of this nonconforming group became increasingly evident as the second war in Iraq unfolded. Many evangelicals opposed President Bush's prowar policies because they believed our invasion of Iraq was outside the bounds of what they considered a just war. When the American economy stagnated and spending on the wars in Afghanistan and Iraq spiraled out of control, leading the Republican administration in Washington to initiate gigantic cuts in desperately needed programs for the poor (i.e., programs for education and public welfare programs), this socially liberal minority began to find its voice. These cuts in social programs, along with the tax breaks for the wealthy that the Bush administration put in place, stimulated a strong reaction. Politically liberal evangelicals perceived that the Republicans were giving tremendous breaks to the rich while delivering few or no benefits to the poor.

Jim Wallis, the leader of the Sojourners Community in Washington, D.C., found, in what he saw as a stab in the back of the poor, the need to call together an array of Christian leaders to form Call to Renewal, a new organization for Christian activists. Claiming to be broad-based across the political spectrum, Wallis's group provided a rallying place for those evangelicals who did not want to be part of the religious right. It remains to be seen how effective Call to Renewal or some other group will be in rallying evangelicals who refuse to buy into the conservative politics of the Republican Party. According to the estimates of some sociologists, as many as 35 percent of evangelicals define themselves as being in opposition to the politics of the religious right and are looking for someplace to go. Their disenchantment with what they see as the right-wing politics that now dominate evangelicalism easily could lead to the establishment of a new and separate movement.

The evangelical establishment is already recognizing these politically liberal Christians as a distinct and separate group, sometimes calling them "neo-evangelicals." Whether that name will stick or this break-off from religious-right evangelicalism will come up with a name of its own, there is strong evidence that a schism in evangelicalism has already begun to happen. Some prominent evangelical leaders are preparing for such a break. Some of them have told me that they want to hold on to the audiences they now have within the mainstream of the evangelical community. But they say that their ability to stay quiet is failing as evangelicalism drifts more and more to the right, and that soon the day will come when they will have to declare themselves as part of a new movement that is not wedded to the Republican Party.

CONFLICT OVER DISPENSATIONALISM

Politics is not the only force at work dividing evangelicals. The growing conflict over dispensationalist theology is another factor creating schism. Dispensationalist theology is a system for interpreting Scripture that is relatively recent in the history of Christianity. It made its first appearance in the middle of the nineteenth century with the teachings of a one-time Anglican preacher named John Darby, in Plymouth, England. Darby's teachings became the official theology of a new movement he founded called the Plymouth Brethren. Though small in number, this emerging Christian denomination exerted incredible influence throughout Protestantism among many who have never heard the name of John Darby or paid any attention to the Plymouth Brethren. Neither the ancient church fathers nor the great Reformers of the church (i.e., Martin Luther, John Calvin, and Ulrich Zwingli) gave the slightest hint of dispensationalism in their preaching and teaching. Nevertheless, a significant proportion of Protestant Christians worldwide have absorbed the dispensationalist perspectives for interpreting Scripture, especially with respect to the second coming of Christ. Certainly the apostle Paul's teachings about the second coming of Christ and, for that matter, Jesus's own predictions about His return did not anticipate what dispensationalists would have to say about this eschatological event.

The way that dispensationalism, the theology of this small sectarian group from Plymouth, England, came to play such an import role in modern evangelicalism was through the publishing and extensive use of *The Scofield Reference Bible*. This particular study Bible, first published in 1909, has been sold to Christians almost everywhere on earth. Those who use the Scofield Bible usually employ the study notes at the bottom of each page as a major source of instruction when trying to interpret Scripture. To many, the Scofield notes ring with almost the same quality of infallibility as the scriptural texts at the top of the page. What most of those who use this study Bible fail to grasp is that the dispensationalist theology they are absorbing would be only a blip on the oscilloscope of Christian history were it not for C. I. Scofield, whose clever notes went into the best-selling study Bible of all time. Oxford University Press, which still prints hundreds of thousands of these study Bibles annually, will admit that the sale of Scofield Bibles is what has kept them in business through hard times.

A second reason why dispensationalism became so widespread is that it was at the core of the curriculum for many of the Bible colleges and institutes that sprang up across America in the early part of the twentieth century. Prestigious institutions such as Moody Bible Institute and Philadelphia College of Bible, along with the highly academic Wheaton College, embraced the dispensationalist theology of John Darby. Dallas Theological Seminary, one of America's most influential institutions for training preachers, became a strong promoter of this school of thought. These dispensationalist institutions produced most of the fundamentalist preachers and missionaries during those years when liberal churches, with their "modernist" theologies, threatened to undermine the basic beliefs of Christianity. The impact that the graduates of these schools have had upon evangelicalism has been enormous.

THE CENTRAL DOCTRINES OF DISPENSATIONALISM

I would not go into an outline of what dispensationalists believe, except that it is hard to understand what is going on in evangelicalism without having some understanding of what this important group of Christians teaches. Their doctrines are a major factor in determining a far-ranging set of consequences that include American policies regarding militarism, the emergence of evangelical Zionism, attitudes toward Palestinians, and the role of American geopolitics. I am not exaggerating when I say that dispensationalism has become a major force in molding American domestic and foreign policies.

According to John Darby, in order to understand the Bible the reader must be properly equipped to "rightly divid[e] the word of truth" (2 Tim. 2:15). To be so equipped, Darby believed, was to accept his particular method, which requires that we divide up the Bible into seven distinct plans of salvation. As we read the Bible, we are supposed to recognize the following historical stages, or dispensations, each one of which offers a different way of living out the will of God. These stages are as follows:

1. *The Dispensation of Innocence:* It begins with the Creation when Adam and Eve were innocent and ends with their being expelled from Eden (Gen. 1:28–3:22).

2. *The Dispensation of Conscience:* People are possessed with the knowledge of both good and evil, and it is their living according to what conscience prompts them to do that will bring salvation (Gen. 3:22–7:23). This dispensation ends with extreme wickedness on the part of humanity and God's sending the Flood.

3. *The Dispensation of Human Government:* In this dispensation, humanity is

given the responsibility of establishing a government that will institute just living. This dispensation ends in ungodly behavior and the confusion of tongues at Babel (Gen. 8:20–11:9).

4. The Dispensation of Promise: In this dispensation, which stretches over four hundred years, extending from the call of Abraham to the giving of the Law at Sinai, salvation belongs to the Jews and is contingent upon God's chosen people living according to the covenant "to walk before the Lord." This dispensation ends with the Jews in bondage in Egypt (Gen. 12:1–Exod. 19:8).

5. The Dispensation of Law: This is a period that extends from Sinai until the sacrificial death of Christ. It is a time wherein people are saved by keeping the Torah given by God to Moses. According to Lewis Sperry Chafer, a one-time professor of systematic theology at Dallas Theological Seminary and a primary exponent of dispensationalism, this period extends through the beginning of the Great Tribulation on earth. The church age, according to Chafer, is parenthetical within the age of Law.

6. The Dispensation of Grace: This is a time when salvation comes through faith in Christ and trusting in His sacrificial work on the cross. This is the dispensation in which we now live. In it we are saved by trusting in the sacrificial death of Christ on the cross. His death is a substitute for the punishment we deserve. Salvation is a free gift for those who believe in Him. This is considered a parenthetical period and was unanticipated in the broad scheme of history as understood by the ancient Hebrew writers of Scripture.

7. The Dispensation of the Kingdom: This will begin when Christ returns to reign over the earth "from the throne of David" for a thousand years.

To make things even more complicated, Darby and his followers take the so-called parenthetical era called "the time of the church" and, in turn, divide it into seven additional sections. These, they claim, are seven distinct periods of church history. According to the dispensationalists, each of these periods relates to one of the seven churches described in the Revelation of Saint John, chapters 2 and 3. They view these chapters of the Bible as a prophetic vision of what will happen to Christianity following the founding of the church. These stages or eras of church history are as follows:

Ephesus: The second generation of Christians, following the early church described in Acts 2.

Smyrna: The period of persecutions under Roman rulers.

Pergamum: The period wherein the church compromised itself with the rule of Constantine.

Thyatira: The period of the apostate church of the Middle Ages, when the worship of the Virgin Mary dominated.

Sardis: The church period following the Reformation, in which there is spiritual deadness in the church.

Philadelphia and *Laodicea:* These are the churches in the last days, leading up to the coming of Christ. Philadelphia is the faithful remnant of Christians, while Laodicea refers to those contemporary churches that, while healthy with financial resources and beautiful buildings, are spiritually bankrupt.

Dispensationalists make a big thing of their claim that we are now living in the final stage of church history prior to the second coming of Christ. They constantly preach that the church is in this Laodicean stage, wherein Christianity is marked by worldly materialism and a "lukewarm" spirituality that the Lord finds repulsive. Given the condition of so many churches in America and the seeming compromises that they have made with the corrupt values of materialism, the dispensationalists have an easy time making their case.

The Laodicean period is coming to an end, according to the dispensationalists, and we are living in the last days of this period of church history. Hence, to be around them is to hear constant references to our "living in the last days." They point to the degradation of societal morals, the materialistic seduction of Christians, and what they consider to be "the apostate ways of the churches" as evidence of their claim that this era prior to the Second Coming is near completion. They affirm the biblical word *Maranatha,* which means "Come quickly, Lord."

This complicated plan of history gets even more complex, and differences over what happens prior to the kingdom age lead to some bitter differences among dispensationalists themselves. They agree that there are to be seven years of great suffering on earth prior to the final return of Christ, and they refer to these seven years as "the Great Tribulation." The argument among dispensationalists, however, is whether Christians (i.e., those who have separated themselves from the apostate church) will stay here on earth and go through this time of tribulation or be "raptured" out of the world, with all the unbelievers and those in the apostate churches *left behind*—hence the title of the now famous book by Jerry Jenkins and Tim LaHaye. *Left Behind* is only the first of a series of books by Jenkins and LaHaye that have far outsold the popular novels by Stephen King. This series gives great impetus to dispensationalism and has made this relatively new invention in Protestantism more prevalent than ever.

Following the seven years of the Great Tribulation, there will be, according to dispensationalists, a literal thousand-year reign of Christ in which Satan and all of his demons will be imprisoned and the pure righteousness of God will reign on earth. Then, toward the end of the millennium of Christ's rule, Satan again will be released on the world, and evil and havoc will bring terror once more to all on planet Earth. Then Christ will reappear on the scene. Satan and his evil followers will be destroyed by fire (Rev. 20:7–10), and the saints will be caught up into a new heaven and a new earth for eternity.

THE DANGERS OF DISPENSATIONALISM

I want to be careful as I do a critique of dispensationalism. First of all, I need to say that it was in the context of this theology, promoted by the followers of John Darby, that I first came into a personal relationship with Christ. During my teenage years, I was part of a regularly meeting study group steeped in dispensationalist teachings, in which I learned a great deal about the Bible. Without that group and Tom Roop, the wonderful man who led our study of Scriptures, I wonder if I ever would have taken seriously the claim of Christ on my life.

Furthermore, some of the most deeply committed Christians I know interpret the Bible with the system devised by Darby and set forth by Scofield in his reference Bible. The congregations primarily responsible for perpetuating dispensationalist theology are some of the most diligently Christian churches I have ever encountered, and out of these congregations have come a host of Christian teachers who are serving throughout Christendom in nondispensationalist churches and organizations. Such realities make my critique of dispensationalism all the more difficult.

Nevertheless, this movement, which has done so much to promote the gospel and win people to Christ, has impacted the evangelical community in ways that have had a variety of negative consequences. It has promoted attitudes, dispositions, and practices evident among Christians in our involvement with the rest of society that hinder our ability to deal properly and relevantly with some of the pressing issues of our day.

As the dispensationalist outline of the history of the world is described, while it seems a bit convoluted and strangely complex, one might react by saying it appears to be harmless enough. But such is not the case. Dispensationalism has resulted in a variety of consequences, which, depending on your politics and views about Christian social action, can be extremely detrimental. Let me list these.

1. Dispensationalism supports a negative view of the church. What dispensationalists say about the church denigrates its divinely ordained character. The church is the "now" body of Christ. It is not simply a period of time to be referred to as a parenthesis.

Christ always was and always will be. Christ is the second member of the Trinity, and before Jesus was born, Christ was with the Father. It was Christ who created the heavens and the earth (John 1:1–3). But two thousand years ago, the eternal Christ took on human flesh and was born in Bethlehem's manger. He took on a body and grew up in the small town of Nazareth. At the age of thirty, He went out to preach, teach, and heal. He declared that the kingdom of God was at hand. It was in and through the body of Jesus that the eternal Christ did His saving work among us.

After the death, resurrection, and ascension of Jesus, the Christ who was incarnated in Him returned, even as He promised (John 14:25–26), and became a mystical presence in all who would receive Him (John 1:12). Those in whom Christ now lives in the world are the *now* body of Christ. It is this high designation that the apostle Paul gave to the church. It is through this *now* body that Christ is at work in the world.

The church is the means through which the eternal Christ is establishing the kingdom of God within human history. It marches on through time until that day when Jesus will physically return. That day, which theologians call "the eschaton," will be the time in which He will bring under His rule all principalities and powers and thrones—*through the church!* To reduce this glorious church to what the dispensationalists call a parenthetical period that appears as an afterthought to the main unfolding of God's plan does a disservice to the body of Christ.

On the other hand, dispensationalists never have had a theologically high view of the church. As a boy growing up in dispensationalist Christianity, I saw the church as little more than a body of believers who got together from time to time to worship and to be deployed in the world for the winning of souls to Christ. There was no sense that there was a mystical presence in the church and that the Holy Spirit, through the church, would be revealing the truths of Scripture and guarding against erroneous interpretations. Unknown to dispensationalists was the doctrine that said being Christian necessitated being a part of the body of Christ, and that no member could say of this body, "I have no need of you" (1 Cor. 12:21; see verses 13–22).

Dispensationalism made being a Christian a very individualistic thing for me. I was brought up to believe that, in these last days, the church had taken on the characteristics of the Laodicean stage of history. I was taught that most congregations of institutionalized religion were "apostate," and that I, along with my dispensationalist friends, were admonished to "come out from among them and be separate." The church had become worldly, I was told, and rejecting its Laodicean fellowship was an obligation of true Christians.

The Roman Catholic Church was the worst example of Laodicean religion, said the dispensationalists, and it was only a matter of time before the growing ecumenical movement would join Protestant denominations to Catholicism. Needless to say, dispensationalists were violently opposed to the ecumenical movement and had declared war on it. To belong to a congregation that was a member of the National Council of Churches—which in turn was a member of the World Council of Churches—was to be labeled either as ignorant of truth or as a coworker with demonic forces. The Antichrist, I was told, would have control over this emerging universal ecclesiastical system and would use its power to suppress true Christianity.

Obviously, such a perspective on mainline Christianity generated a lot of controversies in local congregations and nurtured schismatic tendencies everywhere dispensationalism spread. I think it is fair to say that this movement has done great harm to the traditional denominational mainline churches.

2. Dispensationalism fails to cultivate social action in the church. Not only does dispensationalism promote a negative theology of the church, but it also leaves little room for a theology of social action. If you believe, as dispensationalists do, that the world is on an inevitable downward-spiraling path toward total corruption and chaos, you have little motivation for trying to improve it. Dispensationalists view the world out there as a sinking ship and say we ought to use all of our energies to rescue people out of it, before it's too late. For them, trying to improve the social and economic conditions of society is futile, as demonstrated in this quote from Lewis Sperry Chafer's book *Major Bible Themes:* "In the present age, never is the individual believer (much less the Church) appointed of God to a world improvement program; but the believer is called to be a witness in all the world to Christ and His saving grace, and through this ministry of Gospel-preaching, the Spirit of God will accomplish the supreme divine purpose in the age."

If anyone suggests joining a peace movement to end hostilities in such places as the Middle East or Northern Ireland, that person is likely to hear that such efforts are a waste of time. Dispensationalists will be quick to quote Scripture and remind such "peaceniks" that there will always be "wars and rumours of wars" (Matt. 24:6) and that nothing can change that. Furthermore, there is no way to stop the escalation of conflicts, which will go on until the great Battle of Armageddon, as foretold in the book of Revelation.

If there is any idea that such thinking is harmless, consider the fact that dispensationalist clergymen, such as Jerry Falwell, advised former president George H. W. Bush, as they did former president Ronald Reagan, to embrace a worldview in which America was deemed the instrument of God to raise up an army to fight against the demonic force of the Evil Empire. President Reagan was convinced that he was called to build up the military power of the United States so as to make its army the inevitable victor at Armageddon. Now there is growing evidence that President George W. Bush may be falling into this same kind of thinking as he talks about the need to destroy those nations that make up what he has called "the axis of evil." Many of us fear that if the leaders of our country embrace this kind of "last days" theology, they just might create a self-fulfilling prophecy. We tremble at the possibility that we might have a president who, under the guidance of dispensationalist preachers, believes that it is God's will to get us into a war that could leave the world in shambles.

Another instance of how dispensationalism can impact social action is something encountered by anyone who tries to live out a commitment to end world hunger. Dispensationalists will give an okay to feeding hungry people only if, in so doing, the needy are rendered sufficiently grateful that they become open to the gospel. The idea of doing good for goodness' sake is lost in this kind of thinking. I have also heard dispensationalists say that the time, effort, and money spent on such social action programs would be better spent on evangelizing the lost. The former is acceptable, they say, as long as it does not take resources away from the really important work of evangelism. Sometimes they hold up Mother Teresa as an example of how Christians can be distracted by feeding the hungry from their calling to save the lost. I have actually heard her condemned because she did not make the receiving of food from her Sisters of Charity contingent upon the hungry having first accepted the gospel.

When it comes to changing geopolitics and trying to restructure economic systems to better facilitate helping the poor, dispensationalists do not oppose these efforts but see them as producing nothing that is significant. Believing that we live in the Laodicean era, they usually believe that little if anything can be done to hold back the growing suffering of this present age. They often quote Jesus, who said, "You will have the poor with you always" (see Mark 14:7), citing this verse as evidence of the futility of such efforts. Attempts to cancel Third World debts or to create fair trade relations between poor countries and rich countries may be well intentioned, but according to dispensationalists, these will not accomplish much in the long run. Why work for such things, they argue, when they interpret current events in the newspapers to be the fulfillment of biblical prophecy that predicts progressive doom? Most dispensationalists I know will be surprised if the Rapture does not occur in the next few years to bring an end to this disintegrating world that social activists are trying to save.

As a boy, I attended prophecy conferences with my mother and heard detailed explanations of how predictions about world events, according to the dispensationalists' scheme of things, were being fulfilled and that the Rapture was to be any day. I remember hearing a woman seated behind me muttering with a degree of satisfaction, "Thank You, Jesus!" as the preacher explained how evil the world was getting. As the preacher went on to talk about how crime rates, divorce rates, premarital pregnancy rates, and a host of other indicators of the evil conditions of society were all going up, and why these things pointed to a rapid disintegration of anything good in the world, this woman seemed increasingly pleased. When I asked my mother what this lady was so thrilled about, my mother told me that the woman was happy because the world was getting so bad that Jesus was certain to come again soon. You would have to agree that such beliefs hardly contribute to creating a positive disposition toward trying to change the socioeconomic order so that hunger can be eliminated.

3. Dispensationalists see government as a weak tool for instituting righteousness. It is not surprising that dispensationalists tend to line up with right-wing politics. They have little if any confidence that the governments of this world can be instruments of God for improving social conditions and moving society toward greater justice for the poor and oppressed. Dispensationalists sometimes become extreme in believing the old adage that "the government that governs best is the government that governs least." For them, government can accomplish little. At best they see its role solely as restraining things such as abortion and homosexual behavior, which they see as evils contrary to the teachings of Scripture.

When it comes to "supergovernments" such as the United Nations, dispensationalists react with intense negativism. Many of them view the United Nations as an instrument the Antichrist will use, as the book of Revelation describes, to dominate the world, creating an illusion of world peace while increasing restraints on true Christianity and eventually persecuting God's people. The idea that governments can make the world a better place is ludicrous in their minds. If you believe, as I do, that governments can improve and, in many cases, already have improved social conditions and moved the world toward being more just, you are likely to see the attitude dispensationalists generate toward governments as quite troubling.

4. Dispensationalists' impact on geopolitics can lead only to war. If you think that dispensationalists are a hindrance to world peace because of their abhorrence of the United Nations, consider how their doctrines about Israel are presently impacting geopolitics. Every major political problem in the world today, according to Tony Blair, the prime minister of the United Kingdom, is in one way or another connected to the Israeli/Palestinian conflict in the Middle East. Reflect on that thought as you consider the *Newsweek* magazine report that those it calls "evangelical Zionists" may be the greatest barrier to President Bush in the implementation of his peace plan, designed to bring an end to Jews and Arabs killing each other. While listening to dispensationalists on a variety of other issues, the president still holds, contrary to their beliefs, that his "road to peace" in the Middle East requires the creation of a Palestinian state.

Evangelical Zionists are Christians who are committed to the doctrines of the Second Coming that arise out of dispensationalism. According to their understanding of Scripture, the Jews must return to Palestine, reestablish the State of Israel, and rebuild Solomon's Temple on Mount Zion before Christ can return. This plan requires the displacement of the Arab people who presently occupy parts of the land that the dispensationalists say were promised to the Jewish people. Dispensationalists would never call this "ethnic cleansing," but that is exactly what they propose. They are more committed to this plan than most of the Jews living in Israel. They will work against any politician who does not support this plan, and the likes of Jerry Falwell and Pat Robertson have sent a clear message to President Bush on this matter as the president endeavors to work out his peace plan.

Obviously, the dispensationalists' plan can be carried out only if UN proposals about Palestinian land rights are ignored, causing a war that is likely to bring the whole Arab world into conflict with America. When it comes to rebuilding Solomon's Temple, it is likely that the billion-plus Muslims of the world would join in battle to prevent their mosque on Mount Zion from being torn down to make way for the reconstruction of the Jewish temple that evangelical Zionists have in mind. This site is the third holiest place in the world for Muslims. It is the place from whence they believe Mohammed ascended into heaven, and they are unlikely to surrender it without a horrific battle.

While evangelical Zionists believe that the temple must be rebuilt before Christ's return, there is little in the Bible to support this view. Certainly the apostle Paul never made it a precondition for Christ's return. He taught the early Christians to live in their day with the expectancy of the impending return of Christ (1 Cor. 15:50–58). Jesus Himself gave no indication that such events must occur prior to His coming to set up His kingdom here on earth. What Jesus said was that His disciples should expect His return at any time following His ascension to sit on the right hand of the heavenly Father. When His followers asked Him about the time of His return, Jesus told them that their generation would not die off before all the things that were supposed to happen prior to His return would be fulfilled. All of those prophecy preachers who seem to have figured out how and when Christ will return to set up His kingdom might find it helpful to consider what Jesus Himself said about all of this: "Verily I say unto you, This generation shall not pass, till all these things be fulfilled. Heaven and earth shall pass away, but my words shall not pass away. But of that day and hour knoweth no man, no, not the angels of heaven, but my Father only" (Matt. 24:34–36).

As incredible as it might seem, some evangelicals armed with Scofield Bibles might become a major factor in creating a massive war in the Middle East. Needless to say, a good number of evangelicals are afraid of dispensationalists, and many find the issue so important that they have parted ways with those who are into dispensationalist evangelical Zionism.

5. Dispensationalism leads to environmental ravaging. Another example of how dispensationalism can influence public policy is apparent in the policies of U.S. Secretary of the Interior James Watt, who served during the administration of President Ronald Reagan. Secretary Watt advocated the unrestrained exploitation of oil deposits on government land, even in such places as Yellowstone National Park. This was because he was convinced by "the signs of the times," as dispensationalist prophecies outlined, that the end of the world would very likely occur within the next few decades. Therefore, he reasoned that there was no need to protect these lands for the future, since there would be no extended future for either America or the rest of the world: We need the oil now, so why not drill for it now? After all, does not the Bible say that the end times are at hand?

6. Dispensationalists discount the Sermon on the Mount. I suppose that my biggest concern with dispensationalism is with what it says about the Sermon on the Mount. Dispensationalists contend that the way of life that this crucial portion of Scripture proposes, and the moral teachings that Jesus gave in this sermon, were not meant for people living in this present age. They have no objection to a claim that when Jesus says, "Blessed are the merciful: for they shall obtain mercy" (Matt. 5:7), He eliminates the possibility of capital punishment. Nor would they object to the idea that the equitable justice Moses established in the Torah is transcended by Jesus's teaching in Matthew 5:38–41, where He said:

> Ye have heard that it hath been said, An eye for an eye, and a tooth for a tooth: But I say unto you, That ye resist not evil: but whosoever shall smite thee on thy right cheek, turn to him the other also. And if any man will sue thee at the law, and take away thy coat, let him have thy cloak also. And whosoever shall compel thee to go a mile, go with him twain [two miles].

Dispensationalists entertain little doubt that the Sermon on the Mount, as recorded in Matthew 5–7, would, if taken literally as by Mennonite and Brethren in Christ Christians, lead to pacifism. Strict adherence to what it says in the Sermon on the Mount would have kept us from invading Iraq and required us to deal with Saddam Hussein by trying to overcome his evil with good.

Dispensationalists readily recognize the radical nature of the lifestyle the Sermon on the Mount prescribes, but they escape from having to live out these teachings by claiming that Jesus intended them for people in the next dispensation. They teach that Jesus meant the Sermon on the Mount for people who will live in the Millennium—the thousand-year reign of God's kingdom that Christ will establish when He returns. Until then, they say, the rules Jesus laid down in that sermon do not apply.

To say that what dispensationalists do with the Sermon on the Mount upsets me is a gigantic understatement. This sermon is at the heart of what Jesus's teachings are all about, and to dismiss it in such a cavalier fashion seems, to me, to be obscene. It is this new morality put forth by Jesus in the Sermon on the Mount that sets Christianity apart as a way of life, lifting it above all the other religions of the world. To declare that this sermon is irrelevant to this present age is worse than wrong.

Even non-Christians recognize the greatness and significance of the Sermon on the Mount. Mahatma Gandhi used it as the basis for his movement of nonviolent resistance against British rule. Nelson Mandela found in these words of Jesus the moral basis for overcoming hostility toward those who had oppressed him and the other black people of South Africa. To shove this sermon into another dispensation and declare it nonbinding on present-day Christians is a monumental flaw in the way dispensationalists think.

OPPOSITION TO DISPENSATIONALISM

The most serious opposition to dispensationalism comes from what I believe to be the most dynamic Christian movement of our time. It comes from those Pentecostals and charismatics who exercise what they call "the gifts of the Spirit." All around the world, a vibrant form of spirituality is emerging from charismatic Christianity in which people are experiencing ecstatic infillings of the Holy Spirit that are manifested as speaking in tongues, supernatural healings, and prophesying.

In Latin America, the charismatic movement has become the dominant form of Christianity. So much is this the case that the Roman Catholic churches in places such as Brazil have embraced the movement as a requirement for their survival. While there was much fanfare heralding the advent of liberation theology in Latin America as the Christianity for the poor and oppressed, the real religion of the economically and politically disposed people of the southern hemisphere has become charismatic Christianity. While by no means confined to the lower classes of Latin society, the charismatic movement has had its greatest appeal among the peasant classes of these countries. The poor and disinherited find escape from the privations and sufferings of their mundane existences in the ecstatic joys of charismatic experiences that lift them to incredible emotional highs. Often lacking the financial means to secure essential medical services, these poor people who are stricken with physical maladies find hope in the promise of miraculous healings. "Praying in tongues" offers them an assurance of salvation and a connectedness with God that goes beyond anything that traditional Catholicism offers.

In Honduras, the number of people who now claim membership in Protestant charismatic churches will soon outnumber those who claim affiliation with Catholicism. In Brazil, the people who attend Sunday services at Protestant charismatic churches now outnumber those who attend mass. In Africa, there are variant forms of Pentecostalism, each of which has distinctly African cultural characteristics, and any observer of religion will report that the charismatic movement is sweeping the continent.

In Europe, the same holds true. The only forms of Christianity that seem to have any vitality are charismatic in nature. This is certainly the situation in the United Kingdom, where this movement is breathing new life into formerly lethargic institutional Anglican churches. It is also giving birth to an array of independent churches that are growing beyond any sociological expectations.

In spite of all of these manifestations of spiritual revival under the auspices of the charismatic movement, dispensationalist Christians will have none of it. According to their rigid understanding of what they call "God's plan for the ages," all such forms of religiosity came to an end with the completion of the New Testament canon. They believe that "gifts of the Spirit," such as speaking and praying in tongues, prophesying, and the exercising of healing ministries, belonged to the days of the early church and are not meant for our present time. They say that when Paul told us that all these gifts will cease when "that which is perfect is come," as he wrote in 1 Corinthians 13:10, he was specifically referring to the finalizing of the writing of the books of the New Testament. This is the way dispensationalists understand 1 Corinthians 13:8–10: "Charity never faileth: but whether there be prophecies, they shall fail; whether there be tongues, they shall cease; whether there be knowledge, it shall vanish away. For we know in part, and we prophesy in part. But when that which is perfect is come, then that which is in part shall be done away."

The future of Christianity, I believe, belongs to the charismatic movement, regardless of what dispensationalists may think or say. According to Harvey Cox of Harvard, author of a book on the Pentecostal movement entitled *Fire from Heaven*, by the middle of the twenty-first century charismatic Christianity will be the only significant form of Christianity left. Already a sociological analysis of changing religious affiliations reveals that fundamentalist dispensationalist churches are losing members to the new charismatic congregations that are springing up everywhere. The gigantic Southern Baptist Convention, which has more than its share of dispensationalists, is showing significant leakage of members to these charismatic churches.

Dispensationalists are not about to go down without a fight. Their Bible colleges often expel students who dare to speak in tongues. It is nearly impossible to be in good standing with the Southern Baptist Convention if you show any signs of being Pentecostal. Dispensationalists declare that, in this present age, those miraculous manifestations of the Holy Spirit that charismatics claim are a normative part of their church life are counterfeit or inauthentic.

Many evangelicals who do not employ spiritual gifts (as listed in 1 Corinthians 12 and in Ephesians 4) are willing to admit that exercising these gifts can be a legitimate expression of the work of the Holy Spirit, but dispensationalists are not ready to make that concession. The followers of Darby and Scofield make no room for these charismatic gifts in the church of today. Given this significant difference between them, it seems inevitable that dispensationalists and charismatics (along with those who are sympathetic to the charismatic movement) are doomed to go their separate ways. This schismatic inevitability is bound to become more and more evident in evangelical Christianity as years go by, and as the differences between these two groups become intolerable to those on both sides.

While strict dispensationalists give no quarter to charismatics, the charismatics give some leeway to dispensationalists. There are evidences that some charismatic and Pentecostal churches are modifying dispensationalist charts to allow for the exercising of spiritual gifts, even after the closing of the New Testament canon (i.e., upon the completion of the writing of the New Testament). Who knows? Perhaps something can be worked out to synthesize the beliefs of these two opposing groups.

IS IT TIME FOR A NEW MOVEMENT?

The tensions that arise from some of the new theological ideas are becoming evident in the ranks of evangelicals, as some of its people look for new and creative ways to engage the secularists around them in dialogue. There was a time when evangelicals felt unequal to the task of intellectually conversing with serious non-Christian thinkers. During the first part of the twentieth century, evangelicals lacked the academic firepower to stand up against the ridicule of academia, whose members had more questions to ask than evangelicals were able to answer effectively. The answer to this situation was for evangelicals to retreat from such encounters and carry on their theological discussions only with each other.

Things have changed dramatically over the last twenty-five years, as evangelicals have produced more than their share of intellectuals who are ready and willing to test their beliefs against the arguments of their skeptical friends. But, as in all real dialogue, there has to be as much listening as there is talking, and in their listening to the ideas of others, evangelicals often find their own ideas challenged. In formulating responses to such challenges, evangelicals sometimes modify their theologies and may find them evolving into forms that their more rigid fundamentalist friends find dangerous. Given this reality, we can expect that those evangelicals who deviate from the "official" fundamentalist line of thinking may no longer feel at home within an evangelicalism that seems increasingly to be dominated by rigid fundamentalism.

Some believe that there is a need to start a new movement that differentiates itself from evangelicalism as it is presently understood. That is because fundamentalists have been taking control of evangelical organizations all across the country and are squeezing out any who do not yield to their doctrinaire positions. There is nothing wrong with believing in the fundamentals of the Christian faith that are core to being evangelical. It is just that these particular fundamentalists require more than a belief in the Apostles' Creed, a commitment to the Bible as being an infallible guide for faith and practice, and a personal transforming relationship with Christ for salvation. These fundamentalists are putting pressure on the rest of us evangelicals to believe other things exactly as they do. They demand that we adhere absolutely to their belief in a six-day creation. They act as though any of us who do not buy into their dispensationalist theology, with its Pretribulation Rapture, are not bona fide evangelicals.

Politically, right-wing evangelicals tend to view those who believe in the right of Palestinians to have a homeland as being against the will of God, and they suggest that to have anything to do with the Democratic Party is to make one's Christian commitment suspect. Formerly, such beliefs and commitments were common among these fundamentalist brothers and sisters, but those who held such views did not make them requisites for the rest of us who identified ourselves as evangelicals. But increasingly, fundamentalists are demanding that all who would go under the banner of evangelicalism agree with them, even when to do so means to take positions such as negating the right of women to be preachers and supporting discriminatory policies against gays and lesbians that are contrary to our convictions. Fundamentalists are calling into question more and more of us who do not go along with their beliefs, declaring that if we are not where they are on such issues, we are outside the evangelical fold. These particular fundamentalists tend to see a necessary connection between being theologically evangelical and politically conservative, and when they meet somebody like myself, who holds to a conservative theology while being committed to so-called liberal social issues, they grow angry and condemning.

For instance, upon hearing my belief that justice requires that the Palestinians have a homeland of their own along with the right of self-government, even while strongly affirming the right of Israel to exist as a secure nation free from terrorist threats, some have labeled me a kind of blaspheming agent of the Antichrist. I am attacked even as I plead that the Jews also are entitled to have a safe and secure nation of their own.

I wish that such opinions among my fundamentalist brothers and sisters were rare, but unfortunately for me, that is not the case. The fact that I say that gay men do not choose their sexual orientation, and that most of them sustain a homosexual orientation even after they undergo psychotherapeutic counseling, concerted prayer, and genuine spiritual conversion, makes me *persona non grata* at many evangelical gatherings. My calls for social justice on behalf of gays and lesbians, even as I hold to a theologically conservative position on homosexual behavior, have led to groups canceling after they had invited me to speak. Furthermore, those evangelical groups that do have me as a speaker sometimes have to endure harassment from my critics. No matter that I say loud and clear that while sexual orientation is *not* chosen, behavior *is*—and that I call gay and lesbian people to some form of a celibate lifestyle. If I refuse to say things that I do not believe are true about my gay brothers and lesbian sisters (i.e., that they have *chosen* to be the way they are), then my fundamentalist detractors declare that I have no right to say I am an evangelical.

Another defining issue that has arisen over the last few decades is abortion. If I say that I have pro-choice friends who are, nevertheless, committed Christians, I regularly face the accusation that I must not understand what being a Christian is all about. I agree that we should question the Christianity of anyone who knowingly and willingly commits murder, but my pro-choice Christian friends are convinced in their own minds that killing the unborn is not murder, especially in the early stage of pregnancy.

I take a stand against abortion, especially in cases of late-term abortions, but I am not willing to say that those who differ with me are not Christians. If there is a common allegiance to Christ, then I believe that the discussion between pro-life and pro-choice Christians should continue with civility, rather than with the name-calling that I too often hear from both sides on this hot and extremely important issue. I believe that little dialogue will take place and little progress will be made as long as the pro-choice people call the pro-life people "Nazis," and the pro-life people call the pro-choice people "murderers."

AN ANSWER

Over the past thirty-five years, I have taught at Eastern University in St. Davids, Pennsylvania. This school has a doctrinal statement that, with the exception of what it says about baptism, carefully delineates what could be the theological basis for a new Christian movement, which, for lack of a better label right now, could be called progressive evangelicalism. Every full-time faculty member who teaches at Eastern makes a commitment to this doctrinal statement.

DOCTRINAL STATEMENT

We believe that the Bible, composed of the Old and New Testaments, is inspired of God and is of supreme and final authority in faith and life.

We believe in the supernatural as the vital element in the revelation and operation of the Christian faith.

We believe in one God eternally existing in three Persons—Father, Son, and Holy Spirit.

We believe that Jesus Christ was begotten of the Holy Spirit and born of the Virgin Mary, and that He is true God and true man and is the only and sufficient Mediator between God and humankind.

We believe in the personality of the Holy Spirit and that His ministry is to reveal Christ to humankind in the regeneration and sanctification of their souls.

We believe that man and woman were created in the image of God, and that they sinned and thereby incurred spiritual death.

We believe in the vicarious death of the Lord Jesus Christ for our sins, in the resurrection of His body and His ascension into Heaven, His personal and visible future return to the earth and that salvation is received only through faith in Him.

We believe that baptism is immersion of a believer in water, in the name of the Father and of the Son, and of the Holy Spirit; setting forth the essential facts in redemption—the death and resurrection of Christ; also essential facts in the experience of the believer—death to sin and resurrection to newness of life; and that the Lord's Supper is a commemoration of the Lord's death until He comes.

We believe that a New Testament church is a body of believers thus baptized, associated for worship, service, the spread of the gospel, and the establishing of the Kingdom in all the world.

In addition to these core beliefs, any progressive evangelical movement of which I was a part would have to hold to the following:

- That we continue to talk about, pray about, and intensely discuss the issues of homosexuality and abortion, but that we regard people who disagree with those who hold conservative views on these issues as brothers and sisters in Christ, as long as they trust in salvation through the grace of God that is offered through Christ. In other words, we will not use one's opinions or convictions on the issue of abortion or homosexuality to define who is, or who is not, a Christian.

- That we preach a Christ who transcends all political parties. That we welcome Christians of various political persuasions and that we carefully consider the platforms of each party to determine those parts that are in harmony with the teachings of Scripture and those parts that we find in conflict with biblical teachings.

- That we be agreed that Christ is now at work in the world, changing the world that *is* into the kingdom of God. That we be convinced that being Christian is to be called to join Christ in what He is doing here and now, which means that we are to work with Christ to eliminate poverty, provide justice to the oppressed, bring about global peace, and struggle against racism, sexism, and any other forms of destructive, dehumanizing discrimination. That we believe Scripture requires us to embrace a personal economic lifestyle of simplicity so that others in our world might simply live. That we do this, always mindful of the ultimate importance of sharing the salvation story with the lost.

- That we be committed to adopting a prophetic role. This would involve critiquing the policies of our government when it (1) evidences a less-than-adequate response to the ecological crisis that faces our planet, (2) gives uneven support for justice to either Israelis or Palestinians in the Middle East, (3) establishes any trade policies that contribute to the suffering of people in Third World countries, (4) supports domestic policies that leave the poor in America without medical coverage, or (5) ignores the fact that we have the highest level of illiteracy among the industrialized nations of the world.

- That we reject any triumphalistic spirit that would engender the imposition of Christianity on others or seek special privileges or favored positions for Christians in those arenas of public affairs where the government holds sway. That we also reject any claim that our country be defined as a Christian nation and affirm that ours is a pluralistic society that should provide a level playing field for all and any religions, as well as for those who would promote agnosticism or atheism.

Furthermore, in working for the justice and well-being of all people, neo-evangelicals would cooperate with those of other religions with a respectful attitude, listening to what men and women of other faith traditions can teach us, even as we testify, without compromise, to the gospel of Jesus Christ. I am convinced that Christianity would do more than hold its own in such circumstances.

While the preceding definition of this so-called progressive evangelical movement is rudimentary, I am hoping to find a network of Christians who share these commitments, convictions, attitudes, and core values. Should you choose to be part of such a movement and share in the developing of our mission, I invite you to write to me at

The Evangelical Association for the Promotion of Education
PO Box 7238
St. Davids, PA 19087-7238

I believe that there are many people like me who really want to stay in the evangelical fold, and I am beginning to realize that, if we do not hang together, they will hang us separately. Perhaps a new movement, such as the one I have been describing, would enable evangelicalism to develop into a form that provides a place for us, and perhaps the more traditionally fundamentalistic evangelicals will find room in their hearts to continue to deem us their Christian brothers and sisters. This is my hope and prayer.

14

There Is Hope for Better Days

The future looks bright for us evangelicals who once were ridiculed because of our talk about being "born again" and having a personal relationship with Christ. We now live in a postmodern era in which there is a growing acceptance of belief in realities that transcend a world that limits truth to scientific empiricism and the canons of reason. As Blaise Pascal, the philosopher/mathematician of a bygone day, once said, "The heart has reasons that reason can never know!"

Just fifty years ago, almost every sophisticate assumed that religion based on the kind of mystical invasion of persons by a transcendent spiritual power that evangelical Christians claim to experience was nothing more than self-delusion. Today, more than fifty-five million Americans, including recent presidents of the United States, claim to have had "born-again" experiences and to have personal relationships with the spirit of the resurrected Jesus. Who could have predicted such a turn in events?

According to sociologists, from the German Max Weber to the American Peter Berger, the so-called magical-mystical types of religion were supposed to have disappeared under the impact of what they called "the increasing tendency toward rationalization." By that, they meant to tell us that belief in miracles and mystical experiences belong to the earliest stages in the development of a religion and that, over an extended period of time, people move from that kind of religion to one that appeals to reason. They called this latter stage, toward which they believed all of Christianity to be moving, "rational-moral religion."

In 1950, it appeared that there was no basis for questioning what Weber and Berger had predicted. It looked as though those sociologists had gotten it right.

Those in the pulpits of mainline churches seldom invited their listeners to come down church aisles and experience a mystical encounter with a living Jesus who would become their personal Savior. Instead, they admonished their congregations to take stands against racism, oppose "the military industrial" complex, and pressure government to take better care of the poor. The moral teachings many mainline churches advocated were commonly little more than the moral teachings of secular humanists, legitimated with a sprinkling of biblical references.

GIVE ME THAT OLD-TIME RELIGION

Then the unexpected happened! The so-called magical-mystical religion made an incredible comeback. Some say the comeback of "that old-time religion," so characteristic of nineteenth-century revivalism, was the result of a growing awareness of the limitations of both the science and the rationalism that society once looked upon as the agents that would bring in the brave new world. To many, science had failed them. It had failed to deliver on its promise for progress, and the rationalism that was the hallmark of scientific thinking had failed to answer the most urgent questions of human existence.

Science did not find a cure for cancer, as we had assumed it would, and the harnessing of atomic energy did not bring in an era of economic well-being, but rather an era of fear of the possibility of a nuclear holocaust. Instead of initiating a utopia, the rationalism of modernity only created uneasiness among many who previously had found hope and help in faith. Secular humanism, the adopted child of scientific rationalism, has not proven to be the cure for the foibles of humanity as its advocates promised. Far from being the cure, it is now seen as the disease.

People facing death found no consolation in rationalism. A person told that he or she had a terminal illness found more disappointment than hope in science. Those who sought answers about the meaning of their lives in secular humanism too often found only despairing nihilism in the prevailing philosophies of a society that had allowed religion to be ridiculed in the halls of academia. Not surprisingly, there were those who, upon discovering the bankruptcy of modernity, looked for gratification in that mishmash of Eastern religion, Native American spiritualism, and medieval magic that come together in what is called the New Age movement. Others sought escape in drugs and alcohol from the sense of alienation that accompanied modernity. But increasingly, the lostness that marked the lives of those who embraced secularism drove them to take up the once-discarded faith of their fathers and mothers. In the face of the collapse of morality that always accompanies the ethical relativity that goes with abolishing God from societal consciousness, many of them looked for absolutes to give order and stability to their lives in evangelical Christianity.

Another possible explanation for the encroaching spiritual openness of the twenty-first century is that science, which was supposed to obliterate metaphysical speculation, has actually opened up possibilities for transcending itself. The paradigms of positivism that once ruled have been challenged in more ways than anyone could have imagined a half-century ago. With modern physics raising doubts about its own a priori assumptions regarding realities as basic as the nature of time and space and exploring the ways in which faith influences the healing processes of our bodies, the scoffers of religion find themselves increasingly on the defensive.

Drew University professor Leonard Sweet has pointed out that, not too long ago, if a scientist had been asked if he or she believed God, the answer would have been, "Of course not. I'm a scientist!" Today, if that same scientist were asked if he or she has any room for faith in God, the answer would likely be, "Of course I do! I'm a scientist!"

Perhaps the best explanation for the resurgence of the mystical spiritual evangelicalism that defies the assumptions of scientism is that it comes closest to expressing both the ultimate truths about God and the salvation story and meeting personal needs. It just may be that people are turning increasingly from a purely moral-rational religion to evangelicalism because the latter is better suited to meeting their spiritual hungers. When people look for deliverance from the guilt that comes from sin and seek purpose to deliver themselves from the meaninglessness that so often has given them sleepless nights, they are more likely to find their solace in the biblical preaching of Billy Graham than in the prophetic preaching of social gospel pulpiteers. Not only might the growing popularity of evangelicalism be the result of its inherent truth, it also may be that—pragmatically speaking—it works!

EVANGELICALISM ON THE ROAD TO SELF-IMPROVEMENT

What is very encouraging these days is that evangelicalism is more and more open to critiques and increasingly faces up to its own inadequacies. More and more, it is ready to confront its shortcomings and try to correct them. Of course, there will always be those in its ranks who cling to the past and try to use the Bible to legitimate the oppression of women and gays. But I observe among evangelicals today signs of changing attitudes that can lead to gender egalitarianism and empathy for those with homosexual orientations.

I see signs of the impact of Anabaptist thinking upon evangelicals. From the Mennonites and the Church of the Brethren come voices calling into question the militaristic mind-set that has dominated in many parts of the evangelical community.

While many evangelicals once considered environmentalism synonymous with the New Age movement, now they almost always welcome it as a dimension of their social ethics.

In short, I sense that a growing proportion of the evangelical community is developing a holistic doctrine of salvation, declaring that the salvation being wrought by Jesus not only delivers sinners from condemnation but also provides the vision and hope needed to work for a world marked by social justice and ecological well-being. Of course, there will be a significant reaction against these hopeful tendencies, but I believe that history is on the side of those progressive evangelicals who are increasingly evident, especially within Generation X (i.e., those who are in their twenties and thirties).

Yes, there may be a split in the evangelical community, and there will be those who cling to rigid fundamentalism and continue to assert those values and practices that they have made sacred within their subculture, even though some of those values and practices lack biblical credibility. Many good Christians will fear the uncertainties that go with being on the cutting edge of a dynamic Christianity with new ways of thinking, but I believe that in the long run, progressive evangelicalism will become the more dominant expression of American Christianity.

I believe that the progressive evangelicalism of the future will bring together those members of independent evangelical churches who are discontented with any fundamentalism that advocates such things as a sexual hierarchy with male dominance, simplistic answers to the struggles of gays and lesbians, and a patriotism that is more committed to nationalistic chauvinism than to the values of the kingdom of God, with those evangelicals who are in mainline denominational churches. We must remember that most people who are now members of these mainline churches really are evangelicals, regardless of whether or not the leaders of their respective denominations agree with them. I believe that these two cohorts of evangelicals will come together, embracing much of the dynamism and new forms of worship that are coming to the church through the charismatic movement, and forge the kind of creative spirituality needed for the twenty-first century. I very much want to be part of all of this. That is why I proudly call myself a progressive evangelical.

WHY I BELIEVE I AM AN EVANGELICAL

The first reason I offer for continuing to embrace the evangelical label is that I believe, literally, all the doctrines of the Apostles' Creed. Allow me to remind you of what that creed posits as prepositional truth:

> I believe in God the Father Almighty, Maker of heaven and earth: and in Jesus Christ his only Son our Lord, who was conceived by the Holy Ghost, born of the Virgin Mary, suffered under Pontius Pilate, was crucified, dead, and buried, he descended into hell; the third day he rose again from the dead, he ascended into heaven, and sitteth at the right hand of God the Father Almighty; from thence he shall come to judge the quick and the dead. I believe in the Holy Ghost, the holy catholic church, the communion of saints, the forgiveness of sins, the resurrection of the body and the life everlasting.

This ancient creed, which goes back at least fifteen hundred years, summarizes almost everything that is essential to the belief system of those who would call themselves evangelicals. It affirms the deity of Jesus, establishes His place in human history, asserts our need for His salvation from sin, states the way that salvation becomes available to us, proclaims our certainty that history is moving toward a meaningful triumph by Jesus, and tells us the importance of that fellowship of believers that we call the church.

There is one essential doctrine not contained in the Apostles' Creed to which I adhere. The creed says nothing about the nature of Scripture. Evangelicals believe that the Bible is an infallible message from God, who inspired and guided the writers, and therefore it is the ultimate guide for faith and for living out the Christian life. Most evangelicals even use the word *inerrant*. Whether one declares Scripture to be an inspired, infallible guide for faith and practice or goes all the way to believing it to be the result of verbal dictation by the Holy Spirit, evangelicals share a unified belief that the Bible is a trustworthy book and that in developing theology and ethics, eventually we must answer to what it says. That which we teach and preach must be credible in light of what the Bible tells us.

Finally, we evangelicals contend that correct doctrine and faith in the veracity of the biblical revelation are not enough. We believe that to be "saved" and to have a right relationship with God, we must have a personal relationship with a risen and living Jesus. This is *the* essential mystic dimension of being a Christian.

We hold to the conviction that the historical Jesus is personally present in the world today and that mystically He will enter into the mind and soul of anyone who is willing to yield to Him. This invasion of the surrendered person by the Spirit of Christ, whether sudden or gradual, constitutes what evangelicals mean by being "born again."

A DAILY INVASION

I emphasize especially my own born-again experience. For me, this did not come as a result of what is called in one old hymn "a sudden rending of a veil of clay." For me, there was nothing like what Paul experienced when God confronted him on the road to Damascus. Instead, the invasion of my personhood by the Holy Spirit occurs almost daily in the context of contemplative prayers. Unless I am somehow suffering from delusions, I can say that the Holy Spirit is a felt reality in my life.

Sometimes people question me about the source of my intense passion for the poor and oppressed. My students regularly inquire about the basis of my commitment to social justice. Most of all, people ask how I am able to keep up an exhausting speaking schedule, preaching a message that calls the church to work for justice for the poor. To all of them, I have a simple answer: "My zeal comes from the Lord during my morning times of prayerful quietude. As the psalmist once said, 'My strength cometh from the Lord.'"

Jesus's historical accomplishments in His death and resurrection saved me from the punishment for my sins (which I know I justly deserve), and I sense that I am reborn through His Spirit at the start of each day in times of quietude. I believe His saving work was finished for me two thousand years ago, but daily I experience a renewing of His Spirit within me when I take time each morning to yield to becoming holy.

For me, sanctification is an ongoing process. That is why my favorite Bible verses are Philippians 3:13–14: "Brethren, I count not myself to have apprehended: but this one thing I do, forgetting those things which are behind, and reaching forth unto those things which are before, I press toward the mark for the prize of the high calling of God in Christ Jesus."

ISSUES THAT CONCERN US ALL

I have tried here to address those questions and issues that concern us evangelicals, troubling us, and even leading some to abandon the faith. I have done so in the hope of persuading both inquiring minds outside our faith, and shaky believers within our ranks, that being an evangelical need not involve rigidity in thinking or a refusal to venture into unknown intellectual territories. It is my hope that there is room for innovative and even revolutionary thinking within the evangelical Christian community.

What I have to say should not be taken as some kind of *summa theologica*, but rather as a challenge to my sisters and brothers to be willing, for the sake of eternal truth, to endure the heat that will come from those in our evangelical community who think the most important thing in life is to play it safe. This book is my attempt to do the kind of theologizing that can help to keep evangelicalism alive and well.

One of my Jewish friends told me that fundamentalism scared him for the same reason that he was afraid of Dracula. "I'm afraid of anything that comes back from the dead."

What he did not realize is that, during the first half of the twentieth century, fundamentalism was only wounded. It was not dead. It only needed time to recover. It could be said of fundamentalism, in the words of an almost forgotten poet, Sir Andrew Barton, "I am hurt, but I am not slain, / I'll lay me down and bleed awhile, / And then I'll rise and fight again."

That part of fundamentalism that has been challenged by social justice issues into being activist has changed its name to evangelicalism, and in its progressive expression, it is changing its character to become a movement that is prepared to face the new millennium with confidence. As progressive evangelicalism increasingly emerges out of fundamentalism over the next fifty years, the rest of the world will encounter Christians who are more than ready to struggle with the tough issues that await us, and to do so with open minds and open hearts. Such will be the case if God answers our prayers—and I have faith that God will do just that.

Appendix

OPPORTUNITIES TO HELP THE POOR

1. CHILD SPONSORSHIP

When you sign up to sponsor a child, you receive a photograph and a biographical sketch of the particular child, and you regularly receive letters from him or her. If you saw the movie *About Schmidt*, starring Jack Nicholson, you got a glimpse of what a difference the sponsorship can mean to a child, and how meaningful being a sponsor can prove to be.

I have heard the criticisms of these child-support agencies and have done some firsthand investigating of the two organizations I support to see if those criticisms are justified. They are not!

The first and most common criticism is that only a small portion of the money given ever gets to the sponsored child. Not true! Actually, almost eighty cents out of every dollar given goes directly to help the child and the child's family. The other twenty cents is needed to cover the cost of administering the program and delivering the money to the specific child.

Children in Third World countries, especially orphans, are constantly on the move. An orphan might be with one aunt one week and with another aunt the next. A child might be adopted by one family one month, but then move on to be with another family the next. The sheer logistics of keeping track of where children are, and making sure that the money being given to the adults in charge is actually being spent on keeping the child, are such that full-time staff workers have to maintain constant vigilance. And that is where most of the other twenty cents of the dollar you give is spent.

Another criticism is that in a given village, a few children might have sponsors while others do not. The fear is that sponsored children in a given village might be fed and clothed while others are left out—looking in on schools where the "chosen" children are being cared for, educated, and evangelized. Again, this is not the case. Insofar as it is possible, sponsorship is made available to all the needy children in any village that is targeted for a child-support system.

I personally am deeply committed to recruiting sponsors for Third World children through Compassion International and World Vision, because I know what they do. Having worked in Third World countries such as Haiti, the Dominican Republic, and Zimbabwe, I have seen their work and have been very favorably impressed.

Why not sign up with one of these organizations today and adopt a needy child? It's the first step in helping to end Third World poverty.

Compassion International
PO Box 65000
Colorado Springs, CO 80962
1-800-336-7676
www.compassion.com

World Vision
PO Box 78481
Tacoma, WA 98481
1-800-434-4464
www.worldvision.com

2. LITERACY PROGRAM

There are many features of the Beyond Borders ministry that I appreciate. First and foremost, they have a major emphasis on developing indigenous leadership. The teachers in each of their literacy centers are Haitians. Beyond Borders locates Haitians who can read and write and then puts them into Haitian-run training programs that develop their teaching skills. Each of the ninety-five literacy centers Beyond Borders presently sponsors has its own board of directors made up of Haitian leaders from the respective villages where these little schools are located.

Developing leadership skills and decision-making abilities among indigenous people in these villages is just as important to the Beyond Borders missionaries as the literacy programs themselves. Even the international board, which oversees the entire operation of Beyond Borders, has enough Haitians on it to give Haitians a decisive voice in developing the organization's policies.

Second, the cost of this program is remarkably low. An entire literacy center, which can serve as many as fifty *restavecs* (see p. 134), costs only two hundred dollars a month—that's twenty-four hundred dollars a year. It is possible for a church youth group, Sunday school class, men's group, or women's group to sponsor one of these little schools.

The sponsoring group receives a photograph of the school and the children who are being blessed through its giving. Haiti is close enough to the United States so that sponsors can visit the school being supported. My wife and I support one of these schools ourselves. Our own children are grown and Peggy and I find it very meaningful to know that our gift of two hundred dollars a month is giving some other children the opportunity for a better life. Why not consider funding one of these literacy centers?

Beyond Borders
PO Box 2132
Norristown, PA 19404
1-866-424-8403 (toll free)
mail@beyondborders.net
www.beyondborders.net

3. ENTREPRENEURIAL PROJECT

In the Dominican Republic, Opportunity International provided start-up funding for a small factory that provided employment for a dozen women. The whole thing got started in a Bible study group taught by a local Catholic priest. The women in this group bonded over a period of months, and they began to share their personal problems. One common issue was that most of their husbands were unreliable providers. Even when these men did have work, they often failed to bring their paychecks home to their families. Little by little, these women came to the conclusion that they themselves would have to do something to feed and clothe their families.

With the help of the priest, they established a small factory that manufactured sandals made out of worn-out and discarded automobile tires. The women got a loan from Opportunity International for the few hundred dollars they needed to buy tools and to rent a garage to house this new microindustry. They paid children in the barrio where they lived and worked fifty cents for each discarded tire they brought to the factory. It wasn't long before they had every worn-out tire in Santa Domingo. Then they started getting a lot of *new* automobile tires, and they had to devise another source for their raw materials!

This particular project was so successful that the women were able to pay back the loan with interest within a year, and since then, they have not only supported their families, but also earned enough money to build better housing for themselves.

In another project in Haiti, a handful of women bought a solar panel with their loan money from Opportunity International. Then, with some clever engineering, they were able to use their solar panel to recharge batteries. Since there was no commercial electricity in their village, the people used batteries for everything from radios to flashlights, and these women were soon earning a small fortune by Haitian standards. With a second loan, they bought a television set and a receiving dish. Using the electricity from their solar panel, they were able to set up a village theater where the local people, for a small fee, could watch TV shows each evening.

One of the great things about the loan program of Opportunity International is that it has a 96 percent payback rate. This means that whatever money you give not only will create jobs for one group of workers, but also upon repayment of the loan, there will be resources for still another group—and another and another. Your gift can go on creating jobs for poor people indefinitely.

Consider contacting Opportunity International and becoming a sponsor for a microbusiness in the Third World. With a relatively small investment of a few hundred dollars, you can enable a large number of people not only to escape from grinding poverty, but also to be able to say to their friends and neighbors, "We did it ourselves." Why not get in touch with Opportunity International now?

Opportunity International
and the Women's Opportunity Fund
2122 York Road, Suite 340
Oak Brook, IL 60523
1-800-793-9455
getinfo@opportunity.org
www.opportunity.org

4. POLITICAL ORGANIZATION

Call to Renewal endeavors to be a political-action alternative to the Christian Coalition, which it views as overly committed to the Republican Party. Call to Renewal unifies Christians for the purpose of impacting political policies related to helping the poor. It is a broad-based organization that endeavors to overcome the old dichotomies of liberal and conservative, embracing Christians ranging from Roman Catholics to evangelicals.

> Call to Renewal
> 2401 15th St. NW
> Washington, D.C. 20009
> 202-328-8745
> *ctr@calltorenewal.org*
> *www.calltorenewal.org*

5. GRASS-ROOTS ORGANIZATION

Get in touch with Habitat for Humanity, and the good people there will connect you to a work group near where you live. They welcome women and men with building skills as well as those who are beginners.

> Habitat for Humanity
> 121 Habitat St.
> Americus, GA 31709
> 1-800-422-4828
> *www.habitat.org*
> *publicinfo@hfhi.org*

Notes

CHAPTER 6

1. George MacDonald, *Creation in Christ,* ed. Rolland Hein (Wheaton, IL: Harold Shaw, 1976), 7–8.
2. Ibid.
3. Ibid., 7.
4. H. Richard Niebuhr, *The Kingdom of God in America* (New York: Harper and Row, 1937), 193.

CHAPTER 9

1. Zbigniew Brezezinski, on back cover of Samuel P. Huntington, *The Clash of Civilizations and the Remaking of World Order* (Carmichael, CA: Touchstone Books).

CHAPTER 12

1. Philip Elmer-Dewitt, "Now for the Truth About Americans and Sex," *Time,* October 17, 1994, 64.